# The History of the Origins of Christianity

## Book VI - Comprising the Reigns of Hadrian and Antonius Pius (A.D. 117-161)

### By Joseph Ernest Renan

#### Edited by Anthony Uyl

Devoted Publishing
Woodstock, Ontario, 2017

# The History of the Origins of Christianity Book VI - Comprising the Reigns of Hadrian and Antonius Pius (A.D. 117-161)

## By Joseph Ernest Renan

Member of the French Academy, and of the Academy of Inscriptions and Fine Arts.

## Edited by Anthony Uyl

Originally Published by:
London: Mathieson & Company 25 Paternoster Square, E.C. London.

The text of The History of the Origins of Christianity Book VI - Comprising the Reigns of Hadrian and Antonius Pius (A.D. 117-161) is all in the Public Domain. This edition is published by Devoted Publishing a division of 2165467 Ontario Inc.

**What kind of philosophies do you have? Let us know!**

Contact us at: devotedpub@hotmail.com
Visit us on Facebook: @DevotedPublishing
Get more products via our website: www.devotedpublishing.com

**Published in Woodstock, Ontario, Canada 2017**

For bulk educational rates, please contact us at the email address above.

ISBN: 978-1-988297-74-3

# Table of Contents

# PREFACE

I thought at first that this Sixth Book would finish the series of volumes which I have devoted to the history of the origins of Christianity. It is certain that at the death of Antoninus, circa A.D. 160, the Christian religion had become a complete religion, having all its sacred books, all its grand legends, the germ of all its dogmas, the essential parts of its liturgies; and in the eyes of most of its adherents, it was a religion standing by itself, separated from and even opposed to Judaism. I, however, thought it right to add a last work, containing the ecclesiastical history of the reign of Marcus Aurelius, to the preceding books. In the truest sense, the reign of Marcus Aurelius belongs to the origins of Christianity. Montanism is a phenomenon of about the year 170, and is one of the most notable events of early Christianity. After more than a century had elapsed since those strange hallucinations which had possessed the apostles at the Last Supper at Jerusalem, suddenly in some remote districts of Phrygia there sprung up again prophecy, the glossolalia, those graces which the author of the Acts of the Apostles praises so much. But it was too late: under Marcus Aurelius, religion, after the confused manifestations of Gnosticism, had more need of discipline than of miraculous gifts. The resistance that orthodoxy, as represented by the episcopate, was able to offer to the prophets of Phrygia, was the decisive act of the constitution of the Church. It was admitted that, above individual inspiration, there existed the average judgment of the universal conscience. This average opinion, which will triumph in the course of the history of the Church, and which, representing as it did relative good sense, constituted the power of that great institution, was already perfectly characterised under Marcus Aurelius. A description of the first struggles which thus took place between individual liberty and ecclesiastical authority, seemed to me to be a necessary part of the history which I wished to trace of rising Christianity.

But besides that, there was another reason that decided me to treat the reign of Marcus Aurelius in its relations to the Christian community in the fullest detail. It is partial and unjust to represent the endeavours of Christianity as an isolated fact, as a unique, and, in a manner, a miraculous attempt at religious and social reform. Christianity was not alone in attempting what it alone was able to carry out. Timidly still in the first century, openly and brilliantly in the second, all virtuous men of the ancient world were longing for an improvement in morals and in the laws, and piety thus became a general requirement of the time. With regard to high intellectual culture, the century was not what the preceding age had been; there were no men of such large minds as Cæsar, Lucretius, Cicero and Seneca, but an immense work of moral amelioration was going on in all directions, and philosophy, Hellenism, the Eastern creeds and Roman probity, contributed equally to this. The fact that Christianity has triumphed is no reason for being unjust towards those noble attempts which ran parallel with its own, and which only failed because they were too aristocratic, and did not possess enough of that mystic character which was formerly necessary in order to attract the people. In order to be perfectly just, the two attempts ought to be studied together, allowances ought to be made for both, and it ought to be explained why one has succeeded whilst the other has not.

The name of Marcus Aurelius is the most noble among all that noble school of virtue which tried to save the ancient world by the force of reason, and thus a thorough study of that great man belongs essentially to our subject. Why did not that reconciliation between the Church and the Empire, which took place under Constantine, take place under Marcus Aurelius? It is all the more important to settle this question, as already in this volume we shall see that the Church identifies her destinies with those of the Empire.

In the latter half of the second century, some Christian doctors of the highest authority seriously faced the possibility of making Christianity the official religion of the Roman world, and it might almost be said that they divined the great events of the fourth century. Looked at closely, that resolution by which Christianity, having entirely changed its past, has become the protégé, or perhaps we had better say the protector, of the State, from having been persecuted by it, ceases to be surprising. St Justin and Melito foresaw this quite clearly. St Paul's principle, "All power is of God," will bear its fruits, and the Gospel will become, what Jesus certainly did not foresee, one of the bases of absolution. Christ will have come into the world to guarantee the crowns of princes, and in our days a Roman Pontiff has tried to prove that Jesus Christ preached and died to preserve the fortunes of the wealthy, and to consolidate capital.

As we advance in this history, we shall find that documents become more certain, and preliminary discussions less necessary. The question of the Fourth Gospel has been so often treated in the preceding volumes, that we need not return to that subject now. The falseness of the Epistles to Timothy and Titus, which are attributed to St Paul, has been already demonstrated, and the apocryphal character of the Second Epistle of St Peter is shown by the few pages which are devoted to that work. The problems of the epistles attributed to St Ignatius, and of the epistle attributed to St Polycarp, are absolutely identical, and attention need only be drawn to what has been said in the introduction to our preceding work. Nobody has any further doubt about the approximate age of the Pastor of Hermas. The account of Polycarp's death bears the same characteristics of authenticity as the epistle to the faithful at Lyons and Vienne, which will be mentioned in our last book, and to discriminate between the authentic and the supposititious works of St Justin, does not require the same lengthy explanation as the introductions to the former volumes naturally did. It can plainly be seen, and all signs seem to point to the fact, that we are approaching the end of the age of origins. Ecclesiastical history is about to begin. The same interest is felt in it, but everything takes place in the full light of day, and for the future, criticism will no longer encounter those obscurities which can only be got over by hypotheses or bold speculation. Hic cestus artemque repono. After Irenæus and Clement of Alexandria, our old works on Ecclesiastical History of the seventeenth century are almost sufficient. Any one who reads in Fleury the two hundred and twenty pages that correspond to our seven volumes, will perceive all the difference. The seventeenth century only cared to know what was quite clear, and all origins are obscure; but for the philosophic mind, they are of unequalled interest. Embryogeny is from its very essence the most interesting of sciences, for by it we can penetrate the secrets of nature, its plastic force, its final aims, and its inexhaustible fecundity.

# CHAPTER I

### HADRIAN

Trajan's health was daily growing worse, and so he set out for Rome, leaving the command of the army at Antioch to Hadrian, his second cousin, and grand-nephew by marriage. He was forced to stop at Selinus, on the coast of Cilicia, by inflammation of the bowels, and there he died August 11, 117, at the age of sixty-four. The condition of affairs was very unfortunate: the East was in a state of insurrection; the Moors, the Bretons, the Sarmatians were becoming menacing, and Judea, subjugated but still in a state of suppressed agitation, appeared to be threatening a fresh outbreak. A somewhat obscure intrigue, which appears to have been directed by Plotina and Matidias, bestowed the Empire on Hadrian, under these critical circumstances.

It was an excellent choice, for though he was a man of equivocal morals, he was a great ruler. Intellectual, intelligent, and eager to learn, he had more greatness of mind than any of the Cæsars, and from Augustus down to Diocletian, no other Emperor did so much for the constitution as he did. His administrative capacities were extraordinary, as, although he administered too much, according to our ideas, he nevertheless administered well. He was the first to give the Imperial Government a definite organisation, and his reign marked a principal epoch in the history of Roman law.

Up till his time, the house of the sovereign had been the house of the highest personage in the land,--an establishment composed like any other of servants, freemen, and private secretaries. Hadrian organised the palace, and for the future it was necessary to be a knight in order to arrive at any office in the household, and the servants in Cæsar's palace became public functionaries. A permanent council of the prince, composed chiefly of jurisconsults, undertook all definite public powers; those senators who were specially attached to the government already were made comtes (counts); everything was done through regular offices, in the constitution of which the senate took its proper share, and not through the direct will of the prince. It was still a state of despotism, but of despotism which was analogous to that of the old French royalty, kept in check by independent councils, law courts, and magistrates.

The social ameliorations which took place were still more important, for everywhere a really good and great spirit of liberalism was manifested; the position of slaves was guaranteed, the condition of women was raised, paternal authority was restricted within certain limits, and every remaining vestige of human sacrifices was abolished. The Emperor's personal character responded to the excellence of these reforms, for he was most affable towards those of lowly station, and never would allow himself to be deprived of his greatest pleasure--that of being amiable--under the pretext of his imperial greatness.

In spite of all his failings, he was a man of a quick, unbiassed, original intellect. He admired Epictetus and understood him, without, however, feeling obliged to follow out his maxims. Nothing escaped him, and he wished to know everything; and as he did not possess that insolent pride and that fixed determination which altogether excluded the true Roman from all knowledge of the rest of the world, Hadrian had a strong inclination for everything that was strange, and would wittily make fun of it. The East, above all, had strong attractions for him, for he saw through Eastern impostures and charlatanism, and they amused him. He was initiated into all their absurd rites, fabricated oracles, compounded antidotes, and made fun of the medicine; and, like Nero, he was a royal man of letters and an artist, while the ease with which he learnt painting, sculpture, and architecture was surprising. Besides this, he also wrote tolerable poetry, but his taste was not pure, and he had his favourite authors and singular preferences; in a word, he was a literary smatterer, and a theatrical architect. He adopted no system of religion or of philosophy, but neither did he deny any of them, and his distinguished mind was like a weather-cock, which moves its position with every wind; his elegant farewell to life, which he murmured a few moments before his death,

"Animula, vagula, blandula,"

gives us his measure exactly. For him, whatever he examined into ended in a joke, and he had a smile for everything that was an object of his curiosity. The sovereign power itself could not make him more than half serious, and his bearing always had that easy grace and negligence of the most fluctuating and changeable man that ever existed.

All that naturally made him tolerant. He did not indeed abrogate the laws which indirectly struck

6

at Christianity, and so put it continually in the wrong, and he even allowed them to be applied more than once, but he personally very much modified the effect of them. In this respect he was superior to Trajan, who, without being a philosopher, had very fixed ideas about State affairs, and to Antoninus and Marcus Aurelius, who were men of high principle, but who thought that they did right in persecuting the Christians. In this respect Hadrian's laxity of morals was not without a good effect, for it is the peculiarity of a monarchy that the defects of sovereigns serve the public good even more than their better qualities. The immorality of a really witty man, of a crowned Lucian, who looks upon the whole world as some frivolous game, was more favourable to liberty than the serious gravity and lofty morality of the most perfect Emperors.

Hadrian's first care was to settle the difficulties of the accession which Trajan had left him. He was a distinguished military writer, but no great general. He clearly saw how impossible it would be to keep the newly conquered provinces of Armenia, Mesopotamia, and Assyria, and so he gave them up. That must have been a very solemn hour, when, for the first time, the Roman eagles retreated, and when the Empire was obliged to acknowledge that it had exceeded its programme of conquest, but it was an act of wisdom. Persia was as inaccessible for Rome as Germany, and the mighty expeditions which Crassus, Trajan, and Julian had led into that part of the world failed, whilst less ambitious expeditions--those of Lucius Verus and of Septimus Severus, whose object was not to attack the very foundations of the Parthian Empire, but to detach the feudatory provinces which bordered on the Roman Empire, from it-- succeeded. The difficulty of relinquishing conquests, which was so humiliating to the Roman mind, was increased by the uncertainty of Hadrian's adoption by Trajan. Lucius Quietus and Marcus Turbo had an almost equal right to adoption with him, from the importance of the last commission that they had carried out. Quiltus was killed, and it may be supposed that, eager as they were to find out the deaths of their enemies, in order to discover in them a token of celestial vengeance, the Jews saw in this tragic death a punishment for the new evils which the fierce Berber had inflicted on them.

Hadrian was a year on his return journey to Rome, thus at once beginning those roaming habits which were to make his reign one continual rush through the provinces of the Empire. After another year devoted to the gravest cares of government administration, which was fertile in constitutional reforms, he started on an official progress (tour) and successively visited Gaul, the banks of the Rhine, Britain, Spain, Mauritania and Carthage, and his vanity and antiquarian tastes made him dream of becoming the founder of cities, and the restorer of ancient monuments. Moreover, he did not approve of the idleness of garrison life for soldiers, and he found a means of occupying them in great public works, and that is the reason for these innumerable constructions--roads, ports, theatres--temples which date from Hadrian's reign. He was surrounded by a crowd of architects, engineers, and artists, who were enrolled like a legion. In each province where he set his foot, everything seemed to be restored and to spring up afresh. At the Emperor's suggestion, enormous public companies were formed to carry out great public works, and generally the State appeared as a shareholder. If any city had the smallest title to celebrity, or was mentioned in classical authors, it was sure to be restored by this archæological Cæsar; thus he beautified Carthage and added a new quarter to it; and in all directions towns which had fallen into decay rose up from their ruins, and took the name of Colonia Ælia Hadriana.

After a short stay in Rome, during which he extended the circumference of the pomoesium (the symbolical, not actual wall of the city), he started, during the course of the year 121, on another journey, which lasted nearly four years and a half, and during which he visited nearly the whole of the East. This journey was even more brilliant than the former, and it might have been said that the ancient world was coming to life again beneath the footsteps of a beneficent deity. Thoroughly acquainted with ancient history, Hadrian wished to see everything, was interested in everything, and wished to have everything restored that had existed formerly. Men sought to revive the lost arts, in order to please him, and a neo-Egyptian style became the fashion, as did also a neo-Phoenician. Philosophers, rhetoricians, critics, swarmed about him, and he was another Nero without his follies. A number of ancient civilisations which had disappeared, aspired after their resuscitation, not actually, but in the writings of historians and archæologists. Thus Herennius, Philo of Byblos, tried--very likely under the direct inspiration of the Emperor himself--to discover ancient Phoenicia. New fêtes, the Hadrianian Games, which the Greeks introduced--recalled for the last time the splendour of Hellenic life; it was like a universal restoration to life of the ancient world, a brilliant restoration indeed, but it was hardly sincere, and rather theatrical, and each country found, in Rome's comprehensive bosom, its former titles of nobility again, and became attached to them. Whilst studying that singular spectacle, one cannot help thinking of that and of resurrection from the dead which our own century has witnessed, when, in a moment of universal goodwill, it began to restore all things, to rebuild Gothic churches, to re-establish pilgrimages which had fallen into neglect, and to reintroduce fêtes and ancient customs.

Hadrian, the turn of whose mind was more Greek than Roman, favoured this ecclectic movement, and contributed powerfully towards it, and what he did in Asia Minor was really prodigious. Cyzicus, Nicaea, Nicomedia, sprang up again, and everywhere temples of the most splendid works of architecture, immortalised the memory of that learned sovereign, who seemed to wish that another world, in all the freshness of its youth, should date from him. Syria was no less favoured. Antioch and Daphne became the most delightful places of abode in the world, and the combinations of picturesque architecture, the imagination of the landscape painter, and the forces of hydraulic power, were exhausted there. Even Palmyra was partially restored by the great imperial architect, and, like a number of other towns, took the name of Hadrianople from him.

Never had the world had so much enjoyment or so much hope. The Barbarians beyond the Rhine and the Danube were hardly thought about, for the liberal spirit of the Emperor caused a sort of feeling of universal contentment; and the Jews themselves were divided into two parties. Those who were massed at Bether, and in the villages south of Jerusalem, seemed to be possessed by a sort of sombre rage. Their one idea was to take the city, to which access was denied them, by force, and to restore to the hill which God had chosen for his own, its former honours. Hadrian had not at first been obnoxious to the more moderate party, especially to the half-Christian, half-Essenian survivors of the Egyptian catastrophe under Trojan. They could imagine that he had ordered the death of Quietus to punish him for his cruelty towards the Jews, and perhaps for a moment they conceived the hope that the ecclectic Emperor would undertake the restoration of Israel, as another caprice amongst so many. In order to inculcate these ideas, a pious Alexandrian took a form of thought that had already been consecrated by success. In his poem he supposed that a Sybil, sister of Isis, had had a disordered vision of the trials which were reserved for the latter centuries.

Hatred for Rome bursts out at the very beginning:--

O Virgin, enervated and wealthy daughter of Latin Rome, who hast joined the ranks of slavery whilst drunk with wine, for what nuptials hast thou reserved thyself! How often will a cruel mistress tear these delicate locks!

The author, who is a Jew and a Christian at the same time, looks upon Rome as the natural enemy of the saints, and to Hadrian alone he pays the homage of admiring him thoroughly. After enumerating the Roman Emperors, from Julius Cæsar to Trajan, by the nonsensical process of ghematria, the Sybil sees a man ascend the throne--

Who has a skull of silver, who will give his name to a sea. He will be unequalled in every way and know everything. Under thy reign O excellent, O eminent and brilliant sovereign, and under thy offspring, the events which I am about to mention shall take place.

According to custom, the Sybil now unfolds the most gloomy pictures; every scourge is let loose at the same time, and mankind becomes altogether corrupt. These are the throes of the Messianic child-birth. Nero, who had been dead for more than fifty years, was still the author's nightmare. That destructive dragon, that actor, that murderer of his own relations, and assassin of the chosen people, that kindler of numberless wars, will return to put himself on an equality with God. He weaves the darkest plots amongst the Medes and Persians who have received him; and, borne through the air by the Fates, he will soon arrive to be once more the scourge of the West. The author vomits forth an invective, fiercer still than that with which he began:--

Unstable, corrupted, reserved for the very lowest destinies, the beginning and end of all suffering, because in thy bosom creation perishes and is born again continually, source of all evil, scourge, the point where everything ends for mortal men, who has ever loved thee? who does not detest thee internally? what dethroned king has ended his life in peace within thy walls? By thee the whole world has been changed in its innermost recesses. Formerly there existed in the human breast a splendour like a brilliant sun; it was the rays of the unanimous spirits of the prophets, which brought to all the nourishment of life, and thou hast destroyed these good gifts. Therefore, O imperious mistress, origin and cause of all these great evils, sword and disaster shall fall on thee . . . Listen, O scourge of humanity, to the harsh voice which announces thy misfortunes.

A divine race of blessed Jews, come down from heaven, shall inhabit Jerusalem, which shall extend as far as Jaffa, and rise to the clouds. There shall be no more trumpets or war, but on every side eternal trophies shall rise, trophies consecrating victories over evil.

Then there shall come down from heaven once more an extraordinary man, who has stretched out his hands over a fruitful wood, the best of the Hebrews, who formerly stopped the sun in his course by his beautiful words and his holy lips.

This is doubtlessly Jesus, Jesus, in an allegorical manner, by his crucifixion, playing the part of Moses stretching out his arms, and of Joshua the saviour of the people.

Cease at length to break thy heart, O daughter of divine race, O treasure, O only lovely flower, delightful brightness, exquisite plant, cherished germ, gracious and beautiful city of Judea, always filled with the sound of inspired hymns. The impure feet of the Greeks, their hearts filled with plots, shall not tread thy soil under them, but thou shalt be surrounded by the respect of thy illustrious children, who shall deck thy table in accord with the sacred muses, with sacrifices of all kinds, and with pious prayers. Then the just who have suffered pain and anguish will find more pleasure than they have suffered ills. These, on the contrary, who have hurled their sacrilegious blasphemies towards heaven will be reduced to silence and to hide themselves till the face of the world changes. A rain of burning fire shall descend from heaven, and men shall no longer gather in the sweet fruits of the earth; there shall be no more sowing, no more labour, till mortals recognise the supreme, immortal, eternal God, and till they leave off honouring mortals, dogs, and vultures, to which Egypt wishes men to offer the homage of profane mouths and foolish lips. Only the sacred soil of the Hebrews will bear those things that are refused to other men; brooks of honey shall burst from the rocks and springs, and milk like ambrosia shall flow for the just, because they have hoped, with ardent piety and lively faith, in one only God, the Father of all things, One and Supreme.

At last the runaway parricide, who has been announced three times, enters upon the scene again. The monster inundates the earth with blood, and captures Rome, causing such a conflagration as has never been seen. There is a universal overturning of everything in the world; all kings and aristocrats perish, in order to prepare peace for just men--that is to say, for Jews and Christians, and the author's joy at the destruction of Rome breaks out a third time.:--

Parricides, leave your pride and your culpable haughtiness, for you have reserved your shameful embraces for children and placed young girls, who were pure up till that time, in houses of ill-fame where they have been subjected to the vilest outrages . . . Keep silence, wicked and unhappy city, thou that wast formerly full of laughter. In thy bosom the sacred virgins will no longer find again the holy fire that they kept alive, for that fire, which was so preciously preserved, went out of its own accord, when I saw for the second time another temple fall to the ground, given up to the flames by impure hands, a temple which flourishes still, a permanent sanctuary of God, built by the saints, and incorruptible throughout eternity . . . It is not, indeed, a god made of common clay that this race adores; amongst them the skilful workman does not shape marble; and gold, which is so often employed to seduce men's souls, is no object of their worship, but by their sacrifices and their holy hecatombs they honour the great God whose breath animates every living thing.

A chosen man, the Messiah, descends from heaven, carries off the victory over the Pagans, builds the city beloved of God, which springs up again more brilliant than the sun, and founds within it an incarnate temple, a tower with a frontage of several stadii, which reaches up to the clouds, so that all the faithful may see the glory of God. The seats of ancient civilisation--Babylon, Egypt, Greece, Rome-- disappear one after the other; above all, the giant monuments of Egypt fall over and cover the earth; but a linen-clad priest converts his compatriots, persuades them to abandon their ancient rites, and to build a temple to the true God. That, however, does not arrest the destruction of the ancient world, for the constellations come in contact with each other, the celestial bodies fall to the earth, and the heavens remain starless.

Thus we see that under Hadrian there existed in Egypt a body of pious monotheists for whom the Jews were still pre-eminently the just and holy people, in whose eyes the destruction of the Temple of Jerusalem was an unpardonable crime, and the real cause of the fall of the Roman Empire; who entertained a cause for hatred and calumny against Flavius; who hoped for the restoration of the Temple and of Jerusalem; who looked on the Messiah as a man chosen of God; who saw that Messiah in Jesus, and who read the Apocalypse of St John. Since then, Egypt has for a long time made us grow accustomed to great singularities in all that concerns Jewish and Christian history, and its religious development did not proceed pari passu with that of the rest of the world. Accents such as we have just heard could hardly find an echo either in pure Judaism or in the Churches of St Paul. Judea, above all, would never have consented, even for an hour, either to regard Hadrian as the best of men, or to found such hopes upon him.

# CHAPTER II

### THE RE-BUILDING OF JERUSALEM

During his peregrinations in Syria, Hadrian saw the site where Jerusalem had stood. For fifty-two years the city remained in its state of desolation, and offered to the eye nothing but a heap of immense blocks of stone lying one on another. Only a few groups of miserable houses, belonging to Christians for the most part, stood out from the top of Mount Sion, and the site of the Temple was full of jackals. One day, when Rabbi Aquiba came on a pilgrimage to the spot with some companions, a jackal rushed out of the place where the Holy of Holies had stood. The pilgrims burst into tears, and said to each other: "What! is this the place of which it is written that any profane person who approaches it shall be put to death, and here are jackals roaming about in it!" Aquiba, however, burst out laughing, and proved to them the connexion between the various prophecies so clearly, that they all exclaimed: "Aquiba, thou hast consoled us! Aquiba, thou has consoled us!"

These ruins inspired Hadrian with the thought with which all ruins inspired him, namely, the desire to rebuild the ruined city, to colonise it, and to give it his name or that of his family Thus Judea would become once more restored to cultivation, and Jerusalem, raised to the rank of a fortified place in the hands of the Romans, would serve as a check upon the Jewish population. All the towns of Syria, moreover,--Gerasae, Damascus, Gaza, Peah,--were being rebuilt in the Roman manner, and were inaugurating new eras. Jerusalem was too celebrated to be an exception to this movement of historical dilettantism and of general restoration.

It is very probable that if the Jews had been less unanimous in their views, if some Philo of Byblos had existed amongst them to represent to him the Jewish past as nothing but a glorious and interesting variety amongst the different literatures, religions, and philosophies of humanity, the curious and intelligent Hadrian would have been delighted, and re-built the Temple, not exactly as the Doctors of the Law would have wished it, but in his ecclectic manner, like the great amateur of ancient religions that he was. The Talmud is full of conversations between Hadrian and celebrated rabbis, which of course are fictitious, but which correspond very well with the character of this Emperor, who had a great mind, and was a great talker, very fond of asking questions, curious about strange matters, anxious to know everything, that he might make fun of it afterwards. But the greatest insult that can be shown to absolutists is to be tolerant towards them, and in this respect the Jews resembled exactly the enthusiastic Catholics of our days. Men of such convictions will not be satisfied with their reasonable share; they want to be everything. It is the highest indignity for a religion which looks upon itself as the only true one to be treated like a sect amongst many others; they would rather be outside the pale of the law, and be persecuted; and this violent situation appears to them a mark of divinity. The faithful are pleased at persecution, for in the very fact that men hate them, they see a mark of their prerogative, for the wickedness of men, according to them, is naturally an enemy to truth.

There is nothing to prove that when Hadrian wished to rebuild Jerusalem, be consulted the Jews, or wished to come to any agreement with them. Nothing either leads us to believe that he entered into any relations with the Christians of Palestine, who, externally, had less to distinguish them from the Jews than Christians of other countries. In the eyes of the Christians, all the prophecies of Jesus would have been overthrown if the Temple had been rebuilt, whilst amongst the Jews there was a general expectation that it would be rebuilt. The Judaism of Jabneh, without Temple, without worship, had appeared as a short interregnum, and all uses which presupposed a still existing Temple, were preserved. The priests continued to receive the tithe, and the precepts of Levitical purity were still strictly observed. The obligatory sacrifices were adjourned till the Temple should be rebuilt, but Jews alone could rebuild it; the slightest deviation from any injunction of the Law, would have been quite enough to cause the cry of Sacrilege to be raised. It was better in the eyes of pious Jews, to see the sanctuary inhabited by beasts of prey, than to owe its re-building to a profane jester, who afterwards would not have failed to utter some epigram about those extraordinary gods whose altars he nevertheless restored.

For the Jews, Jerusalem was something almost as sacred as the Temple itself. In fact, they did not distinguish one from the other, and at that time they already called the city by the name of Beth hammigdas. The only feeling which the hasidim felt when they heard that the city of God was going to be rebuilt without them, was one of rage. It was very shortly after the extermination which Quietus and Turbo had carried out, and Judea was weighed down by an extraordinary terror. It was impossible to move, but from that time forward it was allowable to foresee in the future a revolution that should be even more terrible than those which had preceded it,

About 122, probably, Hadrian issued his orders, and the reconstruction commenced. The population consisted chiefly of veterans and strangers, and no doubt it was not necessary to keep out the Jews, as their own feelings would have been enough to have caused them to flee. It seems that, on the other hand, the Christians returned to the city with a certain amount of eagerness, as soon as it was habitable. It was divided into seven quarters or groups of houses, each with an amphodarch over it. As the immense foundations of the Temple were still in existence, that seemed the fittest spot on which to place the principal sanctuary of the new city. Hadrian took care that the temples which be erected in the Eastern Provinces should call to mind the Roman religion, and the connection between the provinces and the metropolis. In order to point out the victory of Rome over a local religion, the temple was dedicated to Jupiter Capitolinus, the god of Rome, above all others a god whose attitude and grave demeanour recalled Jehovah, and to whom, since the time of Vespasian, the Jews had paid tribute. It was a tetrastyle building, and like in most of the temples erected by Hadrian, the entablature of the pediment was broken by an arch, under which was placed a colossal figure of the god.

The worship of Venus was no less intended than that of Jupiter by the choice of the founder of the colony. Everywhere Hadrian built temples to her, the protectress of Rome, and the most important of his personal edifices was that great temple of Venus and Rome, the remains of which can still be seen near the Coliseum, and so it was only natural that Jerusalem should have, by the side of its temple of Jupiter Capitolinus its temple of Venus and Rome. It happened that this second temple was not far from Golgotha, and this fact gave rise, later on, to singular reflections on the part of the Christians. In this close approximation they thought that they discerned an insult to Christianity, of which Hadrian certainly never thought. The works proceeded but slowly, and when, two years later, Hadrian retraced his steps towards the West, the new Colonia Ælia Capitolina was still more a project than a reality.

For a long time a strange story went about amongst the Christians, to the effect that a Greek of Sinope, called Aquila, who was nominated overseer of the works for the rebuilding of Ælia by Hadrian, knew the disciples of the Apostles at Jerusalem, and that, struck by their piety and their miracles, he was baptised. But no change in his morals followed on his change of religion. He was given to the follies of astrology; every day he cast his horoscope, and was looked upon as a learned man of the first order in such matters. The Christians regarded all such practices with an unfavourable eye, and the heads of the Church addressed remonstrances to their new brother, who took no notice of them, and set himself up against the views of the Church. Astrology led him into grave errors on fatalism and man's destiny, and his incoherent mind tried to associate together things which were utterly opposed to each other.

The Church saw that he could not possibly merit salvation, and he was driven outside the pale, in consequence of which he always entertained a profound hatred for her. His relations with Adrian may have been the reason why that Emperor seems to have had such an intimate acquaintance with the Christians.

# CHAPTER III

### THE RELATIVE TOLERANCE OF HADRIAN--THE FIRST APOLOGISTS

The period was one of toleration. Colleges and religious societies were on the increase everywhere. In A.D. 124, the Emperor received a letter from Quintus Licinus Silvanus Granianus, Pro-consul of Asia, which was written in a spirit very much the same as that which dictated to Pliny that beautiful letter of his, so worthy of an upright man. Roman functionaries of any weight all objected to a procedure which admitted implicit crimes that individuals were supposed to have committed, because of the mere name they bore. Granianus showed how unjust it was to condemn Christians on the strength of vague rumours, which were the fruit of popular imagination, without being able to convict them of any distinct crime, except that of their Christian profession. The drawing by lot for the appointments to the Consular Provinces having taken place a short time afterwards, Caius Minutius Fundanus, a philosopher and distinguished man of letters, a friend of Pliny and of Plutarch, who introduces him as asking questions in one of his philosophic dialogues, succeeded Granianus, and Hadrian answered Fundanus by the following rescript

Hadrian to Minicius Fundanus. I have received the letter which Licinius Granianus, an illustrious man whom you have succeeded, wrote to me. The matter seemed to me to demand inquiry, for fear lest people who are otherwise peacefully disposed may be disquieted, and so a free field be opened to calumniators. If therefore the people of your province have, as they say, any weighty accusations to bring against the Christians, and if they can maintain their accusation before the tribunals, I do not forbid them to take legal steps; but I will not allow them to go on sending petitions and raising tumultuous cries. In such a case, the best thing is for you yourself to hear the matter. Therefore if anyone comes forward as an accuser, and proves that the Christians break the laws, sentence them to punishments commensurate to the gravity of the offence. But, by Hercules, if anybody denounces one of them calumniously, punish the libeller still more severely according to the degree of his malice.

It would seem that Hadrian gave similar replies to other questions of the same nature. Libels against the Christians were multiplying everywhere, and they paid very well, for the informer got part of the property of the accused if he were found guilty. Above all, in Asia the provincial meetings, accompanied by public games, almost invariably ended in executions. To crown the festivities, the crowd would demand the execution of some unfortunate creatures. The redoubtable cry:--The Christians to the lions, became quite common in the theatres, and it was a very rare occurrence when the authorities did not yield to the clamour of the assembled people. As has been seen, the Emperor opposed such wickedness as far as he could; the laws of the Empire were really alone to blame for giving substance to vague accusations which the caprice of the multitude interpreted according to its own pleasure.

Hadrian spent the winter of 125-126 at Athens. In this meeting-place for all men of culture he always experienced the greatest enjoyment. Greece had become the plaything to amuse all Roman men of letters. Quite reassured as to the political consequences, they adopted, the easy liberalism of restoring the Pnyx, the popular assemblies, the Areopagus; of raising statues to the great men of the past, of giving the ancient constitutions another trial, and of setting up Pan-hellenism--the confederation of the so-called free states-- again. Athens was the centre of all this childish folly. Enlightened Mæcenases--especially Herod Atticus, one of the most distinguished spirits of the age, and those Philopappuses, the last descendants of the Kings of Commagene and of the Seleucidæ, who about this time raised a monument on the hill of the Museum, which still exists,--had taken up their abode there.

This world of professors, of philosophers, and of men of enlightenment, was Hadrian's real element. His vanity, his talent, his taste for brilliant conversation, were quite at their ease amongst colleagues whom he honoured by making himself their equal, without, however, the least yielding his royal prerogative. He was a clever arguer, and thought that he only owed the advantage, which of course always remained with him, to his own personal talent. It was an unlucky thing for those who hurt his feelings or who got the better of him in an argument. Then the Nero whom, though carefully hidden, he always had in him, suddenly woke up. The number of new professorial chairs that he founded, or of literary, pensions that he bestowed, is incalculable. He took his titles of archon and agonothetes quite seriously. He himself drew up a constitution for Athens, by combining in equal proportions the laws of Draco and of Solon, and wished to see whether they would work satisfactorily. The whole city was restored. The temple of the Olympian Jupiter, near the river Ilisus, begun by Pisistratus, and one of the wonders of the world, was finished, and the Emperor took the title of Olympian. Within the city, a vast square, surrounded by temples, porticos, gymnasia, establishments for public instruction, dated from him. All that is certainly very far from possessing the perfection of the Acropolis, but these buildings excelled anything that had ever been seen, by the rarity of their marbles and the richness of their decorations. A central Pantheon contained a catalogue of the temples which the Emperor had built, repaired or ornamented, and of the gilts which he had bestowed on Greek or barbarian cities; and a library, open to every Athenian citizen, occupied a special wing. On an arch, which remains to our day, Hadrian was made equal to Theseus, and one of the Athenian quarters was called Hadrianopolis.

Hadrian's intellectual activity was sincere, but he lacked a scientific mind. In those meetings of sophists all questions, human and divine, were discussed, but none were settled, nor does it seem that they went so far as complete rationalism. In Greece the Emperor was looked upon as a very religious and even as a superstitious man. He wished to be initiated into the mysteries of Eleusis, and, on the whole, Paganism was the only thing that gained by all this. As, however, liberty of discussion is a good thing, good always results from it. Phlegon, Hadrian's secretary, knew a little about the legend concerning Jesus, and the wide expansion which the spirit of controversy assumed under Hadrian gave rise to an altogether new species of Christian literature, the apologetic, which sheds so much brightness over the century of the Antonines.

Christianity, preached at Athens seventy-two years previously, had borne its fruit. The Church at Athens had never had the adherents nor the stability of certain others; its peculiar character was to produce individual Christian thinkers, and so apologetic literature naturally sprang from it.

Several persons, who were specially called philosophers, had adhered to the doctrine of Jesus. The name philosopher implied severity of morals, and a distinguishing dress,--a sort of cloak, which sometimes made the wearer the subject of the jokes, but more often, the respect, of the passers by. When they embraced Christianity, the philosophers took care neither to repudiate their name nor their dress, and from that there proceeded a category of Christians unknown till then. Writers and talkers by profession, these converted philosophers became, from the very first outset, the doctors and polemical members of the sect. Initiated into Greek culture, they were far greater dialecticians, and had greater aptitude for controversy, than purely apostolic preachers, and from that moment Christianity had its advocates. They disputed, and others disputed with them. In the eyes of the government they were much more likely to be taken seriously than those good people without any education who were initiated into an eastern superstition. Up till then Christianity had never ventured to address a direct demand to the Roman authorities to have the false position in which it found itself rectified. Certainly the characters of some of the preceding Emperors did not by any means invite any such explanations, and any petition would have been rejected unread. Hadrian's curiosity, his facile mind, the idea that he was pleased when some new fact or argument was presented to him, now encouraged overtures which would have had no object under Trajan. To this was added an aristocratic feeling, which was alike flattering to the sovereign and the apologist. Christianity was already beginning to let the policy be seen which it was to follow from the beginning of the fourth century, and which consisted, above all, in treating with sovereigns over the heads of the people. "We will dispute with you, but it is too much honour for the common herd to give it our reasons."

The first attempt of this sort was the work of a certain Quadratus, an important personage of the third Christian generation, and of whom it was said that he had even been a disciple of the Apostles. He sent an apology for Christianity to the Emperor, which has been lost, but which was very highly thought of during the first centuries. He complained of the annoyances to which wicked people subjected the faithful, and proved the harmlessness of the Christian faith. He went still further, and tried to convert Hadrian by arguments drawn from the miracles of Jesus. Quadratus alleged that even in his time some of those whom the Saviour had healed or raised from the dead were known to be alive. Hadrian would certainly have been very much amused to see one of those venerable centenarians, and his freedman Phlegon would have embellished his treatise on cases of longevity with the fact, but it would not have convinced him. He had witnessed so many other miracles, and the only conclusion he drew from them was that the number of incredible things in this world is infinite. In his teratological collections, Phlegon had introduced several of the miracles of Jesus, and certainly Hadrian had conversed with him more than once on this subject.

Another apology, written by a certain Aristides, an Athenian philosopher and a convert to Christianity, was also presented to Hadrian. Nothing is known about it, except that amongst the Christians it was held in as high repute as the one of which Quadratus was the author. Those who had the opportunity of reading it, admired its eloquence, the author's intellect, and the good use he made of passages from heathen philosophers to prove the truth of the doctrines of Jesus.

These writings, striking as they were by their novelty, could not be without their effect upon the

Emperor. Singular ideas with regard to religion crossed his mind, and it seems that more than once he showed Christianity marks of true respect. He had a large number of temples or basilicas built, which bore no inscription, nor had they any known purpose. Most of them were unfinished or not dedicated, and they were called hadrianea, and these empty, statueless temples lead us to believe that Hadrian had them built so purposely. In the third century, after Alexander Severus had really wished to build a temple to Christ, the Christians spread the idea that Hadrian had determined to do the same, and that the hadrianea were to have served to introduce the new religion. They said that Hadrian had been stopped because, on consulting the sacred oracles, it was found that if such a temple were built the whole world would turn Christian, so that all the other temples would be abandoned. Several of these hadrianea, especially those of the Tiberiad and Alexandria, became, in fact, churches in the fourth century.

Even the follies of Hadrian with Antinous possessed an element of the Christian apology. Such a monstrosity seems the culminating point of the reign of the devil. That recent God, whom all the world knew, was made great use of to beat down the other gods, who were more ancient and so easy to lay hold of. The Church triumphed, and later the period of Hadrian was looked upon as the luminous point in a splendid epoch in which the truths of Christianity shone without any obstacle in all eyes. They owed some thanks to a sovereign whose defects and good qualities had had such favourable results. His immorality, his superstitions, his empty initiation into impure mysteries were not forgotten; but in spite of all, Hadrian remained, at any rate in the opinion of part of Christianity, a serious man, endowed with rare virtues, who gave to the world the last of its beautiful days.

# CHAPTER IV

### THE JOHANNINE WRITINGS

It would appear that about this time a mystical book was heard of, of which the faithful thought a great deal; it was a new Gospel, far superior, as was said, to those which were already known; a really spiritual Gospel, as much above St Mark and St Matthew as mind is above matter. That Gospel was the production of that disciple whom Jesus loved,--of St John, who, having been his most intimate friend, naturally knew much that others were ignorant of, so as even to be able on many points to rectify the manner in which they had represented matters. The text in question was a great contrast to the simplicity of the first Evangelical narratives; it put forward much higher pretensions, and certainly it was the intention of those who propagated it that it should replace those humble accounts of the life of Jesus with which men had been contented hitherto. The writer, who was still spoken of in a mysterious manner, had leant upon the Master's breast, and alone knew the divine secrets of his heart.

This new work came from Ephesus, that is to say, from one of the principal homes of the dogmatic elaboration of the Christian religion. It is quite possible that John may have passed his old age and finished his days in that city. It is at least quite certain that in the early ages of Christianity there were those at Ephesus who claimed St John as their own, and did all they could for his aggrandisement. St Paul had his Churches which ardently cherished his memory, and St Peter and St James had also their families by spiritual adoption. The adherents of St John, therefore, wished that he should be in the same position; they desired to make him St Peter's equal; and it was maintained, to the detriment of the latter, that he had held the first rank in the Gospel history, and as the existing accounts did not bear out these pretensions sufficiently, recourse was had to one of those pious frauds which, in those days, caused nobody any scruples. Thus it may be explained how, shortly after the apostolic age, there emerged obscurely from Ephesus a class of books which were destined to obtain in later times a higher rank than all the other inspired writings in the system of Christian theology.

It can never be admitted that St John himself wrote these words, and it is even very doubtful whether they were written with his consent in his old age, and by any one of his own immediate surroundings. It seems most probable that one of the Apostle's disciples who was a depository of many of his reminiscences, thought himself authorised to speak and to write in his name--some twenty-five or thirty years after his death--what he had not, to his followers' great regret, authoritatively put down during his lifetime. Certainly Ephesus had its own traditions about the life of Jesus, and, if I may venture to say so, a life of Jesus for its own particular use. These traditions dwelt especially in the memory of two persons who were looked upon, in those parts, as the two highest authorities with regard to Gospel history, namely, one man who bore the same name as the Apostle John, and who was called Presbeteros Johannes, and a certain Aristion, who knew many of the Lord's discourses by heart. At about this time Papias consulted these two men as oracles, and carefully noted their traditions, which he intended to insert into his great work, The Discourses of the Lord. One remarkable feature in the Presbuteros was the opinion which he gave regarding St Mark's Gospel. He considered it altogether insufficient, and written in complete ignorance of the exact order of the events of the life of Jesus. Presbuteros Johannes evidently thought that he knew the real facts much better, and, if he really wrote it, his tradition must altogether differ from the plan of that of Mark.

We are inclined to think that the fourth Gospel represents the traditions of this Presbuteros and of Aristion, which might go back as far as the Apostle John. It seems, moreover, that to prepare the way for this pious fraud a preliminary Catholic Epistle, attributed to John, was published preliminarily, which was intended to accustom the people of Asia to the style which it was intended to make them receive as that of the Apostle. In it the attack against the Docetæ--who at that time formed the great danger to Christianity in Asia--was opened. An ostentatious stress was laid on the value of the Apostle's testimony, as he had been an eye-witness of the Gospel facts. The author, who is a skilful writer after his own fashion, has very likely imitated the style of St John's conversation, and that small work is conceived in a grand and lofty spirit, in spite of some Elcesaitic peculiarities. Its doctrine is excellent, and it inculcates mutual charity, love for mankind, and hatred for a corrupt world; and its touching, vehement, and penetrating style is absolutely the same as that of the Gospel; and its faults--its prolixity, and dryness--the results of interminable discourses full of abstruse metaphysics and personal allegations, are far less striking in the Epistle.

'The style of the pseudo-Johannic writings is something quite by itself, no model for which existed before the Presbuteros. It has been too much admired; for whilst it is ardent and occasionally even sublime, it is somewhat inflated, false, and obscure, and it altogether lacks simplicity. The author relates nothing, he merely demonstrates dogmatically, and his long account of miracles, and of those discussions which turn on misapprehensions, and in which the opponents of Jesus are made to play the parts of idiots, are most fatiguing. How preferable to all this verbiose pathos is the charming style, altogether Hebrew as it is, of the Sermon on the Mount, and that clearness of narrative which constitutes the charm of the first Evangelists. No need for them to repeat continually that they that saw it bear record, and that their record is true; for their sincerity, unconscious of any possible objection, has not that feverish thirst for those repeated attestations which go to prove that incredulity and doubt have already sprung up. One might almost say, from the slightly exalted style of this new narrator, that he feared that he might not be believed, and that he sought to dupe the religious belief of his readers by his own emphatic assertions.

Whilst insisting strongly on his qualities as an eye-witness, and on the value of his own testimony, the author of the fourth Gospel never once says I, John, for his name does not appear in the whole course of the work, but only figures as its title; but there is not the slightest doubt that John is the disciple intended or designated in a hidden manner in different passages of the book, nor is there any doubt that the forger intended to cause it to be believed that that mysterious personage was the author of the book. It was merely one of those small literary artifices such as Plato is so fond of affecting, and the result is that the recital is often very elaborate, and contains investigations, observations, and literary pranks which are totally unworthy of an Apostle. Thus John mentions himself without mentioning his own name, and praises himself without doing it openly, and he does not debar himself from that literary method which consists in showing, in a very carefully-managed semi-light, those secrets which one keeps to oneself without revealing them to every chance corner. How pleasant it is to be guessed at, and to allow others to draw conclusions favourable to oneself, to which oneself only gives a half expression.

The two objects which the author had in view were to prove the divinity of Jesus to those who did not believe in Him, but, even more than that, to make a new system of Christianity prevail. As miracles were the proofs, above all others, of His divine mission, he improves on the accounts of the wonders that disfigure the earlier Gospels. It seems on the other hand that Cerinthus was one of the manufacturers of these strange books. He had become almost like John's spectre, and the versatility of his mind now attracted him to, and then repelled him from, those ideas which were agitating religious circles at Ephesus, so that at the same time he was regarded as the adversary whom the Johannine writings were striving to combat, and as the veritable author of those writings; and the obscurity that reigns over the Johannine question is so dense that it cannot be said that it must be wrong to attribute the authorship to him. If it be a fact, it would correspond very well to what we know of Cerinthus, who was in the habit of covering his thoughts under the cloak of an apostolic name, and it would explain the mystery as to what became of that book for nearly fifty years, and the vehement opposition which it encountered. The ardour with which Epphianius combats this opinion would lead us to believe that it is not without foundation, for in those dark days everything was possible; and if the Church, when it venerates the fourth Gospel as the work of St John, is the dupe of him whom she looks upon as one of her most dangerous enemies, it is not, after all, any stranger than so many other errors which make up the web of the religious history of humanity.

It is quite certain, however, that the author is at the same time the father and the adversary of Gnosticism, the enemy of those who allowed the real human nature of Jesus to evaporate in a cloudy Docetism, and the accomplice of those who would make him a mere divine abstraction. Dogmatic minds are never more severe than they are towards those from whom they are divided by a mere shade of difference. That Anti-Christ whom the pseudo-John represents as already in existence, that monster who is the very negation of Jesus, and whom he cannot distinguish from the errors of Docetism, is almost he himself. How often in cursing others, does one curse oneself! and thus in the bosom of the Church, the personality of Jesus became the object of fierce strife. On the one hand there was no checking the torrent which carried away every one to the most exaggerated ideas as to the divinity of the founder of Christianity, and on the other hand it was of the highest importance to uphold the true character of Jesus, and to oppose the tendency which so many Christians had towards that sickly idealism which was soon to end in Gnosticism. Many spoke of the Eon Christos as of a being that was quite distinct from the man called Jesus, to whom it was united for a time, and whom it abandoned at the moment of the crucifixion. Cerinthus had maintained this, and so did Basilides, and to such heresy a tangible Word must be opposed, and this was just what the new Gospel did. The Jesus whom it preaches is in some respects more historical than the Jesus of the other evangelists, and yet he is only a metaphysical first principle, a pure conception of transcendental theosophy. This may shock our tastes, but theology has not the same requirements as æsthetics, and the conscience of Christianity, after trying

16

in vain for a hundred years to settle what right conception it should make to itself of Jesus, at last found rest.

> *In the beginning was the Word, and the Word was with God, and the Word was God.*
> *The same was in the beginning with God.*
> *All things were made by him; and without him was not anything made that was made.*
> *In loin was life; and the life was the light of men.*
> *And the light shineth in darkness; and the darkness comprehended it not.*
> *There was a man sent from God, whose name was John.*
> *The same came for a witness, to bear witness of the Light, that all men through him might believe.*
> *He was not that Light, but was sent to bear witness of that Light.*
> *That was the true Light, which lighteth every man that cometh into the world.*
> *He was in the world, and the world was made by him, and the world knew him not.*
> *He came unto his own, and his own received him not.*
> *But as many as received him, to them gave he power to became the sons of God, even to them that believe on his name Which were born, not of blood, nor of the will of the flesh, nor of the will of man, but of God.*
> *And the Word was made flesh, and dwelt among us (and we beheld his glory, the glory as of the only begotten of the Father), full of grace and truth.*--St John, I. 1-14.

What follows is not less surprising. We have before us a life of Jesus which is very different to that which the writings of Mark, Luke. or the pseudo-Matthew have put before us. It is evident that those three Gospels, and others of the same sort, were but little known in Asia, or at any rate had very little authority there. During his lifetime, John no doubt, was in the habit of relating the life of Jesus on a totally different plan to that slight Galilean outline which the traditionists of Batanea had created, and which served as a model after them. He knew that Jerusalem had been one of the chief centres for Jesus' activity, and he drew persons and details which the first narrators were unacquainted with, or had neglected. As to Jesus' discourses as given in the Galilean tradition, the Church at Ephesus, supposing that they were known there, allowed them to fall into oblivion. According to the spirit of the age, there was no more difficulty in putting discourses into Jesus' mouth which were intended to found such and such doctrines, than the authors of the Thora and the prophets of old found in making God speak according to their own prejudices.

Thus the fourth Gospel came to be produced, and though it is of no value if we wish to know how Jesus spoke, it is superior to the synoptic Gospels in the order of facts. The various visits of Jesus to Jerusalem, the institution of the eucharist, his anticipated agony, a number of circumstances relating to the Passion, the Resurrection and his life after he had risen; certain minute details, e. g., concerning Cana, the apostle Philip, the brothers of Jesus, the mention of Cleopas as a member of his family, are so many features, which assure to the pseudo John an historical superiority over Mark and pseudo-Matthew. Many of these details might be drawn from John's own accounts of events which had been preserved, whilst others sprang from traditions which neither Mark nor he who amplified his narrative under the name of Matthew, knew anything about. In several cases in fact, where pseudo-John deviates from the arrangement of the synoptic narrative, he presents singular features of agreement with Luke, and the Gospel according to the Hebrews. Moreover, several features of the fourth Gospel are to be found in Justin, and in the pseudo-Clementine romance, although neither Justin nor the author of the romance knew the fourth Gospel. It is clear, therefore, that, besides the synoptists, there existed a collection of traditions, and of ready-made expressions, which were, so to speak, scattered about in the atmosphere, which the fourth Gospel partially represents to us; and to treat this Gospel as an artificial composition with no traditional basis is to mistake its character just as seriously as when it is looked upon as a document at first hand, and original from beginning to end.

The discourses which are put into the mouth of Jesus in the fourth Gospel are certainly artificial, and without any traditional basis, and criticism ought to put them on the same footing as the discourses with which Plato honours Socrates. There are two striking omissions in it; it does not contain a single parable, nor a single apocalyptic discourse about the end of the world, and the appearance of the Messiah; and one feels that the hopes of an approaching manifestation in the clouds had partly lost their force. According to the fourth Gospel, Jesus' real return after he had left the world, would be the sending of the Paraclete, his other self, who would comfort his disciples for his departure. The author takes refuge in metaphysics, because material hopes, already at times appear to him mere chimeras, and the same thing seems to have happened to St Paul. The taste for abstraction was the reason why then little weight was attached to what is regarded as the most really divine in Jesus. Instead of that refined feeling of the poetry of the earth which fills the Galilean Gospels, we find here nothing but a dry system of metaphysics and dialectics, which turn on the ambiguity between the literal and the figurative sense. In the fourth Gospel, indeed, Jesus speaks for himself, for he makes use of language which no one could be expected to understand, as he uses words in a different sense to their general acceptation, and then is angry because he is not understood. This false situation produces an impression of fatigue in the end, and at last one thinks that the Jews were excusable for not comprehending those new mysteries which were presented to them in such an obscure fashion.

These defects are the consequence of the exaggerated attitude which the author has given to Jesus, for it is one which naturally excludes anything natural. He declares Himself to be the Truth and the Life, and that he is God, and that no one can come to the Father but by him. Such weighty and solemn assertions could not be made without an air of shocking presumption. In the synoptic Gospels, he does not assert that he is God, but reveals himself by the charm of his impersonal discourses, whereas, in this one, the Deity argues in order that he may prove its Divinity. It is as if the rose were to dispute in order to prove that it is fragrant. The author, in such a case, cares so little for probabilities that at times there is nothing to indicate where the discourses of Jesus finish and the dissertations of the narrator begin. At other times he reports conversations at which nobody could have been present, and one feels that his true object is not to relate words which were really spoken, but that above all he wishes to impress the mark of authority on some cherished ideas of his own, by putting them into the mouth of the Divine Master.

# CHAPTER V

## THE BEGINNING OF A SYSTEM OF CHRISTIAN PHILOSOPHY

That religious philosophy which serves as the basis for all those exemplications which were so foreign to the mind of Jesus, is by no means original. Philo had expounded its essential principles more harmoniously and logically. Both Philo and the author of the fourth Gospel attach very little importance to the fulfilment of the words of the Messiah or to apocalyptic belief. All the imagination of popular Judaism is replaced by metaphysics in the structure of which Egyptian theology and Greek philosophy had their full share. The idea of Incarnate Reason, i.e., of Divine Reason assuming a finite shape, is quite Egyptian. From the earliest ages down to the Hermes Trismegistos books, Egypt proclaimed a God, living alone in substance, but eternally begetting his own likeness, one, and yet twofold at the same time. The Sun is that firstborn, proceeding eternally from the Father, that Word who made everything that exists, and without whom nothing has been made. On the other hand, it had for a long time been the tendency of Judaism, in order to escape from its somewhat dry system of theology, to create a variety of the Deity by personifying abstract attributes, such as Wisdom, the Divine Word, Majesty, the Presence. Already in the ancient books of wisdom, in the Proverbs and in Job, Wisdom personified plays the part of an assessor to the Divinity. Metaphysics and Theology, so severely restrained by the Mosaic law, took their revenge, and would soon invade everything.

The expression dabar, in Chaldean, memara, i.e., "the Word," become especially fruitful. Ancient texts made God speak on all solemn occasions, which justified such phrases as: "God does everything by His word; God created everything by His word." Thus people were led to regard "the Word" as a divine minister, as an intermediary by whom God works on the outer world. By degrees this intermediary was substituted for God in visible manifestations in apparitions, in all relations of the Deity with man. That mode of expression had much greater consequences amongst the Egyptian Jews who spoke Greek. The word Logos, corresponding to the Hebrew dabar, and the Chaldean memara, and having the twofold meaning of The Word, and also of Reason, enabled them to enter into a whole world of ideas in which they reunited, on the one hand, the symbols of Egyptian theology which are mentioned above, and on the other, certain Platonic speculations. The Alexandrine Book of Wisdom, which is attributed to Solomon, already delights in those theories. There the Logos appears as the metationos, the assessor of the Deity, and it soon became usual to attribute to the Logos all that ancient Jewish philosophy, said of the Divine Wisdom. The Breath of God (rouah), which is mentioned at the beginning of Genesis as life giving, becomes a sort of Demiurge by the side of dabar.

Philo combined such forms of expression with his notions of Greek philosophy. His Logos is the Divine in the universe--it is an exteriorised God; it is the legislator, the revealer, the organ of God as regards spiritual man. It is the Spirit of God,--the wisdom of Holy Scripture. Philo has no idea of the Messiah, and establishes no connection between his Logos and the divine being which was dreamt of by his compatriots in Palestine. He never departs from the abstract, and for him the Logos is the place of spirits just as space is the place of bodies; and he goes so far as to call it "a second God," or "the man of God;" that is to say, God, considered as anthropomorphous. The end of man is to know the Logos, to contemplate reason; that is to say, God and the universe. By that knowledge man finds life, the true manna that nourishes.

Although such ideas were, by their origin, as far as possible, removed from Messianic ideas, one can see that a sort of effusion might be brought about between them. The possibility of a full incarnation of the Logos is quite in accordance with Philo's ideas. It was a generally received opinion, that in all the various divine manifestations in which God wished to make Himself visible, it was the Logos who assumed the human form. These ideas were favoured by numerous passages in the most ancient historical books, where "the Angel of Jehovah," Maleak Jehovah, indicates the divine appearance which shows itself to men, when God, who is ordinarily hidden, reveals Himself to their eyes. This Maleak Jehovah frequently does not differ at all from Jehovah himself, and it is a habit with translators of a certain period to substitute that word for Jehovah, whenever God is supposed to have appeared on earth, and thus the Logos came to play the part of an anthropomorphous God. It was therefore natural that the appearance of the Messiah should be attributed to the Logos, and that Messiah should be considered as the incarnate Logos.

Certainly the author of the book of Daniel had no idea that his Son of Man had anything in common with the Divine Wisdom, whom, in his time, some Jewish thinkers were already elevating into a personality; but with the Christians the two ideas were very easily reconciled. Already, in the Apocalypse the triumphant Messiah is called "the Word of God," and in St Paul's later Epistles, Jesus is separated almost altogether from his human nature. In the fourth Gospel, the identification of Christ and the Word is an accomplished fact, and the national avenger of the Jews has totally disappeared under a metaphysical conception; henceforth, Jesus is the Son of God, not by virtue of a simple Hebrew metaphor, but in a strictly theological sense. The very slight reputation in which the writings of Philo were held in Palestine, and amongst the popular classes of Jews, must be the only explanation why Christianity did not bring about such a necessary evolution till such a late period, but this evolution took effect in several directions simultaneously, for St Justin has a theory which is very similar to that of pseudo-John, and yet he did not take it from the gospel that bears his name.

Side by side with the theory of the Logos and of the Holy Spirit was developed that of the Paraclete, who was not kept very distinct from the former. In Philo's philosophy, Paraclete was an epithet of, or an equivalent for, Logos. For Christians he became a sort of substitute for Jesus, proceeding from the Father as he did, and who was to console the disciples for the absence of their Master when he should have left them. That Spirit of Truth, which the world does not know, is to inspire the Church throughout all time. Such a manner of raising abstract ideas into personalities was quite in keeping with the fashion of the time. Allius Aristides, who was a contemporary and a compatriot of the author of the fourth Gospel, expresses himself in his sermon on Athene, in a manner which is hardly distinguishable from that of the Christians:--

She dwells in her father, closely united to his essence; she breathes in him, and is his companion and counsellor. She sits at his right hand and is the supreme minister of his orders, and their wills are so conjoined that to her may be attributed all her father's acts.

It is well known that Isis played the same part with regard to Ammon.

The profound revolution which each idea must introduce into the manner of looking at the life of Jesus is self-evident. For the future he was to have no more human qualities, and would know neither temptation nor weakness. In him everything existed before it happened; everything was settled a priori, nothing happened naturally; He knew his life in advance, and did not pray to God to save him from that fatal hour. One fails to see why he lived this life which was forced upon him, gone through merely as a part, without any sincerity about it. But, however revolting such a change may be to our feelings, it was necessary. The Christian conscience desired more and more that everything in the life of their founder should be supernatural. Marcion, without knowing the writings of pseudo-John, did exactly the same thing as he did, for he manipulated St Luke's Gospel till he had got rid of every trace of Judaism or reality from it. Gnosticism was to go even further, for that school Jesus was to become a mere entity, an won, an eternal intelligence that had never lived. Valentine and Basilides really only go a step further along the road on which the author of the fourth Gospel had gone. They all use the same specific terms: Father (in the metaphysical sense), Word, Arche, Life, Truth, Grace, Paraclete, Fulness, Only Son. The origins of Gnosticism and that of the fourth Gospel meet in the far distance; they both start from the same point in the horizon without our being able, on account of the distance, to point out more precisely the circumstances which attended their common appearance, for in such a thick atmosphere the visual rays of criticism are apt to become confused.

Naturally, the conditions under which a book became known, were so different then to what they are now, that we must not be surprised at singularities which would be inexplicable in these days. Nothing is more deceiving than to imagine to ourselves writings of that date, as a printed book, offered to everybody's reading, with newspapers to review the new work, favourably or otherwise. All the Gospels were written for restricted circles of readers, and no edition aspired to being the last and final one. It was a species of literature which could be practised at will, like the legends of Hasan and Hossein amongst the modern Persians. The fourth Gospel was a composition of the same order. In the first instance the author may have written it for himself and a few friends as his conception of the life of Jesus. There is no doubt that he communicated his work with great reserve to those who knew that such a work could not have originated with John, and up till the end of the second century the work encountered nothing but indifference and opposition. During that time the Gospels which are called synoptic give the outlines of the life of Jesus, and the tone of the discourses attributed to him is that of Matthew and Luke. Towards the end of the second century, however, the idea of a fourth Gospel was accepted, and pious legends and mystic reasons were discovered to support this tetrad.

To sum up, it seems most probable that, several years after the Apostle John's death, somebody or other determined to write in his name, and to his honour a gospel that should represent, or should be supposed to represent, his traditions. The definite success of the book was just as brilliant as its beginning had been obscure. This fourth Gospel, the last to appear, which had been manipulated in so many respects, where Philonian tirades were substituted for the actual discourses of Jesus, took more than half a century to assume its place, but then it triumphed all along the line. It was very convenient for the theological and apologetic requirements of the time, to have a sort of metaphysical drama which could escape from the objections which a Celsus was already preparing, instead of a small, very human history of a Jewish prophet in Galilee. The Divine Word in the bosom of God; the Word creating all things; the Word made flesh, dwelling amongst men, so that certain privileged mortals had the happiness of seeing and even touching him! flaying regard to the especial turn of the Greek intellect, which seized upon Christianity at a very early date, this seemed most sublime, and a whole system of theology after the manner of Plotinus might be extracted from it. The freshness of the Galilean idyl, illuminated by the sun of the kingdom of God, was but little to the taste of true Greeks. They naturally preferred a gospel in which they were transported to abstract dreams, and from which the belief in the approaching end of the world was banished. In the present instance, there was no mention of a material appearance in the clouds, no more parables, no persons possessed of devils, nothing about the kingdom of God or of the Jewish Messiah, no millennium, not even any more Judaism. It was forgotten and condemned; the Jews are held up to reprobation as enemies of the truth, for they would not receive the Word which came amongst them. The author will know nothing of them, except that they killed Jesus; just as amongst the modern Persian Shiies, the name of Arab is synonymous with an impious man and a miscreant, as Arabs slew the holiest amongst the founders of Islam.

The literary faults of the fourth Gospel thus make up its general character. It frees Christianity from a number of its original chains, and gives it free scope for that which is essential for any innovation, i.e., ingratitude towards what has preceded it. The author seriously believes that no prophet ever came out of Galilee. Christian metaphysics already sketched out in the Epistle to the Colossians, and in that which is called the Epistle to the Ephesians, are fully developed in the fourth Gospel. It would be dear to all those who, humiliated at the fact that Jesus was a Jew, would neither hear of Judeo-Christianity, nor of the millennium, and who would have liked to have burnt the Apocalypse. Thus the fourth Gospel takes its stand, in the great work of separating Judaism from Christianity, far above St Paul. He wished that Jesus had abrogated the Law, but he never denies that he lived under the Law. His disciple St Luke, by a certain devout improvement, presents Jesus to our view as fulfilling all the precepts of the Law. St Paul thought that the prerogatives of the Jews were still very great; whilst, on the other hand, the fourth Gospel shows a great antipathy to the Jews, both as a nation and as a religious society. Jesus, speaking to them, says: "Your law," and there is no question now of justification by faith or by works, for the problem has gone far beyond the bounds of those simple terms. The knowledge of the truth and science have now become essential, and men are to be saved by their gnosis, their initiation into certain secret mysteries, so that Christianity has become a sort of hidden philosophy which certainly neither Paul nor Peter ever dreamt of.

The future belonged altogether to transcendental idealism. This Gospel, attributed to the well-beloved disciple, which transports us at first into the pure atmosphere of the Spirit and of Love, which substitutes the love of truth for everything else, and proclaims the sway of Mount Gerizim and of Jerusalem equally at an end, was bound in time to become the fundamental Gospel of Christianity. No doubt it will be said that this was a great historical and literary error; but it was also a theological and political necessity of the first order. The idealist is always the worst revolutionary, and a definite rupture with Judaism was the indispensable condition of the foundation of a new religious system. The only chance of success that Christianity had was, that it should be a perfectly pure form of worship, independent of any material creed. "God is a spirit, and they that worship Him must worship Him in spirit and in truth." If Jesus is understood in such a manner, he is no longer a prophet, and Christianity under that aspect is no longer a sect of Judaism; it becomes the Religion of Reason, and thus it came about that the fourth Gospel imparted consistency and stability to the Apostolic work. Whoever its author was, he was the cleverest of all the apologists. He was, successful in bringing Christianity out of its old beaten tracks that had got too narrow for it; which all the Christian orators of our time have attempted in vain. He betrayed Jesus in order to save him, just as those preachers do who put on a pretence of liberalism, and even of socialism, to win over those who may possibly be seduced by those words through a pious fraud. The author of the fourth Gospel has withdrawn Jesus from the Jewish reality in which he was lost, and has launched him boldly into metaphysics. That purely spiritual philosophical manner of understanding Christianity, to the detriment of facts, and to the profit of the mind, found in this singular book an example to encourage, and authority to justify it.

Only those who are not well acquainted with religious history will be surprised to see such a part filled by an anonymous writer in the history of Christianity. The editors of the Thora, most of the Psalmists, the author of the book of Daniel, the first editor of the Hebrew Gospel, the author of the Epistles to Timothy and Titus, which are attributed to St Paul, gave works of the greatest importance to the world, and yet they are anonymous. If it is admitted that the Gospel and the Epistle which is so closely connected with it are the work of Presbuteros Johannes, it might be thought that it would be all the less difficult to accept those writings as the works of St John, since the forger's name was John, and he appears often to have been confounded with the apostle. He was merely called Presbuteros, and after the falsely so-called Epistle of John, there are two short letters by some one who seems to call himself "The Elder." The style, the thoughts, and the doctrine are very nearly the same as in the Gospel and Epistle said to be written by St John. We believe that Presbuteros was also the author of them; but this time he did not wish to pass off his slight works as those of John; and, like the letters to Timothy and Titus, they ought rather to be called specimens of the pastoral style than Epistles. Thus, in the first, the name of the person for whom it is intended is left a blank, and is filled up with the formula: "To the Elect Lady;" In the second, the person to whom it is written is given as Gaius, which was often the equivalent for our So and so. In these short letters some resemblance to the pseudo-Johannine Epistle, and to those of St Paul, has been discovered, and it is probable that our Presbuteros has sometimes concealed his identity behind these anonymous presbuteroi who had seen the Apostles, and whose traditions Irenæus so mysteriously reproduces.

At the end of the third century two tombs were mentioned at Ephesus, which were held in the highest veneration, and to both of which the name of John was given. In the fourth century when, from the passage in Papias, the idea of the distinct existence of Presbuteros Johannes was being firmly established, one of these tombs was allotted to the Apostle and the other to the Presbuteros. We shall never know the exact truth of those extraordinary combinations in which history, legends, fable, and, up to a certain point, pious fraud were all united in proportions which we cannot separate now. An Ephesian called Polycrates, who was destined to become, one day, with his whole family, the centre of Asiatic Christianity, was converted A.D. 131, and this Polycrates fully admitted the pseudo-Johannine tradition, and cited it most confidently in his old age.

Everybody allows that the last chapter of the fourth Epistle is an appendix which was added after the work had been written, though possibly it was added by the author himself; in any case, the source from which it was drawn is the same. It was desirable to complete all that had to do with the relations between Peter, and John by some touching feature, and the author shows that he is a great partisan of Peter, and does his best to pay homage to him in his rank as supreme pastor which was attributed to him in various degrees. He also makes a point of explaining the views that prevailed about the long life of John, and of showing how the aged Apostle might die without the edifice of the promises of Jesus and of Christian hopes falling into ruins at his decease. Men began to fear that the unequalled privilege of those who had seen the Word during his life on earth might discourage future generations, and already that profound saying, which was attributed to Jesus, "Blessed are those that have not seen and yet have believed," was incorporated into a Gospel anecdote.

With the Johannine writings begins the era of Christian philosophy and of abstract speculation, which had hitherto found but little room in the world, whilst at the same time dogmatic intolerance increased most lamentably. The more fact of saluting a heretic was represented as an act of communion with him. How far we are from Jesus here! He wished us to salute everybody, even at the risk of saluting the unworthy, in imitation of our Heavenly Father, who looks on all with a paternal eye, but yet how it was to be obligatory to ascertain the opinions of anyone before saluting him. The essence of Christianity was transferred to the realm of dogma; gnosis was every thing, and salvation consisted in knowing Jesus and knowing him in a certain manner. Theology, that is to say, a rather unwholesome application of the intellect, was the result of the fourth Gospel, and the Byzantine world, from the beginning of the fourth century, wore itself out by this study, which would have had just as fatal consequences for the West if the demon of subtility had not found firmer muscles and less volatile brains to deal with.

In this matter Christianity decidedly turned its back on Judaism; and Gnosticism, which is the highest expression of speculative Christianity, had some reason for pushing its hatred of Judaism to the highest point. The latter made religion consist in outward observances, and left everything that bordered on philosophic dogma as a matter of private opinion, and the Cabala and Pantheism would naturally find an easy development by the side of observances which were carried to the minutest details. A Jewish friend of mine, as liberal a thinker as can be found, and at the same time a scrupulous Talmudist, said to me, "One makes up for the other. Close observances are a compensation for wideness of ideas, and our poor humanity has not enough intelligence to support liberty in two directions at the same time. You Christians did wrong in insisting that the bonds of communion should consist in certain beliefs, for a man does what he pleases, but he believes what he can, and I would rather go without pork all my life, than be obliged to believe in the dogmas of the Trinity and of the Incarnation."

# CHAPTER VI

## PROGRESS OF THE EPISCOPATE

The progress of the Church in discipline and in her hierarchy was in proportion to her progress in dogma. Like every living body she developed an astonishing instinctive cleverness in completing all that was still wanting for her solid foundation and her perfect equilibrium. As the hopes for the end of the world, and of the reappearance of Messiah become fainter, Christianity obeyed two natural tendencies; the one to reconcile itself with the empire as well as it could, and then to organise itself so that it might become lasting. The first church at Jerusalem, the first churches of St Paul, were not established with any view to their endurance, for they were only so many assemblies of the saints at the end of the world, who were preparing themselves by prayer and divine rapture for the coming of God. The Church felt that now the time had come for her to be an abiding city and a real society.

The strangest movement that ever took place in a democracy took place within the Church. The ecclesia, the voluntary reunion of persons meeting on a footing of equality amongst themselves, is the most democratic thing that can be imagined; but the ecclesia, the club has that fatal defect which causes every association of that kind to fall to pieces, and that defect is anarchy, the ease with which schisms arise. But more fatal still are the contentions for pre-eminence in the midst of small confraternities which have been founded on an altogether spontaneous vocation. That seeking after the highest place was the principal evil which affected the Christian churches, and which caused the greatest trouble to the simple and faithful members of the flock. It was thought that this danger might be prevented by supposing that Jesus, in a similar case, could have taken a child and said to the contending parties, "This is the greatest." On different occasions the Master had, as was said, opposed the ecclesiastical primacy, brotherly as it was, to that of the depositories of worldly authority who were given to assume a masterful manner. But that was not enough, and the association of Christians would soon be menaced by a great danger, if some salutary institution did not rescue it from its own internal abuses.

Every ecclesia presupposes a small hierarchy of its own,--what we call in these days a committee, a president, assessors, and a small body of assistants. Democratic clubs take care that these functions shall be as limited as possible both as to time and privileges, but there is something precarious in that, and the result has been that no club has outlived the circumstances which called it into existence. The synagogues had a much longer continuance, although the personnel was never a clerical body. The reason for that is, the subordinate position which Judaism held for centuries, so that the pressure from without counterbalanced the unwholesome effects of internal divisions. If the Christian Church had suffered from the same want of discretion, she would no doubt have missed her destinies; and if ecclesiastical powers had continued to be regarded as emanating from the Church itself, she would have lost all her hieretic and theocratic character; but, on the other hand, it was fated that the clergy should monpolise the Christian Church, and should substitute itself in her place. Speaking in her name, representing itself in everything as her sole authorised agents, that clergy would constitute her strength, but would at the same time be her canker-worm, and the chief cause of her future decline.

History has no example of a more wonderful transformation. What happened in the Christian Church is just what would happen in a club, if the members were to abdicate all their powers into the hands of the committee, and the committee to abdicate theirs into the hands of the president, so that neither those who were present, nor the seniors in office, would have any deliberative voice; no influence, no control over the management of the funds, so that the president might be able to say "I, alone, am the club." The presbutoroi (the elders), the episcopi (the officers, overseers), very soon became the only representatives of the church, and very shortly after another and even more important revolution took place. Amongst the presbutoroi and the episcopi there was one, who, because he habitually took the principal seat, became presbuteros, or episcopos par excellence. The form of worship contributed very powerfully towards this. Only one priest could be celebrant of the eucharist at the same time, and he obtained an extreme importance; and that episcopos became, with surprising rapidity, the chief amongst the presbyterate and those of the whole church. His seat, placed apart from the others, assumed the shape of an arm-chair, and became the seat of honour--the sign of the Primacy, and from that time such church had only one chief presbyter, who called himself episcopos, to the exclusion of all the rest. By his side were to be seen a number of deacons, widows, a council of presbutoroi, but the great step had been taken; the bishop had become the sole successor of the apostles, the professor of the true religion was altogether thrust aside. The apostolic authority, which was supposed to be transmitted by the imposition of hands, had altogether destroyed the authority of the community, and then, the bishops of the different churches coming to an understanding amongst themselves, will, as we shall see, constitute the universal church into a sort of oligarchy, which will hold synods, censure its own members, decide questions of faith, and, in herself, constitute a real sovereign power.

Within a hundred years the change was almost accomplished. When Hegesippus, during the second half of the second century, travelled throughout the whole of Christendom, he remarked nothing but the bishops; everything for him resolves itself into a question of canonical succession, and the living sentiment of the churches exists no longer. We shall show that that revolution was not accomplished without protest, and that the author of the Pastor, for example, still tried, in opposition to the growing influence of the bishops to maintain the equal authority of the presbutoroi. But aristocratic tendency carried the day; on the one side were the shepherds, on the other, the flocks. The primitive equality existed no longer, and, henceforth the Church was to be nothing but an instrument in the hands of those who directed her; and they held their authority, not from the community in general, but from a spiritual heredity from a pretended transmission which went back in a continuous line to the apostles themselves. It will be seen at once that the representative system could not even in the slightest degree become the system of the Christian Church.

In one sense it may be said that this was a falling off, a diminution of that spontaneity which had hitherto been such a creative power. It was evident that ecclesiastical forms were about to absorb and to destroy the work of Jesus, and that all free manifestations of Christian life would soon be stopped. Under episcopal censorship, the glossolalia, prophecy, the creation of legends, and the production of new sacred books, would be withered-up faculties, and the Christian graces would be reduced to official sacraments. In another sense, however, such a transformation was an essential condition of the strength of Christianity. In the first place, the concentration of their forces became necessary, as soon as the churches became at all numerous, for relations between these small religious societies would have been quite impossible, unless they had an accredited representative who was entitled to act for them. It is, moreover, an incontestable fact that, without episcopacy, the churches which were momentarily drawn together by the recollections of Jesus would have been dispersed again. The divergencies of doctrine, the different turns of thought, and, above all, rivalries and unsatisfied self-love, would have had a vast influence on disunion and dismemberment, and, at the end of three or four centuries, Christianity would have come to an end like the worship of Nithras, or, like so many sects, have ended, being unable to withstand the force of time. Democracy is at times eminently creative, but only on the conditions that conservative and aristocratic institutions spring from it, which prevent the revolutionary fever to be prolonged indefinitely.

That is the real miracle of infant Christianity. It produced order, a hierarchy, authority, obedience from the ready subjection of men's wits; it organised the crowd and disciplined anarchy, and it was the spirit of Jesus with which his disciples were so deeply imbued, that spirit of meekness, of self-denial, of forgetfulness of the present, the pursuit of spiritual joys which destroys ambition, that preference for a childlike mind, these words of Jesus, "Let him who would be first among you become as he that serveth," that worked this miracle. The impression which the apostles left behind them also did its share. They and their immediate vicars had an uncontested power over all the churches, and as episcopacy was supposed to have inherited apostolic powers, the apostles governed even after their death. The idea that the chief officer of the Church holds his mandate from the members of that Church who have appointed does not appear once in the literature of that time, and thus the Church escaped, by the supernatural origin of her power, from anything that is defective in delegated authority. Legislative and executive authority can come from the majority, but the sacraments and the dispensations of divine grace have nothing to do with universal suffrage, for such privileges come only from heaven, or, according to the Christian formularies, from Jesus Christ, who is himself the source of all grace and of all good.

Properly speaking, the bishops had never been nominated by the whole community. It was quite sufficient for the spontaneous enthusiasm of the first churches that he should be designated by the Holy Ghost, that is to say, that electoral means should be employed which extreme simplicity alone could excuse. After the apostolic age, and when it became necessary that that sort of divine right with which the apostles and their immediate disciples were supposed to be invested, should be supplemented by some ecclesiastical decision, the elders chose their president from among themselves, and submitted his name to popular approval. As this choice was never made without the people's opinion having been consulted in the first instance, this approval, or rather the vote by raising the hand, was nothing more than a mere formality, but it was enough to preserve the recollection of the gospel ideal, according to which the spirit of Jesus essentially dwelt in the community. The election of deacons was also of a double nature, for they were nominated by the bishop, but they had to be approved by the community before the choice could be valid. It is a general law of the Church that the inferior never nominates his superior, and this is one of the reasons which still gives to the Church, in spite of the totally different tendency of modern democracy, such a great power of reaction.

In the churches of St Paul this movement towards a hierarchy and an episcopate was particularly felt. The Jewish Christian churches, which had less life in them, remained synagogues, and did not land so immediately in clericalism, and thus, by writings attributed to St Paul, arguments for the doctrine which it was sought to inculcate were created. There was no controverting an epistle of St Paul, and several passages of the authentic epistles of that apostle already taught the doctrine of a hierarchy and of the authority of the elders. For the sake of even more decisive arguments, three short epistles were forged, which were supposed to have been written by Paul to his disciples Timothy and Titus. The author of these apocryphal epistles had not got the Acts of the Apostles, and he only knew the apostolical journeys of St Paul vaguely and not in detail. As very few people had any more precise notions about them, he was not gravely compromised, and, besides, at that period, there was such a lack of critical feeling, that it did not strike any one that texts must necessarily agree. Some passages in those three epistles are also so beautiful, that the question might be asked, whether the forger had not some authentic letters of St Paul in his possession which he embodied in his apocryphal compositions?

These three short works, evidently the production of the same pen, and written most likely at Rome, are a sort of treatise on ecclesiastical duties, a first attempt at false decretals, a code for the use of churchmen. Episcopacy is a grand thing, and the bishop is a sort of model of perfection, set up before his subordinates. He must, therefore, be irreprehensible in the eyes of the faithful and of others; he must be sober, chaste, amiable, kind, just, not proud, given to hospitality, moderate, inoffensive, free from avarice, and earning his livelihood honestly. He may drink a little wine for his health's sake, but he must not marry more than once. His family must be grave like himself, and his sons submissive, respectful and free from any suspicion of dissolute morals. If anyone cannot rule his own house, how can he take care of the Church of God? Orthodox above everything; attached to the true faith, the sworn enemy of error, and he is to preach and to teach. For such functions neither a novice must be taken, lest such a rapid elevation should make him be lifted up with pride, nor a man capable of a sudden attack of rage, nor anyone exercising a calling that is looked down upon, for even unbelievers ought to respect a bishop, and not have anything to say against him.

The deacons must be as perfect as the bishops; serious, not double-tongued, drinking little wine, not given to filthy lucre, holding the mystery of the faith in a pure conscience. So must their wives be grave, not slanderers, sober, faithful in all things. They must be husbands of one wife, ruling their children and their own houses well, and as a trial is necessary for such difficult functions, no one is to be raised to them till after a kind of noviciate.

Widows were an order in the Church, and their first duty was to perform their household duties, if they had any to fulfil. They who were widows indeed, and desolate, ought to trust in God, and continue in supplications and prayers night and day, but such as live in pleasure are dead whilst they live. These interesting but feeble persons were subject to a certain rule; they had a female superior, and every Church had side by side with its deacon also its widow, whose duty it was to watch over the younger widows, and to exercise a sort of female diaconate. The author of the false epistles to Timothy and Titus wishes that the widow thus chosen should not be less than sixty years of age, having been the wife of one man, well reported of for good works, if she have brought up children, if she have lodged strangers, if she have washed the saints' feet. But he instructs Timothy to refuse the younger widows, for they will wax wanton against Christ and marry, and withal they learn to be idle, wandering about front house to house, and not only idle, but tattlers also, and busybodies, speaking things that they ought not. "I will therefore that the younger widows marry, bear children, guide the house, give none occasion to the adversary to speak reproachfully. For some are already turned aside from Satan." (1 Tim. v. passim.) Widows who are without means are to be relieved by the Church, whereas those who have relations are to be kept at their expense.

From all this may be seen what a complete society the church already was. Every class had its own particular functions in it, and represented a member of the social body; all had their duties, were it only slaves, the power of the precepts of Jesus was to be admired by their virtuous life. As examples of this, slaves were particularly relied upon, and they are reminded that none can honour the new doctrine more than they. If their master were a heathen, they were to be counted worthy of all honour, that the name of God and His doctrine might not be blasphemed; and if they had believing masters, they were not to be despised because they were brethren, but they were to be served because they were faithful and beloved, partakers of the benefit. Of course there was no word of emancipation. The aged men were to be sober, grave, temperate, sound in faith; the aged women, in behaviour such as becometh holiness, not false accusers, not given to much wine, teachers of good things, for they should be like catechists and teach the young women to be sober and love their husbands and their children; to be discreet, chaste, keepers at home, good, obedient to their own husbands, that the word of God might not be blasphemed. The young men were to be exhorted to be sober minded.

The married women's part is humble indeed, but still a beautiful one.

In like manner also, that women adorn themselves in modest apparel, with shame-facedness and sobriety, not with plaited hair, or gold or pearls or costly array; but (which becometh women professing godliness) with good works. Let the woman learn in silence with all subjection. But I suffer not a woman to teach nor to usurp authority over the man, but to be in silence. For Adam was first formed, then Eve, and Adam was not deceived, but the woman being deceived was in the transgression. Nevertheless she shall be saved in childbearing, if she continue in faith and charity and holiness with sobriety." (1 Tim. ii. 9-15.)

All should be submissive, as subjects, obedient, gentle, inoffensive, enemies to revolution, interested in the preservation of public peace, which alone would allow them to lead their usual holy life. They need not be surprised if they were persecuted, that was the natural lot of Christians. They ought to be the very opposite to the heathen. A man who only follows the dictates of nature is the slave of his desires, carried away by sensuality, wicked, envious, hating and hateful. The transformation which makes the natural man one of the elect is not the fruit of his own merits, but of the compassion of Jesus Christ, and of the efficacy of his sacraments.

This short Epistle, which is already quite Catholic, is a true type of the ecclesiastical spirit, and for seventeen centuries has been the manual of the clergy, the gospel of seminaries, the rule of that spiritual policy as it is carried out by the Church. Piety, which is the soul of the priest, the secret of his resignation and of his authority, is the foundation of this spirit. But the pious priest has his rights; those of reprimanding and correcting--respectfully, indeed, in the case of old people, but always with firmness. "Preach the word, be instant in season and out of season, reprove, rebuke, exhort with all long-suffering and doctrine" (2 Tim. iv. 2). Simple in his life, asking only for food and raiment, the "Man of God," as our author calls him, was sure to be an austere man, often an imperious ruler. "Rebuke not an elder, but intreat him as a father, and the younger men as brethren; the elder women as mothers, the younger as sisters, in all purity." After that one feels that the Christian society cannot be a free one, for every individual member of it will be watched and censured, and will not have the right to say to his fellow citizen, "What business is my belief or my conduct to you? I am doing you no wrong." The believer will say that in believing differently to what he does, he is being wronged, and that he has the right of protesting. Against such an idea, so totally opposed to liberty, princes and laymen must rightly soon revolt. "A man that is an heretic after a first and second admonition reject." (Titus iii. 10.) Nothing could be less in keeping with the maxims of a man of liberal education. The heretic has his opinions as well as you, and he may be right, and politeness certainly requires you to pretend to believe so in his presence. The world is no monastery, and the advantages, which, as is alleged, are obtained by censure and accusation, bring more evils in their train than they hoped to avoid.

In the Epistles to Timothy and Titus orthodoxy has made as much progress as episcopacy. Already there is a rule of faith, a Catholic centre in existence, which excludes everything that does not receive its life from the parent stem as dead branches. The heretic is a guilty man, a dangerous being, who must be avoided. He has every vice, is capable of every crime, and acts which are even laudable in the Christian priest, such as a wish to direct women on certain matters of internal government, are acts of usurpation on his part. The heretics of whom the author is thinking seem to be the Essenes, the Elkasaites, Jewish Christian sectaries, who occupied their minds with genealogies of æons, who insisted on certain acts of abstinence and on a rigorous distinction between things pure and impure, who condemned marriage, and who yet were great seducers of women, whom they overcame by holding out to them the bait of an easy way of expiating their sins, whilst at the same time they might procure sensual pleasure for themselves. One feels that this is approaching very near to Gnosticism and Montanism, and the proposition, that the resurrection was already an accomplished fact reminds us of Marcion. The expressions concerning Christ's Divinity gain in vigour, though still surrounded by some difficulties. A wonderful amount of good practical sense rules everything, however. The ardent pietist who composed these Epistles, does not for a moment lose himself in the dangerous paths of quietism. He repeats almost ad nauseam that the woman has no right to devote herself to the spiritual life, except when she has no family duties to fulfil; that her principal duty is to bear and bring up children, and that it is a mistake to pretend to serve the Church if everything is not well ordered at home. Besides that, the piety which our author preaches is one of an altogether spiritual kind, and is one of feeling in which bodily exercise (1 Tim. iv. 8) and abstinence profit little. St Paul's influence is felt, a sort of mystic sobriety, and, amidst the strangest aberrations of faith in a supernatural direction, these writings contain a large amount of what is upright and sincere.

The composition of the Epistles to Timothy and Titus most likely coincided with what may be called the publication of St Paul's Epistles. Up till that time those letters had been scattered, and each church had kept those which had been addressed to them, whilst several had been lost. At about the period of which we are now speaking they were collected, and the three short epistles, which were looked upon as a necessary complement of St Paul's writings, were embodied with them. They were most likely published at Rome, and the order which the first editor adopted has always been preserved.

They were divided into two categories, Epistles to churches and to individuals, and in each of these categories the epistles were arranged according to stichometry, that is, according to the number of lines in the manuscript. Certain copies soon contained the Epistle to the Hebrews, and its very place at the end of the volume, out of all order as regards its length, ought to suffice to prove that it was incorporated into St Paul's Epistles at some later period.

# CHAPTER VII

### FORGED APOSTOLICAL WRITINGS.--THE CHRISTIAN BIBLE

Meanwhile, however, the world would persist in not coming to an end, and it required all that inexhaustible measure of patience, self-denial and gentleness which formed the basis of the character of every Christian, when they saw how slowly the prophecies of Jesus were being accomplished. The years went by, and the vast Northern glorious light in the centre of which, it was believed, the Son of Man would appear did not yet begin to dawn in the clouds. Men grew weary of seeking for the cause of this delay, and whilst some grew discouraged, others murmured. St Luke, in his Gospel, announced that he would avenge his Elect speedily, that the long-suffering of God would come to an end, and that, by praying day and night under their persecution, the elect would obtain justice like the importunate widow did over the unjust judge. Nevertheless, they began to be tired of waiting. That generation which was not to have passed away before the appearance of Christ in His Glory must all have been dead. More than fifty years had passed since those events had taken place, which were only to precede the accomplishment of the prophecies of Jesus by a very little. All the towns in Judea had heard Christian preachers, and malicious men began to make this the occasion of mocking. The reply of the faithful was that the first rule of the true believer was not to calculate dates. "He will come like a thief in the night," said the wise; "The appearing of our Lord Jesus Christ, which in his own times he shall show," says the author of the Epistle to Timothy; and, meanwhile, that good and practical pastor laid down rules which, admitting the approaching end of the world, did not contain much sense, and men aspired to escape from that provisional state in which those who believed in the hourly appearance of the Messiah would always have remained enthralled.

Then it was that a pious writer, in order to make these doubts cease, had the idea of disseminating amongst the faithful an epistle that was attributed to Peter. The Churches of St Paul had just collected their master's works, and made important additions to them. It appears that a Christian of Rome, who belonged to that group which wished to reconcile St Peter and St Paul at any price, wished to enlarge the very slight literary legacy which the Galilean apostle had left behind him. Already there was one epistle which bore the name of the chief of the apostles, and by taking it for a foundation, and embodying in it phrases borrowed from all sides, there resulted a "Second Epistle of Peter" which, it was hoped, would circulate on the same footing as the former.

Nothing was neglected in the composition of the second epistle to make it coextensive in authority with the first. Whilst composing this little work, the author certainly had before him the short letter of the Apostle Jude, and, no doubt, supposing that it was very little known, he did not scruple to incorporate it almost wholly into his own writing. He was penetrated by the spirit of St Paul's Epistles, of which he possessed the complete edition; and he also made use of the Apocalypse of Esdras or of Baruch. He even attributed to Peter expressions and direct allusions to gospel facts, and to an allegation in St Paul's Epistles, which certainly never found place in anything that Cyphus dictated. The pious forger's object was to reassure the faithful about the long delay of Messiah's second coming, to show that Peter and Paul were agreed on this fundamental mystery of the Christian faith, and to combat the errors of Gnosticism. In several churches his Epistle was favourably received, but protests were also raised against it, which the orthodox canon of Scripture did not put an end to for a long time.

The teaching of the Epistle, however, is quite worthy of the apostolic age, by its purity and loftiness of thought. The Elect become participators of the divine nature because they renounce the corruptions of the world. Patience, sobriety, piety, paternal love, horror of heresy, to wait, to be always waiting and expecting, is the whole Christian life (2 Peter iii. 1, et seq.).

With the Second Epistle of Peter ended, about a hundred years after the death of Jesus, the cycle of writings, which were called, later on, the New Testament, in contradiction to the Old. This second Bible, which was inspired by Jesus, although there is not a single line of his in it, was far from admitting any settled canon; many small works, all more or less pseudo-epigraphs, were admitted by some and discarded by others. The new writings were, as yet, very little circulated, and very unequally read, and the list was not looked upon as final; and we shall see that other works, such as the Pastor of Hermas, take their place by the side of writings which were already sacred, almost on a footing of equality. Yet the idea of a new revelation was already fully accepted. In the so-called "Second Epistle of St Peter," St Paul's Epistles are ranked amongst the Scriptures, and this was not the first time that such an expression had been used. Christianity had thus its sacred book, an admirable collection, which would be sure to make its fortune in those far ages when the immediate recollection of its origin was lost, and no religions were worth anything except by their written texts.

Of course the Jewish Bible maintained all its authority, and continued to be looked upon as the direct revelation of God. That ancient Canon and the apocryphal writings that had been appended to it (such as the Book of Enoch, the Assumption of Moses, etc., etc.) were looked upon, above all, as the immediate revelation of God. It was not touched; whereas, with regard to the new Scriptures, neither additions nor suppressions, nor arbitrary manipulations were forbidden. Nobody had any scruple in attributing to the Apostles and Christ himself such words and writings as they thought good, useful, and worthy of such a divine origin. If they had not said all those beautiful things, they could have said them, and that was enough. An ecclesiastical usage, that of reading aloud in churches, was an incentive to these sort of frauds, and made them almost necessary. In their meetings, the reading of the prophetical and apostolical writings was to take up all the time that was not occupied by the mysteries and the sacraments. The prophetical and the genuine apostolical writings were soon exhausted, and so something fresh was required: and to provide for the constantly occurring requirements of these readings, any edifying work was eagerly welcomed, as long as it had the slightest appearance of apostolicity, or bore the most distant resemblance to the writings of the ancient prophets.

Thus Christianity had accomplished the first duty of a religion, which is to introduce a new sacred book to the world. Another Bible had been added to the old one, which was much inferior to it in classic beauty, but was very efficacious for the conversion of the world. The old Hebrew language, that venerable aristocratic instrument of poetry, of the feelings of the soul and of passion, had been dead for centuries. The Semetic-Aramean patois of Palestine, and that popular Greek, which the Macedonian conquest had introduced into the East, and which the Alexandrian translators of the Bible raised to the height of a sacred language, could not act as the organs for those literary master-pieces; but although it lacked genius, it possessed goodness; and though it had no great writers, it had men who were filled with Jesus, and who have given us the reflex of his spirit. The New Testament introduced a new idea into the world, that of popular beauty, and in any case there is no book which has dried so many tears and soothed so many hearts as it has.

We cannot speak in a general manner of the style of the New Testament, because its writings are divided into four or five different styles. All these various parts, however, have something in common, and it is just that something which imparts their power and success to them. Though written in Greek, their conception is Semetic. Such phrases, without any circumlocution, that language whose everything is black or white, sunshine or darkness, as, "Jacob have I loved; but Esau have I hated," to express "I preferred Jacob to Esau," have carried away the world by their rugged grandeur. Our races were not used to Oriental fulness, to such energetic partiality, to this manner of procedure, all at once used, as it were, by bounds; and so they were overcome and crushed, and even at this present time that style constitutes the great power of Christianity which fascinates souls and wins them over to Jesus.

The canon of Old Testament Scripture, which the Christians admitted, was, as far as regarded the essential works, the same as that of the Jews. Christians who were ignorant of Hebrew read these ancient writings in the Alexandrine version, which is called the Septuagint, and which they reverenced as equal to the Hebrew text, and where the Greek version adds expansions to the original, as is the case in Esther and Daniel, these additions were accepted. Less severely guarded than the Jewish canon, the Christian admitted besides such books as Judith, Tobias, Baruch, the Fourth Book of Esdras, the assumption of Moses, Enoch, and the Wisdom of Solomon, which the Jewish rabbis excluded from the sacred volume and even systematically destroyed; whilst such books as Job, the Song of Solomon, Proverbs, Ecclesiastes, were very little read by people who looked, above all things, for edification, on account of their bold or altogether profane character. The books of the Maccabees were preserved rather as instructive or pious books, than as sources of inspiration.

The Old Testament, which has been mauled in different ways, and been interpreted with all the latitude that a text without vowels allows of, was the storehouse for the arguments of Christian apologists and Jewish polemics. Most frequently these disputes took place in Greek, and though the Alexandrine versions were used, they daily became more and more insufficient. The advantages which the Christians gained from them made the Jews suspicious of them, and a saying was disseminated, which was reputed to be prophetic, in which some wise men of old had announced all the evil that should some day spring from those accursed versions. The day on which the Septuagint version was made was compared to that on which the golden calf was cast, and it was even asserted that that day was followed by three days of darkness. On the other hand, the Christians admitted the legends which represented this version as having been miraculously revealed. Rabbi Aquiba and his school had invented the absurd principle, that nothing in the whole Bible is insignificant, that every letter was written with some particular purpose, and has some influence on the sense. From thenceforward the

Alexandrine translators who had done their work by human means, like philologists and not like cabalists, did not seem as if they could be of any use in the controversies of the time; unreasonable objections to grammatical peculiarities were brought forward, and they wished for translations of the Bible, in which every Hebrew word, or rather root, should be rendered by a Greek word, even if the translation had no sense in consequence.

Aquila was the most celebrated of those who were devoted to a senseless literal translation. His work dates from the twelfth year of Hadrian's reign. Although he was a mere proselyte, he had very likely been educated by Aquiba, and, in fact, his exegesis is an exact pendant to the rabbi's casuistry. A Greek word corresponds exactly to every Hebrew word, even when nothing but nonsense is the result.

The Christians soon got to know Aquila's translation, and they were much vexed at it, for, as they were accustomed to depend on the Septuagint for their texts, they saw that this new translation would overthrow all their methods and their apologetic system. One passage especially troubled them very much. The churches wished at any price to see the prophetic announcement of the birth of Jesus from a virgin from Isaiah 7, xiv., which indeed means something quite different, but where the word παρθένος, employed for the Hebrew alma, and applied to the mother of the symbolical Emmanuel, God with us, is rather peculiar. Aquila overthrew this little scaffolding by translating alma by νεᾶνις. They declared that it was pure wickedness on his part, and a system of pious calumnies was invented to explain how, having been a Christian, he learned Hebrew and devoted himself to that tremendous work merely for the sake of contradicting the Septuagint, and to do away with the passages that proved that Jesus was the Messiah.

The Jews, on the other hand, delighted at the apparent exactness of the new version, openly proclaimed their preference for it over the Septuagint. The Ebionites or Nazarenes also frequently used it, for the manner in which Aquila had rendered the passage of Isaiah enabled them to prove that Jesus was merely the son of Joseph.

However, Aquila was not the only one who translated Hebrew after Rabbi Aquiba's method. The Greek version of Ecclesiastes, which forms part of the Greek Vulgate, presents the very same peculiarities which Rabbi Aquiba caused the translators of his school to adopt, and yet that version is not by Aquiba.

# CHAPTER VIII

### MILLENARIANISM--PAPIAS

The most different tendencies were apparent in the Church of Jesus, which demonstrated the wonderful fecundity of the newly-awakened conscience in the bosom of humanity; but which at the same time created an immense danger for that newly-born institution. Thousands of hands, so to say, were tearing the new religion to pieces, some wishing to keep it within the Jewish pale, whilst others wished to sever every bond between it and that Judaism from which it had sprung. The second coming of Jesus, and the idea of his rule for a thousand years, were the two questions which brought these two contrary feelings most prominently forward. The Gnostics, and, up to a certain point, the author of the Epistle of St John, no longer paid any regard to the fundamental doctrines of the first century. They did not any longer trouble themselves much about the end of the world: it was relegated to the background, where it had scarcely any meaning, and these lofty dreams ought now to be forgotten by every one. In Asia Minor the greater number of Christians lived upon that idea, and refused to go any further in search of the truth as to the meaning of Jesus; and in close approximation to that school where, it would seem, the Johannistic writings were being thought out, a man who might have some intercourse with the authors of these writings was working on a totally different, or rather I should say on a totally opposite, line of thought.

But we must speak of Papias, Bishop of Hierapolis, the most striking personality at a period when two Christians could still differ from each other to an extent which we cannot picture to ourselves now. It has often been thought that Papias was one of St John's disciples, but this must certainly be a mistake. He never saw any of the Apostles, as he belongs to the third generation of Christians, but no doubt he consulted those who had seen them. He was a very careful man, a searcher after truth in his own fashion, and one who knew the Scriptures thoroughly. He made it his occupation zealously to collect the words of Jesus, to comment on those words in their most literal sense, to classify them according to their matter, and, in a word, to gather together all the traditions of the apostolic age which had already disappeared. He therefore undertook an investigation of vast extent, which he carried on according to rules such as a sound judgment would prescribe. Dissatisfied with the small books which were said to be an exact picture of the life of Jesus, he thought he could do better, and laid claim to giving the true interpretation of Jesus' doctrine. He only believed in original teaching, and so he spent his life in questioning those who might know something about primitive tradition.

"I am not," he says, in his preface, "like most of those who allow themselves to be captivated by a flow of words; all I cared for were those which teach the truth. Full of mistrust for the extraordinary precepts which have got about, I only wish to know those that the Saviour had entrusted to his disciples, and which spring from truth itself. If, for example, I were to meet any one who had been a follower of the elders, I should ask him, What did Andrew say? What did Peter say? What did Philip, Thomas, James, John, or any other of the disciples of our Lord say? What do Aristion and Presbuteros Johannes, disciples of the Saviour, say? For I did not think that all the books could bring me so much profit as data collected from living and permanent tradition."

No Apostle had been alive for some time when Papias conceived this project, but there were still persons living who had known some of the members of that first upper chamber. The daughters of Philip, who had reached an extreme old age, and who were not quite in their right mind, filled Hierapolis with their wonderful stories, and Papias had seen them. At Ephesus and at Smyrna Presbuteros Johannes and Aristion both asserted that they were the depositants of precious traditions which it seems they said they had received from the Apostle John. Papias did not belong to that school which was attached to John, and from which it is said the fourth Gospel proceeded, though it is probable that he knew Aristion and Presbuteros. His was composed, in a great part, of quotations borrowed from conversations of these two persons who in his eyes were evidently the best representatives of the apostolic chain and of the authentic doctrine of Jesus. It is needless to say that the Jewish Christian Papias does not mention the Apostle St Paul, either directly or indirectly.

This attempt to reconstruct the teaching of Jesus by mere oral tradition a hundred years after his death would have been a paradox if Papias had refused to make use of the written texts, and in this respect his method was not so exclusive as he seems to imply in his preface. Whilst preferring oral tradition, and whilst, perhaps, not assigning any absolute value to any of the texts which were in circulation, he read the Gospels of which copies came into his possession. It is certainly vexing that we cannot judge for ourselves how much he knew in this respect. But here Eusebius appears to have been very far-sighted. According to his usual custom, he read the works of Papias pen in hand, to note his quotations from the canonical writings, and he only found two of our Gospels--that of St Mark and of St Matthew--mentioned. Papias noticed a curious opinion of Presbuteros on Mark's Gospel, and the citations by which this latter traditionalist excused, as he imagined, the disorder and the fragmentary character of the compilation of the said Evangelist. As to the Gospel attributed to St Matthew, Papias looked upon it as a free and tolerably faithful translation of the Hebrew work written by the Apostle of that name, and he valued it especially on account of the authentic words of Jesus which were to be found in it. Besides this, he met with an anecdote in Papias, which formed part of the Gospel according to the Hebrews, but he is not sure that the Bishop of Hierapolis took them from that Gospel.

Thus it will be seen that this learned man who was so well acquainted with the Scriptures, who had been in the habit of associating, so it was said, with the disciples of John, and had learnt from them the words of Jesus, did not yet know St John's Gospel, a work which appears to have been produced only a few miles from the town in which he was living. Certainly if Eusebius had found any traces of it in the writings of the Bishop of Hierapolis, he would have mentioned it, just as he tells us that he found quotations from the first Epistle of John. It is a singular fact that Papias, who does not know St John's Gospel, knows the Epistle attributed to him, and which is, in a manner, intended to prepare the way for the Gospel. Perhaps the forgers communicated this Epistle to him, but not the Gospel, as they feared his stringent criticism, or perhaps some time elapsed between the Epistle and the Gospel. One can never touch on this question of the writings said to be John's without meeting with contradictions and anomalies.

From this mass of conscientious research Papias composed five books which he called Exegeses or "Expositions of the Words of the Saviour," and which he certainly looked upon as a correct representation of the teachings of Jesus. The disappearance of this work is the most regrettable loss which the field of primitive Christian literature has ever sustained. If we had Papias' book, no doubt a large number of difficulties which confront us in that obscure history would be removed, and most likely that is the very reason why we do not possess it. His work was written from so personal a point of view that it became a scandal for orthodoxy. The four Gospels had an authority which excluded every other, and in fifty years we shall find mystical reasons why there should be four and why there could not be more than four. No author who declared that he did not think much of those holy texts could possibly be looked upon with favour.

Besides this, Papias, although he seems to be a very severe critic, was really extremely credulous. He added things to the Gospels which, not being protected by the authority of inspiration, seemed shocking and absurd. St Mark, with his ponderous thaumaturgy, appears reasonable beside the extravagant wonders which he alleges. The teaching and the parables which he attributes to Jesus are, to say the least of it. extraordinary and absurd, and the whole had that fabulous character which the Gospel accounts, or at least those of the first three, avoided so carefully. The miracles that he attributed to Philip, on the authority of his old, half-crazy daughters, exceeded everything, and those which he alleged Justus Barsabbas worked, went beyond tradition, whilst his account of the death of St John, and especially that of Judas, was such as nobody had ever heard before. He even seemed to be versed in the dreams of Gnosticism when he asserts that God gave the government of the world to angels, who acquitted themselves badly of their duty.

But his wild millenarianism damaged Papias more than anything else in the mind of all the orthodox. His mistake was that he accepted the apocalypse of the year 68 in the sense that its author meant. With the Seer of Patmos he admitted that after the first resurrection of the dead Christ would reign personally on earth for a thousand years. This is what he makes Jesus say, according to a tradition that had been handed down by the presbuteroi:--

A day will come in which vines shall grow, each of which shall contain ten thousand stems; and each stem shall have ten thousand branches; and each branch, ten thousand shoots; and on each shoot there shall be ten thousand grapes; and each grape, when pressed, shall produce twenty-five thousand hogsheads of wine. And when one of the saints shall seize one of the bunches of grapes, another bunch will cry out, "Take me for I am better; and bless God for me." And each grain of wheat shall produce ten thousand ears; and each ear shall produce ten thousand grains; and each grain, ten thousand pounds of flour. And it shall be the same with the fruit trees as with all cereals, with herbs, according to their different properties. And all animals that live on the simple fruits of the earth shall be peaceful and kind towards each other, obedient and respectful towards men.

It was added that Judas refused to believe all these fine things, and from the day that he heard his Master speak thus he became a semi-unbeliever.

Besides this, Papias did not make use of any great amount of discernment in his choice of the words of Jesus when he attributed to him such which appear to have been scattered about in the Jewish apocalypses, and which may be seen more particularly in the Apocalypse of Baruch. His book was directly opposed to the proposition which the other held so dear, and proved how valuable the written Gospels were, by checking the manner in which the traditional words of Jesus were degraded. Already Montanist ideas, with their simple materialism, were making themselves felt, and, like certain Gnostics, Papias could not understand any perfect innocence of life without a total abstention from animal food. The relative good sense of the Galilean dreams had disappeared to make way for the extravagancies of the far East, and so the impossible was sought after, and a sort of subversive gentleness of humanity, such as India alone, as the price of her political annihilation, has been able to realise in life.

The orthodox Church perceived the danger of these chimeras very quickly, and the millenium, above all, became an object of repugnance for every Christian of common sense. Minds who, like Origen, Dionysius of Alexandria, Eusebius, and the Hellenistic Fathers, saw nothing but a revealed philosophy in Jesus, made it their chief business not to attribute to him or to the apostles an opinion which daily became more self-evidently absurd, and to remove from the very threshold of Christianity that fatal objection that the dominant idea of its founders was a manifest dream. Every possible means were sought for to get rid of the apocalypse, and the fidelity of Papias, who was most strongly imbued of all the ecclesiastical writers with the primitive ideas to tradition, was fatal to him. Men strove to forget him, his works were not copied, and only curious readers cared for his writings: and Eusebius, whilst respecting him, says clearly that he was a man of small mind, without any judgment.

Papias' mistake was that of being too conservative, and by being the friend of tradition he seemed to be behind everybody else. The progress of Christianity would naturally make of him an inconvenient man, and a witness to be suppressed, whilst in his own time he certainly responded to the state of many men's minds. The millennists looked upon him as their principal authority; Irenæus esteems him openly, and places him immediately after the Apostles, on the same footing as Polycarp, and calls him by a name which is very appropriate to his character: "A Father of the Church." [1] The Bishop of Lyon thought that his discourses on the vines of the kingdom of David were beautiful and authentic. Irenæus allows these dreams of a concrete idealism, coarse as they may be, whilst Justin has heard of them, and Tertullian and Commodian exceed the materialism of Papias himself. St Hippolytus, Methodius, Nepos, Bishop of Arsinoe in Egypt, Victorinus Pettavius, Lanctantius, the Apollinarists, St Ambrose, Sulpicius-Severus--or St Martin--believe the old tradition in this respect. Up to the fifth century the faithful who were most oxthodox Christians maintained that after the coming of Antichrist, and the destruction of all the nations, there would be a resurrection of the just only; that those who were then on the earth, good and bad, would be preserved alive: the good to obey the just who had been raised as their princes, and the bad to be altogether subject to them. A Jerusalem, consisting altogether of gold, cypress, and cedar, rebuilt by the nations, who should come, led by their kings, to work at the re-erection of its walls,--a restored Temple, which should become the centre of the world,--crowds of victims around the altar,--the gates of the city open day and night in order to receive the tribute of the people,--pilgrims coming in their due order according as they were allowed to come every week, every month, or every year,--the saints, the patriarchs, and the prophets passing a thousand years in one perpetual Sabbath in perfect agreement with the Messiah, who would give them a hundred fold all that they have given up for him-- this was the essentially Jewish Paradise of which many dreamed, even in the times of St Jerome and St Augustine. Orthodoxy fought against these ideas; but as they were openly expressed in many passages of the Fathers, they were never strictly qualified as heresies. St Epiphanius, who was a man of most strict research, who tried to enlarge his catalogue of heresies by making two or three sects out of one, has not devoted a special chapter to the millenarians--and to be consistent he must first of all have got rid of the Apocalypse of the received Canon of Scripture; and so, in spite of the most ingenious attempts of the Greek Fathers, every attempt to do so was unsuccessful.

Besides this there were degrees in the materialism of those simple believers. Some, like Irenæus, saw in the first resurrection nothing but a beginning of incorruption, a means of becoming accustomed to the sight of God, a period during which the saints would enjoy the conversation and the companionship of the angels, and would treat about spiritual matters with them. Others only dreamt of a gross paradise of eating and drinking. They asserted that the saints would spend all that time in feasts of carnal pleasure, and that children would be born during Messiah's reign; that the lords of that new world would wallow in gold and precious stones, and that every creature would immediately obey their slightest desire.

The ideas of the infinite, of the immortality of the soul, were so far absent from these Jewish dreams that a thousand years seemed enough for the most exacting minds. A man must have been very greedy of life if at the end of that time he had not been surfeited with it. In our eyes, a paradise of a thousand years seems only a small thing, as every year would bring us nearer to the time when everything would vanish. The last years which preceded annihilation would seem to us to be a hell, and the thought of the year 999, would be quite enough to poison the happiness of the foregoing years. But it is no good to ask for logic to try and solve the intolerable destiny which falls to the lot of man.

Carried away irresistibly to believe in what is right, and cast into a world that is injustice itself, requiring an eternity to make good his claims, and stopped short by the grave, what can he do? He clings to the coffin and yields his flesh to his fleshless bones, his life to the brain full of rottenness, light to the closed eye, and pictures to himself chimeras that he would laugh at in a child, so that he may not have to avow that God has been able to mock his own creatures to the extent of laying upon them the burden of duty without any future recompense.

Footnotes:

    1. Ἀρχαῖος ἀνήρ (vide Liddell and Scott in verb:)--Translator.

# CHAPTER IX

### THE COMMENCEMENT OF GNOSTICISM

At this period Christianity was a newborn child, and when it emerged from its swaddling-clothes, a most dangerous sort of croup threatened to choke it. The root of this illness was partly internal, partly external, and in some respects the child had been born with the germs of it. In a great measure, however, the illness came from without, and the unhealthy locality in which the young Church dwelt caused it a sort of poisoning to which it very nearly succumbed.

As the Church grew more numerous and began to develop a hierarchy, the docility and self-denial of the faithful began to have its merit. It seemed to be irksome to walk like a lost sheep amongst the close ranks of the whole herd, and so men wished to leave the crowd and have rules for themselves: the universal law seemed to be a very commonplace matter. In all directions small aristocracies were formed in the Church which threatened to rend the seamless robe of Christ, and two of them were marked by rare originality. One was the aristocracy of piety, Montanism; the other, the aristocracy of science, was Gnosticism.

This latter was the first to develop itself. To minds that were initiated into the philosophical subtleties of the times, the ideas and the government of the Church must have appeared very humble, for the via media of relative good sense to which orthodoxy adhered did not suit all men's minds, and refined intellects asserted that they had loftier ideas about the dogmas and the life of Jesus than the vulgar herd who took matters literally, and gave themselves up without reasoning to the direction of their pastors; and sublimity of doctrine was sought, whereas it ought to have been received with the cheerfulness of a pure heart, and embraced with a simple faith.

Jesus and his immediate disciples had altogether neglected that part of the human intellect which desires to know; with knowledge they had nothing to do, and they only addressed themselves to the heart and the imagination. Cosmology, psychology, and even lofty theological speculations, were a blank page for them, and very likely they were right. It was not the part of Christianity to satisfy any vain curiosity; it came to console those who suffer, to touch the fibres of moral sense, and to bring man into relation not with some one or abstract logos, but with a heavenly Father full of kindness, who is the author of all the harmonies and of all the joys of the universe. Especially towards the end of his life St Paul felt the want of a speculative theology, and his ideas became assimilated to those of Philo, who a century before had striven to impart a rationalistic turn of mind to Judaism. About the same time the Churches of Asia Minor launched forth into a sort of cabala which connected the part of Jesus with a chimerical ontology and an indefinite series of avatars. The school from which the fourth Gospel sprung felt the same need of explaining the miracles of Galilee by theology, and so Jesus became the Divine logos made flesh, and the altogether Jewish idea of the future appearing of the Messiah was replaced by the theory of the Paraclete. Cerinthus obeyed an analogous tendency. At Alexandria this thirst for metaphysics was even more pronounced, and produced strange results, which it is time for us to study now.

In that city a crude and unwholesome mass of all theologies and all cosmogonies had been formed, which, however, was often traversed by rays of genius, and which was a doctrine that set up the pretension of having discovered the formula of the absolute, and gave himself the ambiguous title of Gnosis--"perfect science." The man who was initiated into the chimerical doctrine was called Gnosticos--the man of perfect knowledge. At that time, Alexandria was, after Rome, the spot where men's minds were in the most unsettled state. Frivolity and superficial eclecticism produced altogether unforeseen effects, and everything got mixed up together in those wild and fantastic brains. Thanks to an often unconscious charlatanism, the weightiest problems of life were turned into mere cases of filching, and every question about God and the world were solved by juggling with words and hollow formulas, and real science was dispensed with by tricks of legerdemain. It must be remembered that the great scientific institutions founded by the Ptolomies had disappeared or fallen into complete decay, and the only guide which can prevent mankind from talking nonsense--that is, exact science--existed no longer.

Philosophy did exist still, and was trying to raise its head again, but great minds were scarce. Platonism had gained the upper hand over all the other Greek systems in Egypt, and in Syria, which was a great misfortune, for Platonism is always dangerous, unless corrected by a scientific education. There were no more any men of taste refined enough to appreciate the wonderful art in Plato's Dialogues, for most received those charming philosophical fancies in a clumsy spirit; but instruction such as they conveyed, which rather satisfied the imagination than the reason, would please Eastern ideas. The germ of mysticism which they contained made its impress on those races who could not receive pure and simple rationalism. Christianity followed the general fashion, and already Philo had sought to make Platonism the philosophy of Judaism, and those Fathers of the Church who had any weight were Platonists.

To accommodate itself to this unnatural fusion, Greek genius, healthy and intelligible as it was, had to make many sacrifices. Philosophers were to believe in ecstasies, in miracles, in supernatural relations between God and man. Plato becomes a theosophist and a mystagogue, and the invocation of good spirits is taken as a serious matter, and whilst the scientific spirit disappears altogether, that habit of mind which was fortified by mysteries begins to gain the upper hand. In those small religious assemblies of Eleusius and Thrace, where men were in the habit of throwing dust into their own eyes so as to imagine that they knew the unknowable, it was already asserted that the body was the prison of the soul, that the actual world was a decadence from the divine world; teaching was divided into esoteric and exoteric, and men into spiritual, animal, and material beings. The habit of clothing doctrine in a mythical form after the manner of Plato, and of explaining ancient texts allegorically after the manner of Philo, became general. The highest bliss was to be initiated into pretended secrets, into a superior gnosis. These ideas of a chimerical intellectual aristocracy daily gained ground, and the truth was looked upon as a privilege reserved for a small number of the initiated, and thus every master became a charlatan who sought to increase the number of his customers by selling them the secret of the absolute.

The fields of the propaganda of the gnosis and of Christianity in Alexandria were very closely allied. Gnostics and Christians resembled each other in their ardent wish to penetrate into religious mysteries without any positive science, of which they were both equally ignorant, and this brought about their sublime amalgamation. On the one hand, the Gnostics, who alleged that they embraced every belief, and accustomed as they were to look upon the gods of the nations as divine æons much inferior to the supreme God, wished to understand Christianity, and received Jesus enthusiastically as an incarnate æon to be placed side by side with so many others, giving him a chief place in their formulae of the philosophies of history. On the other hand, Christians who had any intellectual requirements, and who wished to attach the Gospel to some system of philosophy, found what they required in the obscure metaphysics of the Gnostics. Then there happened something quite analogous to what happened about fifty years ago, when a certain philosophical system, whose programme, like that of Gnosticism, was to explain everything, and to understand everything, adopted Christianity, and proclaimed itself to be Christian in a superior sense, and Catholic and Protestant theologians might be seen at the same time adopting a number of philosophical ideas which they thought were compatible with their theology, because they did not wish to appear strange to their century.

The Fathers of the Church insist upon it that all this rank and poisonous growth had its origin in the Samaritan sects which sprang from Simon of Gitto (Simon Magus), and he certainly seems already to have presented most of the features which characterise Gnosticism. The Great Announcement, which he certainly did not write himself, but which most likely represents his doctrines, is an altogether Gnostic work. His followers Menander, Cleobius, and Dositheus seem to have had the same views, and all Catholic writers make Menander to be the father of all the great Gnostics of Hadrian's time. If we are to believe Plotinus on the other hand, a travestied and disfigured Platonic philosophy was the only origin of Gnosticism. Such explanations appear to be altogether insufficient to account for such a complicated fact. There were Christian, Jewish, Samaritan Gnostics, but there were also non-Christian Gnostics. Plotinus, who wrote a whole book against them, never imagined that he had anything to do with a Christian sect. The systems of the Samaritan Gnostics, those of Basilides, of Valentinus, of Saturninus, present such shrinking similarities that one must suppose that they have a common origin, though they do not seem to have borrowed from each other. They must therefore have dipped into an earlier source, to which Philo, Apollos, and St Paul, when he wrote his Epistle to the Colossians, contributed, and from which the Jewish cabala also seems to have proceeded.

It is an impossible task to unravel all that contributed to the formation of that strange religious philosophy. Neo-platonism, a tissue of poetical dreams, the ideas that men had in consequence of apocryphal traditions about Pythagorism, already supplied models for a mythical philosophy bordering on religion. About the very time when Basilides, Valentinus, and Saturninus were developing their dreams, one of Hadrian's pensioned orators, Philo of Byblos, gave to the world the old Phoenician theogonies, mixed up as it seems with the Jewish cabala, under a form of divine genealogies which were very analogous to those of the first Gnostics. The Egyptian religion, which was still in a very flourishing state, with its mysterious ceremonies and its striking symbols, Greek mysteries and classical polytheism interpreted in an allegorical sense, Orphism, with its empty formulas; Brahminism, which had become a theory of endless emanations; Buddhism, oppressed by the dream of an expiatory existence, and by its myriads of Buddhas; ancient Persian Dualism, which was so contagious, and to which perhaps the ideas of the Messiah and of the millenium owed their first existence, all these in turn appeared as profound and seductive dogmas to the imaginations of men who were beside themselves between hopes and fears. India, and, above all, Buddhism, were known in Alexandria, and from them the Egyptians borrowed the doctrine of metampsychosis, learning to look on life as the imprisonment of the soul in the body, and the theory of successive deliverances. Gnosticos has the same meaning as Buddha--"he who knows." Following the Persian view, they took the dogma of two principles independent one of the other,--the identification of matter with evil, the belief that the passions which corrupt the soul are emanations from the body, the division of the world into ministeries or adminstrations which have been entrusted to genii. Judaism and Christianity were mixed up together in this farrago of nonsense, and more than one believer in Jesus thought that he could graft the Gospels on to a ludicrous system of theology which seemed to say something without explaining anything in reality, whilst more than one Israelite was already playing a prelude to the follies of the cabala, which is, as a matter of fact, nothing but Jewish Gnosticism.

As we have said, the Church of Alexandria was soon tinged with these chimeras. Philo and Plato already had many readers amongst the faithful who had any education. Many joined the Church, already imbued with philosophy, and found Christian teaching poor and meagre, whilst the Jewish Bible seemed to them to be still more feeble, and, in imitation of Philo, they saw in it nothing but an allegory. They applied the same method to the Gospel, and in some fashion remodelled it, to which it lent itself easily, on account of its plastic character. All the peculiarities of the life of Jesus regained something sublime, according to these new evangelists; all his miracles became symbolical, and the follies of the Jewish ghemetria were heightened and aggravated. Like Cerinthus, these new doctors treated the Old Testament as a secondary revelation, and could not understand why Christianity should maintain any bond of union with that particular God, Jehovah, who is no absolute being. Could there be any stronger proof of his weakness than the state of ruin and desolation in which he had left his own city, Jerusalem? Certainly, they said, Jesus could see further and higher than the founders of Judaism, but his apostles did not comprehend him, and the texts which were supposed to represent his doctrine had been falsified. The gnosis alone, thanks to secret tradition, was in possession of the truth, and a vast system of successive emanations contains the whole secret of philosophy and history. Christianity, which was the last act of the tragedy that the universe is constantly playing, was the work of the æon Christos, who, by his intimate union with the man Jesus, saved everything that could be saved in humanity.

It will be seen that the Christianity of those sectaries was that of Cerinthus and the Ebionites. Their Gospel conformed to the Hebrew Gospel, and they described the scene of the baptism of Jesus as it was related in that Gospel, and believed, with the Docetm, that Jesus had nothing human but his appearance. The Galilean accounts appeared to them nothing but childish nonsense, altogether unworthy of the Deity, and which must be explained allegorically. For them the man Jesus was nothing, the æon Christos was everything; and his earthly life, far from being the basis of doctrine, was nothing but a difficulty to be got rid of at any price.

The ideas of the first Christians about the appearance of the Messiah in the heavens, about the Resurrection, and the Last Judgment, were looked upon as antiquated. The moment of the Resurrection for every individual was that at which he became a gnosticos. A certain relaxation of morals was the consequence of these false aristocratic ideas; mysticism has always been a moral danger, for it too easily gives rise to the idea that by initiation man is dispensed from the obligation of ordinary duties. "Gold," said these false Christians, "can be dragged through the mire without becoming soiled." They smiled when scruples about meats offered to idols were mentioned to them; they were present at plays and at gladiatorial games; and they were accused of speaking lightly of offences against chastity, and of saying,--"What is of the flesh is flesh, and what is of the spirit is spirit;" and they expressed their antipathy for martyrdom in terms that must have hurt the feelings of real Christians most profoundly. As Christ had not suffered, why should they suffer for him?" The real testimony which they ought to render to God," they said, "was to know him as he is, it is an act of suicide for a man to confess God by his death." According to them, the martyrs were nearly always wrong, and the pains that they suffered were the just chastisement for crimes that would have merited death, and which remained hidden. Far from complaining, they ought to be thankful to the law which transformed their just punishment into an act of heroism, and if there were a few rare cases of innocent martyrs, they were analogous to the sufferings of childhood, and fate only was to be blamed for it.

The sources of piety, however, were not yet corrupted by a proud rationalism, which generally frees itself from material practices. A liturgy, veiled in secrecy, offered abundant sacramental consolation to the faithful of those singular Churches, and life became a mystery, each one of whose acts was sacred. Baptism was a solemn ceremony, and recalled the worship of Mithra. The formula which the officiating minister pronounced was in Hebrew, and immersion there followed the anointing, which the Church adopted later. Extreme unction for the dying was also administered in a manner which would naturally create a great effect, and which the Catholic Church has imitated. Amongst the sectaries, worship, like dogma, was further removed from Jewish simplicity than in the churches of Peter and Paul, and the Gnostics admitted several Pagan rites, chants, hymns, and painted or sculptured representations of Christ.

In this respect their influence on the history of Christianity was of the highest order, arid they formed the bridge by which a number of Pagan practices were introduced into the Church. In the Christian propaganda they played a principal part, for, by means of Gnosticism, Christianity first of all proclaimed itself as a new religion which was destined to endure, and which possessed a form of worship and sacraments, and which could produce an art of its own. By means of Gnosticism, the Church effected a juncture with the ancient mysteries, and appropriated to herself all that they possessed that satisfied popular requirements. Thanks to it, in the fourth century, the world could pass from Paganism to Christianity without noticing it, and, above all, without guessing that it was becoming Jewish. The eclecticism and the ingratitude of the Catholic Church are here shown in a wonderful manner. Whilst repudiating and anathematising the chimeras of the Gnostics, orthodoxy received a number of happy popular devotional inspirations from them, and from the theurgical the Church advanced to the sacramental view. Her feasts, her sacraments, her art were in a great measure taken from those sects which she condemned. Christianity, pure and simple, has not left any material object, for primitive Christian archeology is Gnostic. In those small, free, and inventive sects life was without rule but full of vitality. Their very metaphysics already made themselves felt, and faith was obliged to reason. By the side of the Church there was henceforth to be found the school; by the side of the elder, the teacher.

Moreover, some men of rare talent, making themselves the organs of those doctrines which had hitherto been without authority, withdrew them from that state of individual speculation in which they might have remained indefinitely, and raised them to the height of a real event in the history of humanity.

# CHAPTER X

## BASILIDES, VALENTINUS, SATURNINUS, CARPOCRATES

Basilides, who seems to have come from Syria to live at Alexandria, in Lower Egypt. and in the adjacent departments, was the first of those foreign dogmatisers to whom one hesitates at times to give the name of Christian. He is said to have been a disciple of Menander, and seems to have had two courses of instruction: the one, which was intended for the initiated, was restricted to religions of abstract metaphysics which were more in keeping with those of Aristotle than those of Christ, and the other was a sort of mythology, founded, like the Jewish cabala, on abstractions, which men took for realities. The metaphysics of Basilides remind us of those of Hegel, because of their unhealthy grandeur. His system owed much to the Stoic cosmogony. Universal life is a development of a πανσπερμα. Just as the seed contains the trunk, the roots, the flowers, and the fruits of the future plant, so the future of the universe is only an evolution. Filiation is the secret of everything; the species is the child of the genius, and is only an expansion of it.The aspiration of creatures is towards the good. Progress is made by that mind which stops between two boundaries (Μεθόριον πνεῦμα),--which, having, as it were, one foot in the ideal and the other in the material world, makes the ideal circulate amongst the material, and continually raises it. A sort of universal groaning of nature, a melancholy feeling of the universe, calls us to final repose, which will consist in the general unconsciousness of individuals in the bosom of God, and in the absolute extinction of every desire. "The good tidings" of progress were brought into the world by Jesus, the son of Mary. Already, before him, chosen heathens and Jews had caused the spiritual element to triumph over the material; but Jesus completely separated these two elements, so that only the spiritual element remained. Thus death could take nothing from him. All men ought to imitate him, to attain the same end. They will do so by receiving the "glad tidings," that is to say, the transcendent gnosis, eagerly.

In order to make these ideas more accessible, Basilides gave them a cosmogonic form analogous to those which were common in the religions of Phoenicia, Persia, and Assyria. It was a sort of divine epopæia, having for its heroes divine attributes personified, and whose diverse episodes represented the strife between good and evil. The good is the supreme god, ineffable and lost in himself. His name is Abraxas. That eternal being develops himself in seven perfections, which form with the Being himself the divine ogdoade. The seven perfections, Nous, Logos, Sophia, etc., by pairing together, have produced the orders of inferior angels (æons, worlds), to the number of three hundred and sixty-five, That number is made up by the letters of the word Abraxas added together according to their numerical value.

The angels of the last heaven, whose prince is Jehovah, created the earth, which is the most mediocre of the worlds, the most sullied by matter, on the model furnished by Sophia, but under the empire of necessities, which made a mixture of good and evil out of it. Jehovah and the demiurges divided the government of this world between them, and distributed the provinces and the nations amongst themselves. Those are the local gods of the different countries. Jehovah chose the Jews: he is an invading and a conquering God. The Law, his work, is a mixture of material and spiritual views. The other local gods were obliged to coalesce against this aggressive neighbour, who, in spite of the division that had been agreed upon, wished to subjugate all nations to his own.

To put an end to this war of the gods, the supreme God sent the prince of the æons, the Nous, his first son, with the mission to deliver men from the power of the demiurge angels. The Nous did not exactly become incarnate. At the moment of baptism the Nous attached to itself the person of the man Jesus, and did not leave it till the moment of the Passion. According to some disciples of Basilides, a substitution took place at that moment, and Simon of Cyrene was crucified in Jesus' stead. The persecutions to which Jesus and the apostles were subjected by the Jews arose from the anger of Jehovah, who, seeing that his rule was threatened, made a last effort to avert the dangers of the future.

The place which Basilides attributed to Jesus in the economy of the world's history does not differ essentially from that which is attributed to him in the Epistle to the Colossians and in the pseudo-Johannine Gospel. Basilides knew some words of Hebrew, and had certainly taken his Christianity from the Ebionites. He gave a so-called Glaucias, St Peter's interpreter, as his master. He made use of the New Testament very nearly as it had been formed by general consent, excluding certain books, particularly the epistles to the Hebrews, to Titus and to Timothy, admitting St John's Gospel. He wrote twenty-four books of allegorical Expositions of the Gospel, without our being able to tell exactly what texts he made use of. After the example of all the sects that surrounded the Church, and, in a measure, sucked her, Basilides composed apocryphal books,--esoteric traditions attributed to Matthias; revelations borrowed from chimerical people, Barcabban and Barcoph; prophecies of Cham. Like Valentinus, he seems to have composed sacred psalms or canticles. Lastly, besides the commentary on the received Gospels that he had edited, there was a gospel analogous to that of the Hebrews, of the Egyptians, and of the Ebionites, which differed little from that of Matthew, which bore the name of Basilides. His son, Isidore, carried on his teaching, wrote commentaries on the apocryphal prophets, and developed his myths. Weak Christians easily allowed themselves to be seduced by these dreams. A learned and esteemed Christian writer, Agrippa Castor, constituted himself its ardent adversary as soon as it appeared.

Theurgy is generally the ordinary companion of religious intemperance. The disciples of Basilides did not invent, but they adopted, the magic virtues of the word Abraxas. They were also reproached with a very lax state of morals. It is certain that when so much importance is attached to metaphysical formulas, simple and good morality seems to be a humble and almost indifferent matter. A man who has become perfect by gnosis can allow himself anything. It seems that Basilides did not say that, but he was made to say it, and that was to a certain point the consequence of his theosophy. The saying which was attributed to him,--"We are men, the others are only swine and dogs," was, after all, only the brutal translation of the more acceptable saying,--"I am speaking for one in a thousand." The taste for mystery which that sect had, its habit of avoiding the light and hiding itself from the eyes of the multitude, the silence that was exacted from the initiated, gave rise to those rumours. Many calumnies were mixed up with all that. Thus Basilides was accused of having maintained, like all the Gnostics, that it was no crime to renounce apparently the beliefs for which one was persecuted; to lend oneself to acts indifferent in themselves, which the civil law exacted; even to go so far as to curse Christ, so long as in one's mind one distinguished between the aeon Nous and the man Jesus. Now we have the original text of Basilides, and we find in it a much more moderate criticism of martyrdom than that which his opponents attribute to him. It is true that, attributing no importance whatever to the real Jesus, the Gnostics had no reason to die for him. On the whole they were only semi-Christians. Perhaps the superstitions which sprang from the sect were not the faults of Basilides. Some of his maxims were very beautiful, but his style, from the fragments which we possess, appears to have been obscure and pretentious.

Valentinus was certainly superior to him. Something sorrowful, a gloomy and icy resignation makes a sort of bad dream out of the system of Basilides. Valentinus penetrates everything with love and pity. The redemption of Christ has for him a feeling of joy; his doctrine was a consolation for many, and real Christians adopted, or at least admired him.

That celebrated, enlightened man, born, as it seems, in Lower Egypt, was educated in the schools of Alexandria, and first taught there. He would also appear to have dogmatised in Cyprus. Even his enemies allow that he had genius, a vast amount of knowledge, and rare eloquence. Gained over by the great seductions of Christianity, and attached to the Church, but nourished on Plato, and full of the recollections of profane learning, he was not satisfied with the spiritual nourishment which the pastors gave to the simple: he wanting something higher. He conceived a sort of Christian rationalism, a general system of the world, in which Christianity would have a place in the first rank, but would not be everything. Enlightened and tolerant, he admitted a heathen as well as a Jewish revelation. A number of things in the Church's teaching appeared to him coarse and inadmissible by a cultivated mind. He called the orthodox "Galileans," not without a shade of irony. With nearly all the Gnostics, he denied the resurrection of the body, or rather maintained that, as far as regards those who are perfect, the resurrection is accomplished already,--that it consists in the knowledge of the truth,--that the soul alone can be saved.

If Valentinus had limited himself to cherishing these thoughts internally, to speaking about them to his friends, and to not frequenting the Church except in so far as it answered to his feelings, his position would have been altogether correct. But he wanted more: with his ideas, he wished to have a place of importance in the Church; and he was wrong, for the order of speculation in which he delighted was not one which the Church could encourage. The Church's object was the amelioration of morals and the diminution of the people's sufferings, not science or philosophy. Valentinus ought to have been satisfied with being a philosopher. Far from that, he tried to make disciples, like the ecclesiastics. When he had insinuated himself into any one's confidence, he proposed different questions to him, in order to prove the absurdity of orthodoxy. At the same time, he tried to persuade him that there was something better than that: he expounded that superior wisdom with mystery. If objections were made to him, he would let the discussion drop with an air that seemed to say, " You will never be anything but a simple believer." His disciples showed themselves equally unconceivable. When they were asked questions, they wrinkled their brows, contracted their faces, and slipped away, saying, "O depth" If they were pressed, they affirmed the common faith amidst a thousand ambiguities, then returned to their avowal, baffled their opponent, and escaped, saying, "You do not understand anything about the matter."

Already it was the essence of Catholicism not to suffer any aristocracy,--that of elevated philosophy no more than that of pretentious piety. Valentinus's position was a very false one. In order to make himself acceptable to the people, he conformed his discourses to those of the Church; but the bishops were on their guard, and excluded him. The simple believers allowed themselves to be caught; they even murmured because the bishops drove such good Catholics out of their communion. Useless sympathy! for already the Episcopate had restricted the Church on all sides. Valentinus thus remained in the state of an unfortunate candidate for the pastoral ministry. He wrote letters, homilies, and hymns of a lofty moral tone. The fragments by him that have been preserved have vigour and brilliancy, but their phraseology is eccentric. It resembles the mania which the Saint Simonians had of building up great theories in abstract language to express realities which were almost paltry. His general system had not that appearance of good sense that succeeds with the masses. The pretended Gospel of St John, with its far simpler combinations of the Logos and the Paraclete, had far greater success.

Valentines starts, like all the Gnostics, from a system of metaphysics whose fundamental principle is that God manifests himself by successive emanations, of which the world is the most humble. The world is a work which is too imperfect for an infinite workman t it is the miserable copy of a divine model at the beginning. The Abyss (Bythos), inaccessible, unfathomable, which is also called Proarché, Propator, Silence (Sigè) is its eternal companion. After centuries of solitude and of dumb contemplation of its being, the Abyss wishes at length to appear in the outer world, and with his companion begets a syzygia, Nous or Monogenes and Alethia (Truth); they beget Logos and Zoe, who in their turn beget Anthropos and Ecclesia. Together with the primordial couple those three syzygias form the ogdoade, and with other syzygias emanated from Logos and Zoe, from Anthropos and Ecclesia the divine Pleroma, the plenitude of the divinity which for the future is conscious of its own existence. These couples fall from perfection in measure as they get further and further from the first source; at the same time, the love of perfection, the regret, the desire to return to their first principle, are awakened in them. Sophia especially makes a bold attempt to embrace the invisible Bythos, who only reveals himself by his Monogenes (only son). She continually wears herself out, extends herself to embrace the invisible; drawn away by the sweetness of her love, she is on the point of being absorbed by Bythos, of being annihilated. The whole Pleroma is in confusion. In order to re-establish harmony, Nous or Monogenes engender Christos and Pneuma, who pacify the æons, and make equality reign amongst them. Then, out of gratitude for Bythos, who has pacified them, the moons bring together all their perfections, and form the æon Jesus, the firstborn of creation, as Monogenes had been the firstborn of the emanation. Thus Jesus becomes in the inferior world what Christos had been in the divine Pleroma.

In consequence of the ardour of her insensate passion, Sophia had produced by herself a sort of hermaphrodite abortion without consciousness, Hakamoth, also called Sophia Prunicos, or Prunice, who, driven from the Pleroma, moved about in the void and the night. Moved by compassion for this unfortunate being, Christos, leaning on Stauros (the cross), comes to her aid, gives the erring æon a determinate form and consciousness; but he does not give her knowledge, and Hakamoth, again rejected from the Pleroma, is cast into space. Given up to all the violence of her desires, she brings forth, on the one hand, the soul of the world, and all psychic substances; and on the other, matter. In her, anguish alternates with hope. At one time she feared her annihilation; at other times the recollection of her lost past filled her with joy. Her tears formed the moist element; her smile was the light; her sadness, opaque matter. At last the æon Jesus came to save her, and, in her delight, the poor delivered creature gave birth to the spiritual element,--the third of the elements that constitute the world. Hakamoth, or Prunice, nevertheless does not rest; agitation is her essence; there is a work of God going on in her; she endures a continual flow of blood. The bad part of her activity is concentrated on the demons; the other part, re-united to matter, implants in it the germ of a fire which shall devour it some day.

With the psychic element Hakamoth creates the demiurge, which serves her as an instrument for organising the remaining beings. The demiurge creates the seven worlds, and man in the last of these worlds. But the surprising thing is that a superior and altogether divine principle is revealed in man, and that is the spiritual element, which Hakamoth had imparted to her work from oversight. The creator is jealous of his own creature; he lays a snare for him (the prohibition to eat the fruit of Paradise); man falls into it. He would have been eternally lost except for the love which his mother Hakamoth bore him. The redemption of each world has been accomplished by a special saviour. The saviour of men was the son Jesus, clothed by Hakamoth with the spiritual principle; with the psychic principle by the demiurge; with the material principle by Mary; identified lastly with Christos, who, on the day of his baptism, descended on to him in the form of a dove, and did not leave him again till after his condemnation by Pilate. The spiritual principle will persevere in Jesus till the agony on the cross. The psychic and the material principles alone will suffer, and will rise to heaven through the ascension. There were Gnostics before Jesus, but he came to reunite them and to form them into a Church by the

Holy Spirit. The Church is made up neither of bodies nor of souls, but of spirits: the Gnostics alone form her component parts. At the end of the world matter will be devoured by the internal fire which she hides within herself; Christ will reign instead of the demiurge, and Hakamoth will definitely enter into the Pleroma, which will, thenceforward, be pacified.

Men by their very nature, and independently of their efforts, are divided into three categories, according as the material element, the psychic or animal element, and the spiritual element predominate in them. The heathen are the material men who are irrevocably devoted to the works of the flesh. The simple faithful, the generality of Christians, are the psychic men; in virtue of their intermediate essence, they can rise or fall, lose themselves in matter, or be absorbed into the spirit. The Gnostics are the spiritual men, whether they be Christians, whether they be Jews, like the prophets, or heathens, like the sages of Greece. The spiritual men will some day be joined to the Pleroma. The material men will die altogether; the psychic men will be damned or saved according to their works. External worship is only a symbol, which, though it is good for the psychic mind, is altogether useless for men who give themselves up to pure contemplation. It is an eternal error of the mystic sects who put into their chimeras the initiation above good works, which they leave to the simple. That is the reason why every gnosis, whatever it may do, arrives at indifference to works and contempt for practical virtue, that is to say, at immorality.

There is certainly something grand in these strange myths. When it is a question of the infinite, of things which can only be known partially and secretly, which cannot be expressed without being strained, pathos itself has its charms; one takes pleasure in it, like in those somewhat unhealthy poems whose taste one blames, though one cannot help liking them. The history of the world, conceived like an embryo which is seeking for life, which painfully attains consciousness, which troubles everything by its movements, whilst those movements themselves become the cause of progress and end in the full realisation of the vague instincts of the ideal, such are the ideas which are not very far removed from those which we choose at times to express our views about the development of the infinite. But all that could not be reconciled to Christianity. Those metaphysics of dreamers, that system of morality thought out by recluses, that brahminical pride which would have brought back the rule of castes had it been allowed its own way, would have killed the Church, if the Church had not taken the initiative. It was not without reason that orthodoxy kept a middle position between the Nazarenes, who only saw the human side of Jesus, and the Gnostics, who saw nothing but his divine nature. Valentinus made fun of the simple eclecticism which induced the Church to wish to join two contrary elements together. The Church was right. There is no medium between regulated faith and free thought. Whoever does not admit authority puts himself outside the pale of the Church, and ought to turn philosopher. "They speak like the Church," Irenæus said, "but they think differently." It was a sad game to play. Valentinus was led to hypocrisy and fraud by the same reasons as Basilides was. To free himself from apostolic chains, he claimed to attach himself to secret traditions and to an esoteric teaching which Jesus was said not to have imparted to any except the most spiritually-minded of his disciples. Valentinus said that he had received that hidden doctrine from a pretended Theodades or Theodas, a disciple of St Paul. He appears to have called this the Gospel of Truth. Valentinus' Gospel, at any rate, approximated very closely to that of the Ebionites. In it the duration of the appearances of the risen Jesus was extended over eighteen months.

These despairing efforts to reconcile God and man in Jesus, resulted from difficulties that were inherent in the nature of Christianity. In fact, the travail which was agitating the Christian conscience in Egypt manifested itself also in Syria. Gnosticism appeared in Antioch almost at the same time as it did in Alexandria. Saturninus, or Satorniles, who was said to have been a pupil of Menander, like Basilides was, put forth views which were analogous to those of the latter, though they bore an even stronger impress of Persian dualism. The Pleroma and matter--Bythos and Satan--are the two poles of the universe. The kingdoms of good and evil are the two confines on which they meet. Near those confines the world came into existence, and it was the work of the seven last Eons or demiurges who were wandering in the realms of Satan. Those æons (Jehovah is one of them) divide the government of their work between them, and each appropriates a planet. They do not know the inaccessible Bythos; but Bythos is favourable to them, reveals himself to them by a ray of his beauty, and then hides himself from their admiration. The divine image ceaselessly haunts them, and they create man in the likeness of that image.

Man, as he left the hand of the demiurges, was pure matter. He crawled on the earth like a worm, and had no intelligence. A spark from the Pleroma gives him true life. He thinks, and rises to his feet. Then Satan is filled with rage, and dreams of nothing but of opposing this regenerate man, the mixed work of the demiurges and of God, a man who shall spring entirely from himself. Side by side with divine humanity there is for the future the satanic humanity. To crown the evil, the demiurges revolt against God, and separate creation from that superior principle from which it ought to draw its life. The divine spark no longer circulates between the Pleroma and humanity--between humanity and the

Pleroma. Man is devoted to evil and to error. Christ saves him by suppressing the action of the God of the Jews, but the strife between the good and evil men continues. The former are the Gnostics; the soul is entirely in them, and consequently they live eternally. On the other hand, the body cannot rise again: it is condemned to perish. Whatever propagates the body propagates the empire of Satan, and, consequently, marriage is an evil. It weakens the divine principle in man, by subdividing that principle to infinity.

It will be seen that all those sects were equally incapable of giving a serious basis to morality. They even had difficulty in avoiding the breakers of secret debauches and accusations of infamy. Alexandria could not stop on that slippery ground. That extraordinary city was destined to see, at its most brilliant period, all the evils of the age burst forth within it in all their energy. Carpocrates drew from it the deductions of an unwholesome philosophy, which carried the exaggerations of an intemperate supernaturalism amongst all orders, and tossed men to and fro between asceticism and immorality, rarely leaving him in the golden mean of reason. Carpocrates and his son Epiphanes did not recoil before any of the excesses of sensual mysticism, as they proclaimed the indifference of actions, the community of women, the holiness of all perversions, as means of delivering the spirit from the flesh. That deliverance of the spiritual man which wrests souls from the wicked demiurges to reunite them to the supreme God, was the work of the sages Pythagoras, Plato, Aristotle, Jesus, etc. The statues of those sages were adored,--they were crowned,--incense and even sacrifices were offered to them. According to Carpocrates, Jesus, the son of Joseph, had been the justest man of his time. After having practised Judaism, he recognised its vanity, and by that act of disdain he merited deliverance. Nowhere is it forbidden to aspire to equal and even to surpass him in holiness. His resurrection is an impossibility; his soul alone has been received into heaven; his body remained on earth. The apostles-- Peter, Paul, and the others--were not inferior to Jesus, but if any one could arrive at a more perfect contempt for the world of the demiurges, that is to say, for reality, he would surpass him. The Carpocratians claimed to exercise that power by magical operations, by philtres, by witchcraft. It is clear that they were not true members of the Church of Jesus. Nevertheless, the sectaries took the name of Christians, and the orthodox were in despair at it. As a matter of fact, in their conventicles, abominations, such as the calumniators of the Christians reproached the faithful with, took place, and this usurpation of the name caused deplorable prejudices to take deep root amongst the multitude.

Far from exhibiting the slightest complaisance towards the culpable mysteries, the Church only held them in abhorrence and visited them with the most violent anathemas which she could find in her sacred texts. What was said of the Nicolaitanes at the beginning of the Apocalypse was brought to mind. By the name Nicolaitanes, the Seer of Patmos most likely intends to designate St Paul's partisans: at any rate such a designation has nothing at all to do with the Deacon Nicholas, who was one of the Seven in the Primitive Church of Jerusalem. But that false identification was soon accredited. Scandalous stories were told against the alleged heresiarch which very much resembled those which were told about the Carpocratians. Many aberrations took place on all sides, and no paradox was without its defender. People were found who took the part of Cain, of Esau, of Korah, of the Sodomites, of Judas himself. Jehovah was the evil,--a tyrant filled with hatred, and it had been right to brave his laws. These were kinds of literary paradoxes; just as thirty or forty years ago it was the fashion to set up criminals as heroes, because they were supposed to be in revolt against bad social order. There was a Gospel of Judas. In excuse for this latter, it was said that he had betrayed Jesus with a good intention, because he had found out that his master wished to ruin the truth. The traitor's conduct was also explained by a motive of interest for humanity. The powers of the world (that is to say, Satan and his agents) wished to stop the work of salvation, by preventing Jesus from dying. Judas, who knew that the death of Jesus on the cross was beneficial, broke the charm, by giving him up to his enemies. Thus he was the purest of spiritual men. These singular Christians were called Cainites. Like Carpocrates, they taught that, in order to be saved, it was necessary to have done all sorts of actions, and, in some manner, to have exhausted all the experiences of life: it is said that they placed the perfection of enlightenment in the commission of the darkest deeds. Every act has an angel who presides over it, and they invoked that angel whilst they were doing the act. Their books were worthy of their morals. They had the Gospel of Judas, and some other writings which were made to exhort men to destroy the work of the Creator; one book in particular, called The Ascension of St Paul, into which they seem to have introduced horrible abominations.

These were aberrations without any real object, and which certainly the serious-minded Gnostics rejected just as much as the orthodox Christians. The really grave part about it was the destruction of Christianity, which was at the bottom of all these speculations. In reality the living Jesus was suppressed, and only a phantom Jesus, without any efficacy for the conversion of the heart, was left. Moral effort was replaced by so-called science; dreams took the place of Christian realities, and every man arrogated to himself the right to carve out as he chose a Christianity according to his fancy, from the dogmas and earlier books. This was no longer Christianity, it was a strange parasite which was trying to pass for a branch of the tree of life. Jesus was no longer a fact without analogy; he was one of the apparitions of the divine spirit. Docetism, which reduced all the human life of Jesus to a mere appearance, was the basis of all these errors. Still, moderate with Basilides and Valentinus, it becomes absolute with Saturninus, and with Marcion we shall see that the whole of the Saviour's earthly career is reduced to a pure appearance.

Orthodoxy will be able to resist these dangerous ideas, whilst at times allowing itself to be drawn away by their seductive qualities. Gospels, deeply tinged with new ideas, were spread abroad. The "Gospel of Peter" was the expression of pure Docetism. The "Gospel according to the Egyptians" was a remodelling, after the Alexandrine ideas, of the Gospel according to the Hebrews. The union of the sexes was forbidden in it. The Saviour, on being questioned by Salome when his kingdom would come, answered, "When you tread under foot the garment of shame; when two shall make one; when that which is outside shall be like that which is inside, and the male joined to a female shall be neither male nor female." Interpreted according to the rules of the vocabulary of Philo, these strange words signify that when humanity is no more, the body will be spiritualised and enter into the soul, so that man will be nothing but a pure spirit. The "coats of skins" with which God covered Adam will then be useless; primitive innocence will reign again.

# CHAPTER XI

### THE LAST REVOLT OF THE JEWS

After staying in Jerusalem for two years, Hadrian got tired of doing nothing, and again began to think of his travels. First of all he paid a visit to Mauritania, and then directed his course for the second time to Greece and the East. He stayed at Athens for nearly a year, and consecrated the edifices that he had ordered to be erected during his first journey; and Greece had one long festival, and seemed but to live in him. In every direction classic recollections revived, and Hadrian made them durable by monuments and columns, and founded temples, libraries, and professorial chairs. The ancient world before dying made its pilgrimage to the places from which it had sprung, and seemed as if it were uttering its last eulogy. The Emperor presided like a pontiff at these innocent solemnities, which hardly amused anybody now but those who were empty-headed and idle.

The august traveller then continued his journey through the East, and visited Armenia, Asia Minor, Syria, and Judea. As far as outward appearances went, he was everywhere received as a guardian spirit, and medals which were struck for the occasion bade him welcome in every province. That of Judea is still in existence. Alas; what a falsehood. Below the inscription ADVENTVI AVG. IVDAEAE is to be seen the Emperor in a noble and worthy attitude receiving Judea with kindness, and she is presenting her sons to him. Already the Emperor has the handsome and gentle look of the Antonines, and seems to be the impersonification of calm civilisation educating fanaticism. Children go before him bearing palms, whilst in the middle a Pagan altar and a bull symbolise religious reconciliation; and Judea, a patera in her hand, seems to share in the sacrifice that is being prepared. This is how official optimism instructs sovereigns. The opposition between the East and the West was actually getting more and more accentuated, and the signs of this were so certain that the Emperor could not doubt them--his benevolent eclecticism was, however, at times singularly unsettled.

From Syria Hadrian went to Egypt by way of Petra. His discontent and his ill temper with the peoples of the East increased daily. A short time before Egypt had been in a state of great agitation. The ancient worships, which were springing into life again, caused a certain amount of fermentation, for it was so long since an Apis had been seen that these ancient chimeras were beginning to be forgotten, when suddenly a clamour arose; that miraculous animal had been found, and as everybody wished to possess it, all tried to get it from the others. The hold of Christianity over Egypt was not so strong as it was elsewhere, for many heathen superstitions were mixed up with it. All these follies only served to amuse Hadrian, and a letter which be wrote about that time to his brother-in-law Servian, has been preserved to us:--

I have found that Egypt, my dear Servian, which you praised to me, to be a very flighty country, hanging by a thread, turning round with every breath of fashion. There, those who adore Serapis are Christians at the same time, and men who call themselves bishops of Christ are devoted to Serapis. There is not a president of a synagogue, not a Samaritan, not a Christian priest, who does not supplement his functions by those of the astrologer, of the diviner, and the charlatan. The patriarch himself, when he comes to Egypt, is forced by some to adore Serapis, and by the others to adore Christ. It is a seditious, futile, and irrelevant education, and a rich and productive city, where nobody lives in idleness. Some are glassblowers, others papermakers, others again dyers, and all understand and practise some trade. The gouty can find something to do, the shortsighted can obtain employment, the blind are not without occupation, and even the one-armed are not idle. Money is their only god, the divinity which Christians, Jews, people of all sorts, adore. One regrets to find such a low state of morals in a city which by its manufactures and its grandeur is worthy of being the capital of Egypt. I have granted it everything; I have restored its ancient privileges, and given it new ones, and I forced them to thank me whilst I was there; but I had scarcely left when they began to talk about my son Verus, and to say, what no doubt you know, about Antinous. The only revenge that I wish to have is that they may always be forced to eat their own fowls, fecundated in a manner that I do not like to mention. I have sent you some glasses of prismatic colours, which the priests of the temple offered me; they are specially dedicated to you and to my sister. Have them used on festive occasions, only take care that our Africanus does not make too good use of them.

From Egypt Hadrian returned to Syria, and there he found the people very badly disposed. They were getting bolder. Antioch gave him an unfavourable reception, and so he went to Athens, where he was worshipped. There he heard of some very serious events, for the Jews were having recourse to arms for the third time. Their attack of furious madness of the year 117 seemed as if it were about to recommence, and Israel disliked the Roman government more than ever. Every malefactor who revolted against the State was a saint, and every brigand became a patriot. It was looked upon as an act of treason to arrest a robber. "Vinegar, off-spring of wine," said a rabbi to a Jew, whose business it was to arrest evil-doers, "why do you denounce God's people?" Elijah also met this worthy public officer and exhorted him to give up his odious trade.

It seems that the Roman authority also committed more than one mistake. Hadrian's administration became more and more intolerant towards the Eastern sects, whom the Emperor made fun of. Several lawyers thought that circumcision, like castration, was punishable ill-usage, and so it was forbidden. The cases in which those who had practised epispasm, and had been forced by fanatics to be circumcised over again, would more especially give rise to these prosecutions; and we do not know how far imperial justice advanced along this difficult road which was so opposed to liberty of conscience. Hadrian was certainly not a man given to excessive measures, and in Jewish tradition all the odium of these measures rests on Tineius Rufus, who was the Legate Proprætor of the Province of Judea, and whose name the malcontents changed into Tyrannus Rufus.

These annoyances, which were so easily avoided in the only cases which were of any importance to pious families, namely, the cases relative to the circumcision of infants, were not the chief cause of the war. What really raised the Israelites to revolt, was the horror that they felt at seeing the transformation of Jerusalem, or, in other words, the progress that the construction of Ælia Capitolina was making. The sight of a Pagan city rising on the ruins of the holy city, the rebuilding of the profaned temple, those heathen sacrifices, those theatres raised with the very stones of that venerated building, those foreigners dwelling in the city which God had loved, all this appeared to them to be the very height of sacrilege and of defiance.

Far from wishing to return to this profaned Jerusalem, they fled from it like an abomination, whilst the south of Judea was more than ever a Jewish country. A number of large places had sprung up there which could defend themselves, thanks to the position of their houses, which were massed together on the summit of low hills. For the Jews of that district, Bether had become another holy city, and equivalent to Zion. The fanatics procured arms by a singular stratagem. They were bound to furnish the Romans with a certain number of implements of war, and so they manufactured them badly, on purpose that the rejected weapons might come to them. Instead of visible fortifications, they constructed immense tunnels; and the fortifications of Bether were completed by advanced works of broken stone, and all the Jews who remained in Egypt and Libya hastened to swell the number of the rebels.

We must do that justice to the clear-sighted portion of the nation that they took no part in a movement that presupposed enormous ignorance of the world, and complete blindness as to what they were doing. As a general rule, the Pharisees were defiant and reserved, and many of the doctors of the law fled into Galilee, and into Greece, to avoid the coming storm. Several did not conceal the fact that they were faithful to the Empire, and even attributed a certain legitimacy to it. Rabbi Joshua Ben Hanania seems to have acted in a conciliatory spirit up to his extreme old age; and after him, the Talmudists say, all prudent counsels were lost. Under these circumstances was seen again what had been continually seen for the last hundred years: a nation, which was easily duped at the slightest breath of Messianic hope, would go on in spite of the doctors; they only thought of their casuistry; and if they died, they did not die fighting, but in defending themselves from breaking the law.

The Christians resisted the temptation even better. Although revolt might gratify the hatred of some of them for the Roman Empire, a distinct distrust for all that proceeded from fanatical Israel stopped them on the dangerous descent. They had already chosen their part, and the form of their resistance to the Empire was not revolt but martyrdom. They were tolerably numerous in Judea, and, contrary to the orthodox Jews, they might even live in Ælia. Of course the Jews tried to gain over their quasi-compatriots, but the disciples of Jesus were already very far from all earthly politics, for he had buried for ever the hopes of a material patriotism and Messiah. Hadrian's reign was far from being unfavourable to the Churches, and so they did not move; and some voices were even raised to foretell to the Jews the consequences of their obstinacy, and the extermination that awaited them.

Every Jewish revolt had, more or less, to do with Messianic hopes, but never before had any one given himself out for the Messiah; but this took place now. No doubt under the influence of Christian ideas, and in imitation of Jesus, a man gave himself out for the long-expected heavenly messenger, and succeeded in seducing the people. We have no clear history of that strange episode, for the Jews, who alone could have informed us what were the secret thoughts and the motive secret of these agitators, have left us nothing but confused pictures of them, like those of a man who has been mad. There was no Josephus then, and Barcochebas, as the Christians called him, remains an insoluable problem, and one on which even imagination cannot hope to exercise itself with any hope of reading the truth.

The name of his father, or of the place where he was born, was Coziba, and he was always called "the son of Coziba" (Bar or Ben-Coziba), but his real name is unknown. Perhaps his partisans were induced to conceal his name, and that of his family, purposely in the interests of his part as Messiah. He seems to have been a nephew of Rabbi Eleazar of Modin, an Agadist of the highest renown, who had lived very much with Rabbi Gamaliel II. and his companions. One asks oneself whether the recollection of the Maccabees, who were still living at Modin, did not excite Bar-Coziba's patriotic enthusiasm. There can be no doubt as to his courage, but the scantiness of historical information prevents us from saying more than that. Was he serious? Was he a religious enthusiast or a fanatic? Was he one of those sincere believers in the Messiah who came on to the scene too late? Or are we only to see in this equivocal person a charlatan, an imitator of Jesus, with a totally different object, a common impostor, even a criminal, as Eusebius and St Jerome assert? We cannot tell, for the only circumstance in his favour is that the principal Jewish Doctor of the Law at that period was in his favour, a man who, from his habit of thought, would be far removed from the dreams of an impostor, and that was the Rabbi Aquiba.

For many years he had been the chief authority amongst the Jews, and he was compared to Esdras and even to Moses. As a general rule, the doctors were not at all favourable to popular agitators. Taken up with their own discussions, they thought that the destinies of Israel, dependent on the observance of the Law and Messianic dreams, were limited for them to the Mosaic ideal which those who were scrupulously devout realised. How could Aquiba incite the people, whose confidence he enjoyed, to commit a veritable act of folly? Perhaps the fact of his having sprung from the people, and his democratic tendency to contradict the traditions of the Sadducees, may have helped to lead him astray, and perhaps also the absurdity of his exegesis deprived him of all practical rectitude. One can never with impunity play with common sense, or put such pressure on the springs of the intellect as may threaten to snap them. At any rate the fact appears certain, though it is difficult to believe it, that Aquiba recognised Bar-Coziba's Messianic character. After a fashion he invested him with it before the people when he gave him the commander's baton and held his stirrup for him when he mounted his war-horse to inaugurate his reign as Messiah. His name of Bar-Coziba was an unhappy one, and lent itself to all kinds of unfortunate allusions. Looking on the bearer of it as the predestined Saviour of Israel, it is said that Aquiba applied the verse from Numbers xxiv. 17: "A star shall arise out of Jacob," a verse which was supposed to have a Messianic sense to him, and so his name of Bar-Coziba was changed into Bar-Kokaba, "the son of the star."

Bar-Coziba being thus recognised as the man who, without any official title, it is true, but in virtue of a sort of universal acceptance, passed as the religious guide of the people of Israel, became the chief of the revolution, and war was decided on. At first the Romans neglected the foolish popular agitations. Bether, in its isolated position, far from the great highroads, did not attract their attention; but when the movement had invaded the whole of Judea, and the Jews began to form threatening bands in all directions, they were obliged to open their eyes. They began to attack the Roman forces, and to lie in ambush for them in a murderous fashion. Besides this, the movement, as happened in 68 and in 117, had a tendency to spread over the rest of the East. Arab brigands who lived near the Jordan and the Dead Sea, who were in a state of anarchy through the destruction of the Nabatæan kingdom of Petra, thought they saw a chance of pillage in Syria and Egypt. The confusion was general. Those who had practised epispasm to escape the capitation tax, submitted anew to a painful operation, so that they might not be excluded from the hopes of Israel; and some thought so surely that the time of Messiah had arrived, that they thought themselves authorised to pronounce the name of Jehovah as it is written.

As long as Hadrian was in Egypt and Syria, the conspirators did not let their plans be seen, but as soon as he had gone to Athens the revolt broke out. It appears that the report was spread that the Emperor was ill and attacked by leprosy. Ælia, with its Roman colony, was strongly guarded. The Legio Decima Fratensis was still in garrison there, and no doubt the road between Ælia and Cæsarea, the city which was the centre of the Roman authority, also remained open, and thus ælia was never surrounded by the insurrection. It was easy to keep communications open, thanks to a circle of colonies which were established in the east and north of the city, and especially owing to such places as Nicopolis and Lydda, which were assured to the Romans.

It is therefore probable that the revolt in its northward progress did not go beyond Bether, and did not reach Jerusalem, but all the smaller towns of Judea which had no garrisons proclaimed the independence of Israel. Bether, in particular, became a sort of small capital, a prospective second Jerusalem side by side with the great Jerusalem which they hoped to conquer soon. Its situation was very strong, as it commanded all the valleys of the revolted country, and was made almost impregnable by means of tremendous outworks, the remains of which may be seen even to this day.

The first case of the insurgents was the monetary question. One of the greatest punishments of the faithful Jews was to be obliged to handle money bearing the effigy of the Emperor, and idolatrous figures. For religious purposes, above all, they either sought for coins of the Asmonean princes, which were still current in the country, or else those of the first rebellion, when the Asmonean coinage had been imitated. The new insurrection was too poor and too badly provided with machinery to issue coins of a new mould. They were satisfied with withdrawing the coins bearing the stamp of Flavius and Trajan, and impressing them anew with an orthodox stamp which the people knew, and which had a national meaning for them; and perhaps some ancient coins had been found which facilitated the operation. For this imitation, the handsome coins of Simon Maccabæus, the first Jewish prince who coined money, were especially selected. From their date, which was that of the liberty of Israel or of Jerusalem, those coins seemed to have been struck for the very purpose, and those on which was to be seen a temple surmounted by a star, and those which bore only the impress of the two trumpets which were destined, according to the Law, to summon Israel to the Holy War, were more appropriate still. The stamp upon stamp was done very roughly, and on a great number of coins the first Roman impress is still visible. This coinage was called the money of Coziba, or the money of the revolt, and as it was partly fictitious it lost much of its value later on.

It was a long and terrible war, and lasted for over two years, whilst the best generals seem to have worn themselves out in it. Tineius Rufus, seeing that he was outnumbered, asked for assistance, and though his colleague Publicius Marcellus, Legate of Syria, hastened to bring it him, both failed. In order to crush the revolt, it was necessary to summon the first captain of his period, Sextus Julius Severus, from Britain. He received the title of Legate of the Province of Judea, in the place of Tineius Rufus, and Quintus Lollias Urbicus was his second in command as Hadrian's legate.

The rebels never showed themselves in the open country, but they were masters of the heights, on which they built fortifications, and between their embattled towns they dug out covered ways, subterranean communications, which were lighted from above by air-holes, which gave air as well as light. The secret passages were places of refuge for them when they were driven back, and enabled them to go and defend another point. Unhappy race! Driven from its own soil, it seemed as if it preferred to bury itself in its bowels rather than leave it, or allow it to be profaned. This war of moles was extremely murderous, and fanaticism reached the same height as in 70. Nowhere did Julius Severus venture to come to an engagement with his adversaries, for, seeing their number and despair, he feared to expose the heavy masses of the Romans to the danger of a war of barricades and of fortified hill tops. He attacked the rebels separately, and, thanks to the number of his soldiers, and to the skill of his lieutenants, he nearly always succeeded in starving them out, by surrounding them in their trenches.

Bar-Coziba, driven into a corner by impossibilities, became more violent every day, and his rule was that of a king. He ravaged the surrounding country, and did not recoil before the grossest imposture in order to sustain his part as Messiah. The refusal of the Christians to receive him as such, and to make common cause with him, irritated him greatly, and so he resorted to the most cruel persecutions against them. The Messianic character of Jesus was the denial of his own and the principal obstacle to his plans. Those who refused to deny or to blaspheme the name of Jesus were put to death, scourged, tortured. Jude, who seems to have been Bishop of Jerusalem at that time, may have been one of the victims. Enthusiasts looked upon the political indifference of the Christians, and their loyal fidelity to the Empire, as a want of patriotism; but it seems that the more sensible among the Jews openly gave vent to their displeasure. One day when Aquiba, seeing Bar-Coziba, cried out, "Here is the Messiah!" the Rabbi Johaman ben Torta replied, "Aquiba, the grass will be growing between your jaws before the son of David comes."

As usual, Rome prevailed in the end, and in turn each centre of resistance fell. Fifty improvised fortresses, which the rebels had built, and nine hundred and fifty-five market towns were taken, and turned into ruins. Beth-Rimmon, on the Idumæan frontier, was the scene of a terrible slaughter of fugitives. The siege of Bether was particularly long and difficult; the besieged endured the last extremities of hunger and thirst, and Bar-Coziba was killed there, though nothing is known of the circumstances of his death.

The massacre was terrible. A hundred and eighty thousand Jews were killed in the various engagements, whilst the number of those who perished from hunger, by burning, and from sickness, is incalculable. Women and children were murdered in cold blood.Judea literally became a desert, and howling wolves and hyenas entered into the houses. Many towns of Darom were ruined for ever, and the desolate look which the country wears even now is still a living sign of the catastrophe that happened seventeen and a half centuries ago.

The Roman army had been sorely tried. Hadrian, writing to the senate from Athens, does not make use of the ordinary preamble which emperors were in the habit of using: Si vos liberique vestri valetis, bene est; ego quidem et exereitus valemus. Severus was rewarded as he deserved for this well-conducted campaign, for, at Hadrian's suggestion, the senate decreed him triumphal ornaments, and he was raised to the dignity of Legate of Syria. The army of Judea was overwhelmed with rewards, and Hadrian was hailed as Emperor for the second time.

Whatever was not killed was sold at the same price as the horses, at the annual fair of the 'l'erebinthe, near Hebron. That was the spot where Abraham was supposed to have pitched his tent when he received the visit of the three Divine Beings. The field in which the fair was held, carefully marked out by a rectangular enclosure, exists still. From that time forward a terrible memento was attached to that place, which, up till then, had been so sacred in their eyes, and they never mentioned the fair of the Terebinthe without horror. Those who were not sold there were taken to Gaza and there put up for sale at another fair that Hadrian had established there. Those unfortunate wretches who could not be got rid of in Palestine were taken to Egypt, and many suffered shipwreck, whilst others died of hunger; others, again, were killed by the Egyptians, who had not forgotten the atrocities which the Jews committed in the same parts eighteen years previously. Two brothers who still kept up the resistance at Kafar-Karouba were killed, with all their followers.

The subterranean works of Judea, however, still contained a crowd of unfortunate beings, who did not dare to leave them for fear of being killed. Their life was terrible; every sound seemed to herald the approach of the enemy, and in their mad terror they rushed at and crushed each other. The only means they had of assuaging their hunger was by eating the bodies of their neighbours who had died. It seems that, in certain cases, the Roman authorities forbade the burial of corpses, so as to make the impression of their chastisement even greater. Judea was like a vast charnel-house, and those wretches who succeeded in reaching the desert looked upon themselves as favoured by God.

All certainly had not deserved such severe punishment, and in this instance, as happens so often, wise men paid for fools. A nation is a solidarity, and the individual who has contributed nothing towards the faults of his compatriots, who has even groaned under them, is punished no less than the others. The first duty of a community is to check its absurd elements; and the idea of withdrawing from the great Mediterranean confederation that Rome had created, was absurdity itself. Just as history ought to sympathise with those gentle and pacific Jews who only desired freedom to meditate on the Law, so also our principles oblige us to be severe towards a Bar-Coziba who plunged his country into a abyss of ills, and towards an Aquiba who upheld popular follies by his authority. Every one who sheds his blood for the cause which he considers righteous, is deserving of our respect; but we owe him no approval for that. The Jewish fanatics were not fighting for their liberty, but for a theocracy, for liberty to harass the Pagans, and to exterminate everything that appeared to them to be bad. The ideal which they sought after would have been an unsupportable state of affairs. Analogous, as far as intolerance went, to the miserable Asmonean period, it would have been the reign of zealots, radicals of the very worse sort: it would have been the massacre of unbelievers, a Reign of Terror. All the liberals of the second century looked upon it like that. A very intelligent man, who, like the Jews, belonged to a noble and conquered race, Pausanias, the antiquary, expresses himself thus:--"In my time there reigned that Hadrian who showed such respect for all the gods, and who had the happiness of his subjects so much at heart. He undertook no war without being forced to it; and as for the Hebrews who border on Syria, he subjugated them because they had revolted against him."

# CHAPTER XII

### DISAPPEARANCE OF THE JEWISH NATION

The immediate consequence of this mad act of rebellion was a real persecution of Judaism. The Jews were weighed down by a tribute that was heavier still than the fiscus judaicus imposed by Vespasian. The exercise of the most essential practices of the Mosaic religion--circumcision, the observance of the Sabbath and of feasts, apparently insignificant simple usages were forbidden, under pain of death; and even those who taught the Law were prosecuted. Renegade Jews, who had turned spies, tracked the faithful who met in the most secret places to study the sacred code, and the Jews were reduced to reading it on the roofs of the houses. The doctors of the Law were cruelly persecuted, and rabbinical ordination entailed the death penalty both on the ordainer and on the ordinee. There were many martyrs in Judea and Galilee, and throughout the whole of Syria it was a crime to be a Jew. It was now, it appears, that the two brothers, Julianus and Pappus, who are celebrated in Jewish tradition for having preferred death to an apparent violation of the Law committed in public, were executed, and though water in a coloured glass was offered them so that they might pretend to think that they had drunk Pagan wine, they refused to take it.

About that period the schools of the Casuists were chiefly taken up with the question of those precepts which might be broken in order to avoid death, and those for which martyrdom ought to be suffered. The doctors generally admit that in times of persecution all observances may be renounced as long as three prohibited things, idolatry, fornication (i.e., unlawful unions), and murder are abstained from. This sensible principle was put forward: "It is suicide to resist the Emperor's orders." It was admitted that religious worship might be kept secret, and that the circumcision of children might be announced by the sound of hand-mills instead of with the usual noisy demonstrations. It was also pointed out that, according to Leviticus xviii. 5, the observance of the Law gives life, and so that consequently any one who dies for the Law is responsible for his own death, so that when a man found himself between the two precepts to observe the Law and to preserve his own life, he ought to obey the second, which is the more commanding, at any rate when death is certain, just as, in the case of a serious illness, it is lawful to take remedies which may contain some impure substance. There was another point on which all were agreed, and this was that it was better to suffer death than to violate the slightest commandment publicly; and lastly, they agreed in placing the duty of teaching above all other obligations. At Lydda especially these questions were agitated, and that city had its celebrated martyrs, who were called the murdered of Lydda.

The great doubt about Providence that takes possession of the Jew as soon as he is no longer prosperous and triumphant, made the position of those martyrs a particularly cruel one. The Christian, depending as he does altogether on the future life, is never firmer in his faith than when he is being persecuted; but the Jewish martyr has not the same light. "Where is now your God?" is the ironical question which he constantly fancies that he hears from Pagan lips. To the very last Rabbi Ishmael ben Elischa never ceased to fight against the ideas that sprang up in his mind, and in the minds of his companions, against divine justice. "Do you still trust in your God?" he was asked, and his answer was, "Though he slay me yet will I trust in him," using the words of Job that have been badly translated.

Aquiba, who had been a prisoner for a long time, nevertheless kept up a correspondence with his disciples. "Prepare for death, terrible days are coming," was the sentence always on his lips. He was put to death because the was betrayed to the Romans for imparting profound doctrine. He is said to have been flayed alive with red-hot iron hooks. Whilst he was being torn to pieces he cried incessantly, "Jehovah is our God! Jehovah is our only God!" and he laid a stress on the word "only" (ehad), till he expired, when a heavenly voice was heard saying, "Happy Aquiba, as you died whilst uttering that word only.'"

It was not till late, and by means of successive experiences, that Israel arrived at the idea of immortality. Martyrdom made this belief almost a necessity. Nobody could pretend that those scrupulous observers of the Law who died for it had their reward here below. The answer that sufficed for cases like those of Job and Tobias did not suffice here. How could any one talk of a long and happy life for heroes who were expiring under a terrible death? Either God was unjust, or the saints who were thus tormented were great culprits. In the middle ages there were martyrs who accepted this latter doctrine with a kind of despair, and when they were being led to execution, they would maintain that they had deserved it, for they had been guilty of all sorts of crimes. But such a paradox must necessarily be very rare. The reign of a thousand years which was reserved for the martyrs, was the first solution of that difficult problem which was attempted. Then it came to be a received opinion that ascensions to heaven in heart and mind, that revelations, the contemplation of the divine secrets of the cabala, were the martyr's reward. As the apocalyptic spirit was lost, the tikva, that is, the invincible confidence of man in the justice of God, assumed forms that were analogous to the enduring paradise of Christians. But that article of faith was never an absolute dogma amongst the Jews; no trace of it is found in the Thora; and how could it be supposed that God had expressly deprived the saints of old of such a fundamental dogma?

From thenceforward all hopes of seeing the Temple raised up again were lost, and the Jews had even to give up the consolation of living near the holy places. The species of worship that the Jewish people vowed to the soil which they thought God had given them, was the evil that the Roman authorities wished to cure at any price, so that for the future they might cut off the root of Jewish wars. An edict drove the Jews from Jerusalem and its neighbourhood under pain of death, and the very sight of Jerusalem was refused them. Only once a year, on the anniversary of the taking of the city, did they obtain authorisation to come and weep over the ruins of the Temple, and to anoint a hollow stone, which they thought marked the site of the Holy of Holies, with oil; and even that permission was dearly bought. "On that day," says St Jerome, "you might see a mournful crowd, a miserable people, who received no pity, assemble and draw near. Decrepit women, old men in rags, all are weeping, and whilst their cheeks are covered with tears, and they raise their livid arms, and tear their thin hair, a soldier comes up and calls on them for payment, so that they may have the right to weep a little longer." The rest of Judea was also prohibited ground to the Jews, but not so strictly, for certain localities, such as Lydda, always preserved their Jewish quarters.

The Samaritans, who had taken no part in the revolt, hardly suffered less than the Jews. Mount Gerizim, like Mount Moriah, had its temple of Jupiter; the prohibition of circumcision attacked them in the free exercise of their religion; and the memory of Bar-Coziba seems to have been execrated by them.

The construction of Ælia Capitolina went on more actively than ever, and everything was done to efface the recollection of the past, which had been so threatening. The old name of Jerusalem was almost forgotten, and Ælia took its place throughout the whole of the East, so that a hundred and fifty years later Jerusalem had become a name in ancient geography which nobody knew any more. The city was full of profane edifices, forums, baths, theatres, tetranymphea, etc. Statues were erected in all directions, and the subtle Jewish mind tried to discover mocking allusions in them, which Hadrian's engineers certainly never intended. Thus over the gate leading to Bethlehem there was a piece of sculpture in marble which they thought resembled a pig, and in that they saw a most insulting piece of irony towards the vanquished people, whilst they forgot that the wild boar was a Roman emblem, and figured on the standards of the legions. The circumference of the city was slightly altered towards the south, and became about what it is now. Mount Zion remained outside the enclosure, and was covered with kitchen gardens. Those parts of the city which were not rebuilt afforded a mass of loose stones which served as a stone quarry for the new buildings. The foundations of Herod's temple (the present harâm) excited wonder by their strength, and soon the Christians declared that these tremendous layers of stones would only be dislodged at the coming of Antichrist.

On the site of the Temple, as has been said, was raised the temple of Jupiter Capitolinus. Bacchus, Serapis, Astarte, the Dioscuri were associated there with the principal god. As usual, statues of the Emperor were scattered broadcast, and one of them at least was equestrian; whilst the statues of Jupiter and Venus were also set up near Golgotha. When, in later years, the Christians settled their sacred topography, they were scandalised at this proximity, and looked upon it as an outrage; and in the same way they thought that the Emperor had intended to profane Bethlehem by setting up the worship of Adonis there.

Antoninus, Marcus Aurelius, and Verus occupied themselves in beautifying the city, and improving the highroads that led to it, and these public works irritated the real Jews. "In spite of all, the works of this nation are admirable," said Rabbi Juda bar Ilaï one day to two of his friends who were seated with him. "They build forums, construct bridges, and establish baths." "That is much to their merit!" replied Simeon ben Jochaï; "they do it all for their own benefit: they put brothels into the forums; they have the baths for their own amusement, and they construct the bridges so that they may receive the tolls.

The hatred of Greek life, which was always so active amongst the Jews, was redoubled at the sight of a material renovation which seemed to be its striking triumph. Thus finished the final attempt of the Jewish people to remain a nation which possessed a name and a defined territory. In the Talmud, the war of Bar-Coziba is very rightly called "the war of extermination." Dangerous movements, which seemed to be the rekindling of the flame, appeared again during the first years of Antoninus: they were easily repressed. From that moment Israel had no longer a fatherland, and then it began its wandering life, which for centuries has marked it as the wonder of the world. Under the Roman sway the civil situation of the Jew was lost without recovery. If Palestine had wished it, it would have become a province like Syria, and its lot would have been neither worse nor better than that of the other provinces. In the first century, several Jews played most extraordinarily important parts. Afterwards that will never be seen, and it seems as if the Jews had disappeared underground: they are only mentioned as beggars who have taken refuge in the suburbs of Rome, sitting at the gates of Aricia, besieging carriages, and clinging to the wheels, so as to obtain something from the pity of travellers. They are a body of raïas, having, it is true, their statutes, and their personal magistrates, but who are outside the pale of common law, forming no part of the State, in some measure analogous to the Zingari in Europe. There was no longer a single rich notable Jew of any consideration associating with men of the world. The great Jewish fortunes did not re-appear again till the sixth century, and then it was chiefly amongst the Visigoths of Spain, in consequence of the false ideas with regard to usury and commerce which were spread abroad by Christianity. Then the Jew became, and continued to be during the greater part of the Middle Ages, a necessary personage without whom the world could not accomplish the simplest transactions. Modern Liberalism alone could put an end to this exceptional situation. A decree of the Constituent Assembly in the year 1791 made them again citizens and members of a nation.

In that world which was burnt up by a sort of internal volcanic fire, there were some oases. Some survivors of Sadduceeism, who were treated as apostates by their co-religionists, preserved amidst these mystical dreams the healthy philosophy of Ecclesiasticus. The provincial Jews, who were subject to the Arsaeides, lived tolerably happily, and observed the Law without being interfered with. The composition of a charming book, the date of which is uncertain, and which was not translated into Greek till towards the end of the second century, may be attributed to these provinces. It is a little romance, full of freshness, such as the Jews excelled in, the idyl par excellence of Jewish piety and domestic pleasures.

A certain Tobit, son of Tobiel, who sprung from Cades of Naphtali, was taken captive to Nineveh by Shalmaneser. From his childhood he had been a model of goodness, and, far from participating in the idolatry of the Northern tribes, he regularly went to Jerusalem, the only spot that God had chosen as a place of worship, and offered his tithe to the priests, the descendants of Aaron, according to the rules of the Teruma and of the Maaser scheni. He was charitable, benevolent, and amiable towards all; he abstained from eating the bread of the heathen, and in return God obtained Shalmaneser's favour for him, who made him his purveyor. After Shalmaneser's death. Sennacherib, who had returned furious from his expedition to Jerusalem, began to act very severely towards the Jews; their bodies were lying about unburied in all directions, and were to be seen in heaps outside the walls of Nineveh, and Tobit went and buried them by stealth. The king, surprised at the disappearance of the bodies, asked what had become of them. Tobit was persecuted, hid himself, and lost his property, and only the murder of Sennacherib saved him. He then continued his pious work of burying the Israelites whom he found dead, though his neighbours made fun of him, and asked him what his reward would be. One evening he came back overcome by fatigue; he could not go into his own house, as he was unclean from having touched the dead bodies, so he threw himself at the foot of a wall in the court of his house and went to sleep: an accident deprived him of his eye-sight. Here we have the same problem laid down as in the book of Job, and with the same vigour: a just man not only badly rewarded for his goodness, but struck in consequence of his virtue itself: an act of virtue followed by misfortune resulting from it. How can one allege after that that the servant of Jehovah always receives the reward of his fidelity? His wife asks him where his alms and his good actions are, and what profit he has gained from them.

Tobit persists in the affirmation of a true Israelite that God is just and good, and he even carries his heroism so far as to vilify himself so as to justify God; he declares that he has deserved his lot, firstly on account of the sins and omissions that he has been guilty of through ignorance, then because of the sins of his fathers. Because the ancestors of the then existing generation were guilty, therefore that generation is dispersed and dishonoured. Tobit only begs for one favour, which is to die at once, so that he may return to the earth and go to the eternal place.

Now on that same day, at Ecbatana, another afflicted creature had also asked God for death. That was Sara, the daughter of Raguel, who had been married seven times, and, though she was absolutely pure, had seen her seven husbands strangled on their wedding-night by the wicked demon Aëschmadaëva, who was jealous of her, and killed all those who wished to touch her. Those two prayers were presented at the same time at the throne of God by the Archangel Raphael, who is one of the seven angels that are allowed to penetrate into the sanctuary of the divine glory to carry the prayers of the saints thither. God hears the supplication of these two just and sorely tried persons, and bids Raphael make good the evil.

Everybody knows the charming idyl that follows. It has rightly found a place amongst these sacred fables which, reproduced under many different shapes, never weary us. Gentle morality, family feeling, filial piety, the love and the eternal union of the husband and wife, charity towards the poor man, devotion to Israel, have never been expressed in a more charming fashion. Good will to all, strict honesty, temperance, great care not to do to others what one would not wish to have done to oneself; care in the choice of one's company and to be intimate only with good people, the spirit of order, regularity in one's affairs, judicious family arrangements, that is that excellent Jewish morality which, though it is not exactly that of a nobleman, or of a man of the world, has become the code of the Christian middle classes in its best sense. Nothing is further removed from avarice. That same Tobit, who lives on intimate terms with the persecutors of his co-religionists because it is an advantageous place, lays it down as a principle that happiness consists in a moderate fortune joined to justice; he can put up with poverty with a light heart, and declares that real pleasure consists in giving, and not in laying up treasure.

Above all, the ideas of matrimony as developed here are particularly chaste, sensible, and refined. The Jew, with his recollections always fixed on his ancestors the prophets and patriarchs, and persuaded that his race will possess the earth, marries only a Jewess of good family, whose relatives are honourable and known to be so. Beauty is far from being a matter of indifference; but, before everything else, laws and usages and family convenience must be consulted, so that the fortune may not change hands. The man and woman are reserved for one another throughout all eternity. Marriages founded on sensual love turn out badly, but on the other hand, a union founded on real sentiment is the agglutination of two souls: it is blessed by God when it is sanctified by the prayers of the two lovers, and then becomes friendship full of charm, especially when the man maintains that moral superiority over his companion that belongs to him by right. To grow old together, to be buried in the same tomb, to leave their children well married, to see their grand-children, and perhaps the children of the latter, what more can be requisite for happiness?

The author, separated from the book of Job by nearly a thousand years, has in reality not an idea beyond that of the old Hebrew book. All ends for eth best, as Tobit dies at a hundred and sixty-eight years of age, having had nothing but happiness since his trials, and being honourably buried by the side of his wife. His son dies at a hundred and twenty-seven years of age, in possession of his own and of his father-in-law's property. Before dying, he hears that Nineveh is taken, and rejoices at that good news, for what can be sweeter than to see the chastisement of the enemies of Israel?

Thus God appears like a father who chastises a son whom he loves and then takes pity on him. When the just man suffers, it is as a punishment for his own faults and those of his fathers. But if he humbles himself and prays, God pardons him and restores him to prosperity. Thus to sin is to be one's own enemy: charity preserves from death, almsgiving saves.

What happened to Tobit will happen to Israel. After having chastised it, God will repair its disasters. The Temple will be rebuilt, but not as it was before, and then all those who were dispersed shall be restored to their own country. Israel, thus reunited, will rebuild Jerusalem and the Temple with all the magnificence which was foretold by the prophets, and this time for eternity. It will be a city of sapphires and emeralds; its walls and towers shall be of pure gold; its squares shall be like mosaics of beryl and carbuncle, and its streets shall say Alleluia. All people shall be converted to the true God, and shall bury their idols. Happy shall they be then who have loved Jerusalem and pitied her sufferings.

As soon as it was translated, that little book came into great favour with the Christians. Some of its features were of a nature to shock the delicacy of a few; it was, in some respects, too Jewish; some places in it might be touched up in a still more edifying manner. Hence arose a series of alterations, whence sprang a variety of Greek and Latin texts. The last alteration, that of St Jerome, which was made with remarkable literary feeling, gave that form to the book which it has in the Latin text of the Vulgate. The awkwardness and the clumsiness of the original have disappeared, and the result of those corrections is a small masterpiece which all succeeding centuries have read and admired.

The Jewish people are without an equal when it is a question of accentuating and imparting a charm to an ideal of justice and domestic virtues. The Thora is the first book in the world, regarded as a book of devotion, but it is an impracticable code. No society could have lived under it, and the Jews of the time of Bar-Gioras and Bar-Coziba were defending a Utopia when they defended a nationality founded on such principles. History has that sympathy for them which it owes to all those who have been conquered; but how much more was the peaceable Christian and the author of the Book of Tobit, who thought it quite natural not to revolt against Shalmaneser, imbued with the traditions of Israel.

# CHAPTER XIII

### THE TALMUD

The Law, with that calmness of mind that it produced, acted like a sedative which quickly restored serenity to the troubled spirit of Israel. The Jewish quarters of the West do not appear to have suffered much from the follies of their co-religionists of the East. Even in the East peaceable Israelites had not participated in the strife, and soon became reconciled to the conquerors. Some ventured to believe that heaven was favourable to the Romans, and that, after all, the Law, when it was strictly observed in families, always gave the Jews a modus vivendi. Thus order was re-established in Syria sooner than one might have thought. The fugitives from Jerusalem went either to the East to Palmyra, or else into the South towards Yemen, or else to Galilee. That latter country above all received a new impulse from the emigration, and for centuries afterwards remained an almost exclusively Jewish country.

After the extermination of the year 67, Galilee had been lost to Judaism for some time. Perhaps the revolt of 117 was the reason that the beth-din was transported thither. After the defeat of Bar-Coziba, the inhabitants who had been driven from the South took refuge there in a body and repopulated the villages, and then the beth-din became definitely Galilean. That tribunal had its seat first of all at Ouscha, then in the villages near Sephoris, at Schefaram, at Beth-Shearim, and at Sephoris itself; then it was established at Tiberias, and was not moved till the Mussulman conquest. Whilst Darom was almost forgotten and its schools were declining, whilst even Lydda was falling with wretchedness and ignorance, and was losing the right of fixing the embolismic calculations, Galilee became the centre of Judaism. Meïron, Safat, Gischala, Alma, Casioun, Kafr-Baram, Kafr-Nabarta, Ammouka, were the chief localities of this new development, and were filled with Jewish monuments, and these, nearly all of them reverenced in the Middle Ages as tombs of the prophets, can still be seen in the midst of a country which for the third and fourth time has become desert and desolate. Tiberias was, in a measure, the capital of that kingdom of disputation and subtlety where the last remains of original Jewish activity were exhausted.

In fact, in that tranquil country, restored to its favourite retired and studious life, the family life and that of the synagogue, Israel definitely renounced its earthly visions, and sought the kingdom of God, not like Jesus in the ideal, but in the rigorous observance of the Law. From that time forward proselytism disappears by degrees from amongst that people who had been its most ardent followers. A law of Antoninus put a stop to the restrictive measures of Hadrian, and allowed the Jews to circumcise their children; but Modestinus the lawyer draws attention to the fact that such permission applied only to their own children, and exposed those who should perform that operation on any one who was not a Jew to capital punishment. Only some madmen, the Siccani, continued their religious ambush, and forced the unhappy wretches whom they could surprise in their houses to choose between circumcision and the dagger. The majority knew nothing of these aberrations. It renounced heroism, and made martyrdom useless by those clever distinctions between the precepts which may be transgressed in order to save one's life and those for which one must suffer death. And from this sprung a singular spectacle: Judaism, which had given the first martyr to the world, now left the monopoly of it to Christians, so much so that in certain persecutions Christians might be seen figuring as Jews, so that they might enjoy the immunities of Judaism. The latter only had martyrs whilst it was revolutionary; as soon as it renounced politics it settled down altogether, and was satisfied with that tolerance, so closely bordering on independence, that was accorded to it. On the other hand, Christianity, which never had anything to do with politics, reckoned martyrs amongst its ranks, till it in turn became triumphant and persecuting.

It was the Talmud that created the Jewish people during that long period of repose. The doctors of old had taught the Law without any logical order, solely according to the cases that were brought before them. Then in their teaching they had followed the order of the hooks of the Pentateuch. With Rabbi Ben Aquíba a fresh distribution was introduced, a kind of classification according to matter, necessitating divisions and subdivisions, like a Corpus juris. Thus a second code, the Mischna, was formed side by side with the Thora. The Scriptures were no longer taken as the foundation, and, to speak truly, with that taste for arbitrary interpretation that had been introduced, the Scriptures had become almost useless. It was no longer a question of understanding the will of the legislator clearly, it was a question of finding at any price, in the Bible, arguments in favour of traditional decisions, and verses to which received precepts could be attached. It is the destiny of religions that the sacred books should always be thus destroyed by commentaries. Sacred books alone do not form religions; it is the force of circumstances, involving a thousand wants of which the first originator could not have dreamt. Thus the coincidence between the sacred books and the religious state of any period is never perfect; the coat does not fit well enough, and then the commentator and the traditionalist come and settle matters. Thus it happens that, instead of studying the sacred book by itself, it was thought better, after a certain time, to read it in the codes which have been extracted from it, or rather which have been adapted to it.

The attempt to codify the oral Jewish law was made in different directions at the same time. We have no longer the Mischna of Rabbi Aquiba, nor many others that existed. The Mischna of Juda the Holy, written sixty years later, has thrown those that preceded it into oblivion, but he neither invented all the divisions nor all the titles. Many of the treatises in his compilation had been completely drawn up before his time. Besides that, after Aquiba, the original schools disappeared, and the doctors, full of respect for their predecessors, who seemed to them to be surrounded by the halo of martyrdom, tried no new methods--they were mere compilers.

Thus the Jews made a new Bible for themselves, which rather threw the first one into the shade, at the same time that the Christians did. The Mischna was their Gospel, their New Testament. The distance between the Christian and the Jewish book is enormous. The simultaneous appearance of the Talmud and the Gospel from the same race of people,--of a slight masterpiece of elegance, lightness, and moral subtlety, and of a ponderous monument of pedantry, of miserable casuistry, and religious formalism, is one of the most extraordinary phenomenons of history. These twins are certainly the most dissimilar creatures that ever issued from the womb of the same mother. There is something barbarous and unintelligible, a disheartening contempt for language and form, an absolute lack of distinction and of talent, that make the Talmud one of the most repulsive books that exist. The disastrous consequences of one of the greatest faults that the Jewish people ever committed, which was to turn their back on Greek discipline, which was the source of all classical culture, are clearly felt in it. That rupture with reason itself placed Israel in a state of deplorable isolation. It was a crime to read a foreign book. Greek literature seemed to be a toy, a female ornament, an amusement beneath the notice of a man who was preoccupied with the study of the Law, a childish science which a man ought to teach his son " at an hour which is neither day nor night." As the Thora says, "You shall study the law day and night." Thus the Thora came to be regarded as the embodiment of all philosophy and all science, and dispensing with any other study. Christianity was less exclusive, and took a large portion of Hellenic tradition into its bosom. Separated from that great source of life, Israel fell into a state of poverty, or rather of intellectual aberration, from which it did not emerge till it came under the influence of the so-called Arabian system of philosophy, that is to say, under the influence of a singularly refracted ray of Greek light.

There certainly are in this confused medley of the Talmud some excellent maxims, more than one precious pearl of the kind as those which Jesus adopted and idealised. and which the Evangelists made divine in writing them. From the point of view of the preservation of the individuality of the Jewish people, Talmudism was an heroic party, and such as could scarcely be found in the history of a race. The Jewish nation, dispersed from one end of the world to the other, had no other nationality than the Thora; to maintain this scattered whole, without clergy, bishops, pope, or holy city, without any central theological college, an iron chain was required, and nothing binds men together so firmly as common duties. The Jew, carrying all his religion with him, requiring neither temples nor clergy for his worship, enjoyed incomparable freedom in his emigrations to the end of the world. His absolute idealism made him indifferent to material things; faithfulness to the recollections of his race--the confession of faith (the schema) and the practice of the Law, sufficed him. When one is present at any ceremony in a synagogue, at first sight everything seems modern, borrowed, common-place. In the construction of their places of worship the Jews have never sought a style of architecture which would be peculiar to them. The ministers of religion, with their bands, their three-cornered hat, and their stole, look like parish priests; the sermon is formed on the model of the Catholic pulpit; the lamps, the seats, all the furniture, has been bought in the same shop that supplies the neighbouring parish. Nothing in the singing or the music goes further back than the fifteenth century. Some portions of the worship even are imitations of the Catholic form. The originality and the antiquity suddenly burst forth in the profession of faith: 'Hear, O Israel, Adonai, our God, is One, holy is His name!" This headstrong proclamation, this persistent cry, which in the end has carried away and converted the world, constitutes the whole of Judaism. That people has made God, and yet there never was a people less given to disputing about God.

One very sensible feature, in fact, was to have chosen practice, and not dogma as the basis for religious communion. The Christian is united to the Christian by the same belief; the Jew is united to the Jew by the same observances. By making the union of souls bear on truths of the metaphysical order, Christianity prepared the way for schisms without number; by reducing the profession of faith to the schema, that is to say, to the affirmation of the Divine Unity and to the outward bond of ritual,

Judaism got rid of the logical disputes from its midst. The season for excommunication amongst the Jews was generally acts, not opinions. The Cabala always remained a matter for free speculation, and never became a compulsory article of faith; the immortality of the soul was regarded as a consoling hope, and it was allowed without difficulty that religious practices would be abolished when Messiah came, when Jewish principles would be universally adopted. Even the belief concerning Messiah had a doubt cast upon it by a learned doctor, and the Talmud gives his opinion without blaming it. That was very judicious. It is perfect nonsense to be compelled to believe any particular doctrine, whilst the greatest external strictness may be allied to entire liberty of thought. That is the reason of that philosophical independence which ruled in Judaism during the Middle Ages down to our days. Eminent doctors, the oracles of the synagogue, such as Maimonides and Mendelsohn, were pure rationalists. A book like the Iccarim, (Fundamental Principles) of Joseph Albo, which proclaimed that religion and prophecy are only a form of symbolism which is destined to ameliorate man's moral condition, that all divine laws can be modified, that individual punishments and rewards in the future life are nothing but figures of speech, that such a book, I say, should become celebrated and not incur any anathema, is a fact that is without example in any other religion. And piety did not suffer for it. Those men who had no hope in a future life endured martyrdom with admirable courage, and died accusing themselves of imaginary crimes, so that their death might not be too strong an objection against the justice of God.

Great disadvantages counterbalanced the advantages of that severe discipline to which Israel submitted in order to retain the unity of its race. Their ritual united co-religionists amongst themselves, but separated them from the rest of the world, and condemned them to an isolated life. The chains of the Talmud forged those of the Ghetto. The Jewish people, which up till then had been so devoid of superstition, became its most thorough type, and the mocking allusions that Jesus made to the Pharisees were justified. For centuries their literature turned chiefly on the sacred furniture and vestments, and on slaughter houses. That other Bible became a prison in which the new Judaism carried on its unhappy life of reclusion up to our days. Enclosed in that unwholesome encyclopedia, the Jewish intellect got so sharp that it went wrong. For the Israelites the Talmud became a sort of Organon, in every respect inferior to that of the Greeks. The Jewish doctors put forward the same claims as the jurists who in the sixteenth century declared that they could find a whole system of intellectual culture in Roman Law. In our time, this vast collection, which still serves as the basis for Jewish education in Hungary and in Poland, may be considered as the principal source of the defects which may be remarked occasionally amongst the Jews of those countries. The belief that Talmudic studies supply the place of all others, and make those who devote themselves to them fitted for everything, is the great cause of that presumption, that subtlety, that want of general culture, which so often destroy really fine qualities in the Israelite.

The Jewish mind is endowed with extreme vigour. For centuries it was forced to rave because it was restricted to a narrow and barren circle of ideas. The activity which it displayed was the same as if it had been working in a wide and fertile soil, and thus the result of headstrong work, applied to a thankless dry matter, was mere subtlety. To wish to find everything in texts was to oblige themselves to childish feats of strength. When their natural sense is exhausted, a mystical sense is sought for, and then men set to work to count letters, and to compute them as if they were numbers. The chimeras of the Cabala and of the Notarikon were the last results of that extreme spirit of exactitude and of servile adherence. In such an accumulation of disputes as to the best means of fulfilling the Law, there was the proof of a very ardent religious spirit; but we may be allowed to add that there was in it something of a witticism and of amusement. Ingenious and active men, who were condemned to a sedentary life, driven from public places and from the general society of the time, sought means to get rid of their weariness by combining dialectics with the texts of the Law. Even in our time, in those countries where Jews live exclusively among themselves, the Talmud is, if we may say so, their chief diversion. The meetings which they have to explain its difficulties, and to discuss obscure or imaginary cases, seem to them to be pleasure parties, and those subtleties which we look upon as irksome, have seemed, and still seem, to thousands of men to be the most attractive matter to which human genius can be applied.

From that moment the Jews acquired all the faults of isolated men: they became morose and malevolent. Till that time the spirit of Hillel had not altogether disappeared, and at least some gates of the synagogue were open to converts; but now they would have no more proselytes. They asserted that they had the true, the only Law, and at the same time asserted that that Law belonged to them only. Any one who tried to join God's people was repelled with insults. Certainly it was only right to be discreet, and to inform the neophyte of the dangers and unpleasantnesses that awaited him. But they did not stop there: every proselyte was soon looked upon as a traitor; as a deserter who would make use of Judaism as a short cut to Christianity. It was openly declared that proselytes were Israel's leprosy, and that these intruders ought to be mistrusted to the twenty-fourth generation. The wise distinctions that the Jews of the first century, and the Haggadists, who took their inspiration from Isaiah and Jeremiah, made with regard to ceremonial, that grand concession that the precept of circumcision only applied to the descendants of Abraham, were all forgotten. From that time forward proselytism was forbidden, and the law of Antoninus, which permitted Jewish children alone to be circumcised, became superfluous; for it was evident that neither the Greek nor Roman world would resign itself to an ancient African practice which had its origin in a matter of health, but which was not at all fitted for our climate, and which had become oppressive and senseless for the Jews themselves.

Morals suffered somewhat from so many attacks on nature. Without containing any bad advice, and, even strangely enough, whilst insisting on bashful modesty, the Talmud often mentions lascivious subjects, and takes a tolerably excited imagination on the part of its writers for granted. In the third and fourth centuries, Jewish morals, especially those of the patriarchs and doctors, are said to have been very lax, but, above all things, in this decrepit Israel, reason seems to have been weakened. The supernatural is scattered about lavishly in an insane fashion. Miracles appeared so simple that a hallel, a special prayer, is devoted to them as to one of the most ordinary events of life. There never was any nation which, after a period of extraordinary activity, underwent such a terrible abasement.

A small sect, hedged in by numerous rules which prevent it from living the general life, is unsociable by nature, and is necessarily hated and easily gets to hate others in turn. In a large society which is imbued with great liberal principles, as our modern civilisation is, and as in some respects Arabian civilisation, and that of the first half of the Middle Ages were, that causes no great inconvenience. But in a society like that of the Christian Middle Ages, and like in the East in our time, it is the cause of accumulated antipathies and contempt. The Jewish Talmudist, who, wherever he went, was a stranger without a fatherland, often proved himself a scourge for the country to which chance had taken him. We must remember the Jews of the East and of the coast of Barbary, who are filled with hatred when they are persecuted, and are arrogant and insolent as soon as they feel that they are protected. The noble efforts of the Jews of Europe to improve the moral condition of their Eastern brethren are themselves the best proof of the inferiority of these latter. No doubt the detestable social organisation of the East is the primary cause of the evil, but the exclusive spirit of Judaism has also much to do with it. The regulations of the Ghetto are always disastrous, and, I repeat it, that Pharisaism and Talmudism made that rule of reclusion the natural state of the Jewish people. For the Jew, the Ghetto was not so much a restraint coming from outside as a consequence of the Talmudic spirit. Any race would have perished under it, and the manner in which the Jewish people resisted this deleterious mode of life, speaks highly for its moral constitution.

No one who has any lofty mind can help feeling a profound sympathy for a people which has played so extraordinary a part in this world, that one cannot imagine what would have been the history of the human race if chance had checked the destinies of that small tribe. In judging of that terrible crisis which the Jewish people went through about the beginning of our era, which caused, on the one hand, the foundation of Christianity, and, on the other, the destruction of Jerusalem and the introduction of Talmudism, there are several acts of injustice that have to be repaired. The colours in which the Pharisees are represented in the Gospels have been rather heightened; the Evangelists seem to have written under the influence of the violent ruptures which took place between the Christians and the Jews about the time of the siege of Titus. In the Acts of the Apostles, in all that we know about the Church of Jerusalem, and of James, the Saviour's brother, the Pharisees have a very different part to that which they play in the discourses which the Synoptists attribute to Jesus. Nevertheless, one cannot prevent one's self from being decidedly with Hillel, with Jesus, with St Paul against Sehamaï, or with the Haggadists against the Halachists. It was the Haggada (popular preaching) and not the Halacha (the study of the Law) which conquered the world. Certainly Judaism, serried, resisting, enclosed between the double hedge of the Law and the Talmud which survived the destruction of the Temple, is still grand and imposing. It has done the greatest service to the human intellect; it saved the Hebrew Bible, which the Christians would probably have allowed to be lost, from destruction. Judaism, since it has been dispersed, has given great men to the world, and some of the highest moral and philosophical characters; and on several occasions it has been a valuable auxiliary to civilisation; but it is no longer that grand, fertile Judaism, carrying in its loins the salvation of the world, which the period of Jesus and of the Apostles presents to our view; it is the respectable old age of a man who once upon a time held the destinies of humanity in his hand, and who afterwards lives in obscurity for many years, still worthy of esteem, but for the future without any providential part to play.

St Paul, Philo, the author of the Sibylline verses, and of those attributed to Phocylides, were right then when they rejected the practices of Judaism, whilst they maintained its basis. These practices would have made all conversions impossible, for, scrupulously observed by the majority of the nation, they were, and are still, a real misfortune for it and for those countries which they inhabit in large numbers. The prophets, with their lofty aspirations, and not the Law, with its strict observances, contained the future of the Hebrew people. Jesus is the outcome of the prophets, and not of the Law, whereas the Talmud is the worship of the Law carried to superstition. After having waged relentless war on all idolatries, Israel substituted a fetichism for them, the fetichism of the Thora.

# CHAPTER XIV

### THE MUTUAL HATRED OF JEWS AND CHRISTIANS

The Jewish catastrophe of the year 134 was almost as advantageous for the Christians as that of the year 70 had been. In their eyes, everything that savoured of the law of Moses must have appeared to be abrogated without a chance of return; faith alone, and the merits of the death of Jesus, were all that remained. Hadrian did a signal service to Christianity when he prevented a Jewish restoration of Jerusalem. Ælia, peopled, like all the colonies were, by veterans and common people from different parts, was no fanatical city, but, on the contrary, a centre disposed to receive Christianity. As a rule, the colonies were inclined to adopt the religious ideas of the countries to which they were transported. They would not have thought of embracing Judaism, but Christianity, on the other hand, received everybody. During the whole course of its three thousand years of history, it was only for those two hundred years, from Hadrian to Constantine, that human life had unfolded freely within its bosom idolatrous forms of worship, established on the ruins of the Jewish religion, complacently adopted more than one Jewish practice. The Pool of Bethesda continued to be a place of healing, even for the heathen, and to work its miracles as in the times of Jesus and of the apostles, in the name of the great impersonal God. For their part, the Christians continued, without exciting any feeling except one of pious admiration in the breasts of the worthy veterans who formed the colony, to perform their cures by means of oil and sacred washings. The traditions of that Church of Jerusalem were distinguished by a special character of superstition, and, of course, thaumaturgy. The holy places, especially the cave and the manger at Bethlehem, were shown, even to the heathen. Journeys to those places sanctified by Jesus and the apostles, began within the first years of the third century, and replaced the former pilgrimages to the temple of Jehovah. When St Paul took a deputation of his churches to Jerusalem, he took them to the Temple, and surely he was thinking neither of Golgotha nor of Bethlehem. Now on the other hand, men strove to retrace the life of Jesus, and a topography of the Gospel was formed. The site of the Temple was known, and, close to it, the stela of James, the Martyr, brother of the Saviour, was venerated.

Thus the Christians reaped the fruits of their prudent conduct during the insurrection of Bar-Coziba. They had suffered for Rome that had persecuted them; and in Syria, at least, they found the prize of their meritorious fidelity. Whilst the Jews were punished for their ignorance and their blindness, the Church of Jesus, faithful to the Spirit of her Master, and, like Him, indifferent to politics, was peaceably developing in Judea and the neighbouring countries. The expulsion of the Jews was also the lot of those Christians who were circumcised and kept the Law, but not of those uncircumcised Christians who only practised the precepts of Noah. That latter circumstance made such a difference for their whole life that men were classified by it, and not by faith or disbelief in Jesus. The Hellenistic Christians formed a group in Ælia, under the presidency of a certain Mark. Till then, what was called the Church of Jerusalem had had no priest who was not circumcised, and, more than that, out of regard for the old Jewish nucleus, nearly all the faithful of that Church united the observation of the Law with belief in Jesus. From that time the Church in Jerusalem was wholly Hellenistic, and her bishops were all Greeks, as they were called. But this second Church did not inherit the importance of the former one. Hierarchically subordinate to Cæsarea, she only occupied a relatively humble position in the universal Church of Jesus, and nothing more was heard of the Church of Jerusalem till two hundred years later.

In those countries the controversy with the Jews became an object of paramount importance. The Christians thought them much more difficult to convert than the heathen, and they were accused of subtlety and of bad faith in the discussions. It was alleged that as beforehand they had made up their minds to baffle their antagonists, they only looked at minutiæ, at slight inexactitudes, in which they easily got the better. What was said to them about the life of Jesus irritated them, and no doubt the antipathy that they felt for the accounts of the virginal birth of the pretended Messiah, inspired them with the fable of the soldier and of the prostitute who, according to them, were the real authors of that birth, which was allowed to be irregular. Arguments taken from the Scriptures did not affect them any more, and they lost their patience when certain passages were brought up against them in which it appeared as if God were mentioned in the plural. The passage in Genesis: "Let us make man in our own image," particularly irritated them. A pretty Haggada was invented to guard against that objection:

"When God was dictating the Pentateuch to Moses, and He got to the word naase, let us make,' Moses was very much astonished, and refused to write it down, and vehemently rebuked the Eternal for thus striking a mortal blow at Monotheism. The Eternal, however, maintained his wording, and said, 'Let him who wishes to be deceived, deceive himself!'" The Jews generally admitted that wherever in the Bible there was a passage that was favourable to the plurality of the Divine persons, God, by special providence, has so disposed matters that the refutation is found side by side with it.

The essential matter for the Christians was to prove that Jesus had accomplished all the texts of the prophets and the psalms which were thought to apply to the Messiah. Nothing can equal the arbitrariness with which the Messianic application was carried out. The Christian exegesis was the same as that of the Talmud and of the Midraschim: it was the very denial of the historical meaning. The texts were cut up like so much dead matter, and every phrase, separated from its context, was applied without scruple to the prominent prejudice of the moment. Already the Evangelists who wrote at second hand, especially pseudo-Matthew, had sought for prophetic reasons for all the facts of the life of Jesus. Men went much further than that. Not only did Christian exegetes torture the Septuagint version so as to obtain from it anything that might fit into their thesis and abuse the new translators who weakened the arguments which they drew from it, but they forged some passages. The wood of the cross was introduced into Psalm xcvi. 10, where it had never figured; the descent into hell, into Jeremiah; and when the Jews cried out, protesting that nothing like it was found in the text, they were told that they had mutilated the text out of pure spite and bad faith, and that,. for example, they had cut the account of the prophet being sawn in two by a wood saw out of the book of Isaiah, because that passage brought to mind the crime which they had committed against Jesus, too well. A convinced and ardent apologist finds no difficulty in anything. They referred to the official registers of the returns of Quirinius, which never existed, and to a pretended report of Pilate to Tiberius, that had been forged.

Dialogue seemed to be a convenient form by which to attain to the wished-for object in these controversies. A certain Ariston of Pella, doubtlessly the same from whom Eusebius has borrowed the account of the Jewish war under Hadrian, wrote a discussion that was supposed to have taken place between Jason, a Jew who had been converted to Christianity and Papiscus, a Jew of Alexandria, who obstinately adhered to his ancient faith. As usual, the war was waged by means of Biblical texts; Jason proved that all the Messianic passages were accomplished in Jesus. The admirers of the book asserted that Jason's Hebraic arguments were so strong, and his eloquence so gentle, that there was no resisting it. Papiscus, in fact, at the end of the dialogue, his heart enlightened by the infusion of the Holy Ghost, recognised the truth of Christianity, and asked Jason to baptise him. However, the book was not received with unanimous approval. The author appeared almost too simple-minded, and it was thought what he wrote about the Scripture bordered on the ridiculous. Celsus eagerly seized the opportunity of making fun of it, and Origen only defended it in an embarrassed manner, allowing that it was one of the least valuable books that had ever been written in the defence of religion, and recognising it as more fit to instruct the simple than to satisfy the learned. Eusebius and St Jerome gave it up altogether; it was not copied, and so it was lost.

Another very inferior book that appeared in Judea has preserved for us the echo of these intestine broils. The author made use of the wills or rather of the recommendations that he put into the mouths of the patriarchs, Jacob's sons, as the basis of his writing. The language of the original is that Greek interspersed with Hebraisms which is the language of the greater part of the New Testament writings. The quotations are taken from the Septuagint. The author was a born Jew, but he belonged to Paul's party, for he speaks of the great apostle in a tone of enthusiasm, and he shows himself most severe towards his former co-religionists, whom he accuses of felony and treason. In the work, traces of nearly all the writings in the New Testament are to be found, and the two Bibles are comprehended under the common term of "The Holy Books," and the book of Enoch is quite confidently quoted as being inspired. Never was the divinity of Jesus spoken of in grander terms. It was because they had slain Jesus and denied his resurrection that the Jews were captives, dispersed over the whole world, given up to the influence of Satan and of demons. Since their apostacy, the spirit of God has gone over to the heathen. Israel will again be gathered together from the dispersion, but it will have the disgrace of not associating itself till late with the converted Gentiles.

A striking vision expresses the sentiments of the author with regard to his ancient race. Napthali relates that one day in a dream he saw himself sitting with his brothers and his father on the shore of the lake Jabneh where they saw a vessel sailing at random. It was laden with mummies, and had neither crew nor captain, and its name was The Ship of Jacob. The patriarchal family embarked on it, but soon a terrible tempest arose, and the father, who was holding the rudder, disappeared like a phantom; Joseph saved himself on the mast, the others escaped on ten planks, Levi and Juda on the same one. The shipwrecked men were dispersed in all directions; but Levi, clothed in sackcloth, prayed to the Lord, when the tempest was stilled, the vessel reached the land in the midst of a profound calm, the ship-wrecked men found their father Jacob again, and joy became universal.

The intention of the author of the testaments of the twelve patriarchs had been to enrich the list of the writings contained in the sacred canon; his book is of the same order as the pseudo-Daniel, the pseudo-Esdras, the pseudo-Baruch, the pseudo-Enoch. Its success, however, was not the same. By its declamatory tone and its emphatic commonplaceness, by an exaggerated severity towards the pleasures of love and the luxury of women, by its severe tirades against the Jews, the book was calculated to edify the pious faithful; but the time for great successes with regard to frauds in the Canon of Scripture was passed; already a tolerably strong hedge surrounded the sacred volume and prevented fresh compositions being furtively inserted. so the book was only received in very restricted fractions of the Church. However, as it was altogether Christian and anti-Jewish, it did not share in the reprobation with which the Greek Church visited apocryphal Jewish and Judeo-Christian literature. Copies of it were multiplied, and the original Greek was preserved in a good number of manuscripts.

The philosopher Justin of Neapolis, in Samaria, was a much more valuable defender whom the Church acquired at about that period. His father, Priscus, or his grandfather, Bacchius, doubtlessly belonged to the colony which Vespasian established at Sychem, and which procured for that town the name of Flavia Neapolis. His family was heathen, and gave him a careful Hellenistic education. Justin had more heart and religious requirements than rational faculties. He read Plato, tried the different philosophical schools of his time, and as happens to ardent but not very judicious minds, he found satisfaction in none of them. He required the impossible from those schools. He wanted a complete solution of all the problems which the universe and the human conscience raise. The sincere avowal of powerlessness which his different masters made to him attracted him towards the disciples of Jesus. He was the first man who became a Christian through scepticism, the first who embraced the supernatural, that is to say, the negation of reason, because he was out of temper with reason.

He has related to us, with too much art for his account to be looked upon as an exact autobiography, how he went through all the sects, his errors, the charm which the Jewish revelation exercised on him when he knew it, and the manner in which the prophets led him to Christ. What struck him above all was the eight of the morality of the Christians and the spectacle of their indomitable firmness. The other forms of Judaism, by which he was surrounded, especially the sect of Simon Magus, only filled him with disgust. The philosophical turn which Christianity was already assuming had great attractions for him. He adhered to the dress of the philosophers, that pallium which was nothing but an index of an austere life devoted to asceticism, and which many Christians were fond of wearing. In his eyes his conversion was no rupture with philosophy. He was fond of repeating that he had only begun to be a real philosopher from that day; that he had only abandoned the writings of Plato for those of the prophets, and profane philosophy for a new philosophy--the only sure system, the only one which gives repose and peace to those who profess it.

The attraction which Rome possessed over all the sectaries made itself felt by Justin. Shortly after his conversion he set out for the capital of the world, and there it was that he composed those Apologies, which, by the side of Quadratus and Aristides, were the first manifestation of Christianity to the eyes of a public initiated to philosophy. His antipathy for the Jews, which was inflamed by the recollection of the recent acts of violence of Bar-Coziba, inspired him with another work, whose exegesis was as singular as that of Ariston of Pella, and in which error and injustice have perhaps been pushed even further.

In fact, the parts were changed. The heathen entered the Church in crowds, and became its most numerous members. The two great bonds that attached the new worship to Judaism--the Passover and the Sabbath--were getting looser day by day. Whilst in St Paul's day the Christian who did not observe the law of Moses was hardly tolerated, and was constrained to make all kinds of humiliating concessions, it was now the Judaising Christian whom it was not wished to exclude from the Church. If he was irreproachable in his faith in Jesus Christ and in his obedience to the commandments, if he was persuaded of the inefficacy of the Law, if he only wished to observe a part of it by way of a pious remembrance, if he would not in any way trouble those Gentiles whom Jesus Christ had truly circumcised and brought out of error, if he was not guilty of any propaganda to persuade those latter to submit to the same practices as he did himself, if he did not hold up these practices as obligatory and necessary for salvation, he might be saved. This, at any rate, was what men of large mind admitted. But there were others who neither dared to have intercourse nor to live with those who observed the Law in any shape.

"As for me," Justin says, "I believe that when a person, from weakness of understanding, wishes to observe as much as he can of that Law which was imposed upon the Jews because of the hardness of their heart, when, at the same time, that person hopes in Jesus Christ, and is determined to satisfy all the eternal and natural duties of justice and of piety, that he makes no difficulty in living with other Christians without wishing to induce them to be circumcised or keep the Sabbath. I believe, I repeat, that such a person ought to be received to friendly intercourse in every way. But any Jews who pretend to believe in Jesus Christ and wish to force the faithful Gentiles to observe the Law, I reject absolutely. . . . Those who, after having known and confessed that Jesus is the Christ, abandon their faith because they are persuaded by these obstinate-minded men in order to go over to the Law of Moses, whatever may be their reason for doing so, will find no salvation unless they acknowledge their fault before their death."

Origen looks at matters in a similar fashion. Jews who have become Christians, according to him, have abandoned the Law. Jews who observe the Law as Christians are Ebionites and sectaries, because they value circumcision and practices that Jesus has abolished. Logic accomplished itself. It was inevitable that a duality which prevented Christians from eating together even at Easter, must end in a complete schism.

From the middle of the second century, in fact, the hatred between the two religions was sealed. The quiet disciples of Jesus, and the Jews who were exiled for their territorial fanaticism, became daily more mutually furious. According to the Christians, a new people had been substituted for the ancient. The Jews accused the Christians of apostasy, and subjected them to real persecution.

"They treat us like enemies, as if they were at war with us, killing us and torturing us when they can, just as you do yourselves," Justin said to the Romans.

Women who wished to become converts were scourged in the synagogues and stoned. The Jews reproached the Christians for no longer sharing the anger and the griefs of Israel. The Christians began to inflict a reproach on the whole Jewish nation which certainly neither Peter, nor James, nor the author of the Apocalypse would have addressed to them, that of having crucified Jesus. Up till then his death had been looked upon as Pilate's crime, as that of the High Priests and of certain Pharisees, but not of the whole of Israel. Now the Jews were made to appear as a decided nation, one that assassinated God's envoys and rebelled against the clearest prophecies. The Christians made a sort of dogma out of the non-reconstruction of the Temple, and looked upon those as their most mortal enemies who put forward any pretensions to giving the lie to their prophecies on this matter. As a matter of fact, the Temple was not restored till the time of Omar, that is to say, at the period when Christianity in its turn was conquered at Jerusalem. When Omar wished to be shown the holy site, he found that the Christians had converted it into a place for depositing filth, out of hatred for the Jews.

The Ebionites or Nazarenes, who had for the most part retired to the other side of the Jordan, naturally did not share these sentiments. They were a numerous body, and by decrees gained possession of Paneas, all the country of the Nabateans, Hauran, and Moab. They kept up their relations with the Jews and Aquiba, and the most celebrated doctors were known to them; Aquila was their favourite translator, but the mistakes that they made with regard to the period at which those two teachers flourished, proves that they had only received a vague echo of their celebrity. Besides this, the writers of the Catholic Church speak about two sorts of Ebionites, one of which retained all the Jewish ideas, and only attributed an ordinary birth to Jesus, whereas the other agreed with St Paul in admitting that observances were necessary only for Israelites by blood, and admitted that Jesus had a supernatural birth, such as is recounted in the first chapter of Matthew. The dogmas of the Ebionite school followed the same line of development as those of the Catholic Church; by degrees, even in that direction, there was a tendency to elevate Jesus above humanity.

Although they were excluded from Jerusalem as being circumcised, the Ebionites of the East were always supposed to dwell in the Holy City. The Ebionites of the rest of the world still looked upon the Church of Jerusalem as it had been in the time of Peter and James as the peaceful capital of Christendom. Jerusalem is the universal kibla of Judeo-Christianity; the Elkasaites, who observed that kibla to the letter, only symbolised the general feeling. But such a resistance to evidence could not last long. Soon Judeo-Christianity had no longer a mother, and Nazarene or Ebionite traditions existed no longer except amongst the scattered sectaries of Syria.

Hated by the Jews, almost strangers to the Churches of St Paul, the Judeo-Christians decreased daily. It was not with them as it was with other Churches, which were all situated in large cities, and participated in the general civilisation, for they were scattered about in unknown villages, to which no rumours from the outside world had access. Episcopacy was the product of great cities: they had no Episcopacy. Thus having no organised hierarchy, deprived of the ballast of Catholic orthodoxy, tossed about by every wind, they were more or less lost in Essenism and Elkaism. With them the Messianic belief resulted in an endless theory about angels. The theosophy and the asceticism of the Essenes caused the merits of Jesus to be forgotten; abstinence from flesh, and the ancient precepts of the Nazarites, assumed an exaggerated importance. The literature of the Ebionites, which was all in Hebrew, appears to have been weak. Only their old Hebrew gospel, which resembled that of Matthew, preserved its value. The converted Jews who knew no Greek were fond of it, and still made it their gospel in the fourth century. Their Acts of the Apostles, on the other hand, were more or less sophisticated. The journeys of Peter, which are scarcely mentioned in the canonical Acts, received a large development through their imagination. They added on to them some wretched apocryphas, which were attributed to some of the prophets and apostles, and in which James seems to have played a principal part. Hatred for St Paul breathes out of all those writings, the like of which we shall find written in Greek at Rome.

Such a false position was sure to condemn Ebionism to death. "Wishing to maintain an intermediary position," Epiphanius wittily remarks, "Ebion was nothing, and in him this saying was accomplished: I came near suffering every misfortune, party wall as I am between the Church and the synagogue.'" St Jerome also says that because they wished to be Jews and Christians at the same time, they did not succeed in being either Jews or Christians. Thus at the very birth of Christianity occurred what has happened in nearly all religious movements. The first century of the Hegira witnessed the extermination of the companions, relations, and friends of Mahomet, of all those, in a word, who wished to enjoy the monopoly of that revolution of which they were the authors. In the Franciscan movement, the real disciples of St Francis d'Assisi found, at the end of a generation, that they were dangerous heretics who were given up to the flames by hundreds.

The fact is that in those first days of a creative activity ideas progress with giant strides: the imitator soon becomes retrograde, and a heretic amongst his own sect, an obstacle to its views, which wish to progress in spite of him, and thus often insult and kill him. He does not advance any more, and everything is advancing around him. The Ebionim, for whom the first Beatitude had been pronounced (Blessed are the Ebionim!), were now a scandal for the Church, and their pure doctrine was looked on as blasphemy. Certainly the jokes of Origen, and the insults of Epiphanius towards the real founders of Christianity, have something offensive about them. On the other hand, it is certain that the Ebionim of Kokaba would not have transformed the world if Christianity had remained a Jewish sect; a small Talmud would have been the result, and the Thora would never have been abandoned. In time the relations of Jesus would have become a religious aristocracy, which would have been intolerable and destructive to the work of Jesus. Like nearly all the descendants of great men, they would have laid claim to the inheritance of his genius, or of his sanctity, and would have treated those with disdain whom Jesus would, with much more reason, have taken as his spiritual family. Like the heirs of some celebrated writer, they would have wished to keep what he had thought and felt for the benefit of all to themselves. The lowly Jesus would have become a principle of vanity for some foolish people; the desposyni would have been persuaded that their great-great uncle had preached and had been crucified to obtain religious titles and honours in the synagogue for them. Jesus seems to have feared this serious mistake; one day, stretching out his hand to his disciples, he said with perfect truth,--

Behold, my mother and my brethren. Whoever does the will of my Father which is in heaven, the same is my brother, and sister, and mother.

Ebionism and Nazaraism continued till the fifth or sixth centuries in the more remote parts of Syria, especially in the countries beyond Jordan, which was the refuge of all the sects, as well as in the region of Alep, and in the island of Cyprus. Persecuted by the orthodox emperors, it disappeared in the whirlwind of Islam. In one sense it might be said that it was continued by Islam. Yes, Islamism is, in many respects, the prolongation or rather the revenge of Nazaraism. Christianity, such as the Greek polytheists and metaphysicians had made it, could not suit the Syrians or Arabs, who held strongly to the view of separating God from man, and who required the greatest religious simplicity. The heresies of the fourth and fifth centuries, having their centre in Syria, are a sort of permanent protestation against the exaggerated doctrines of the Trinity and the Incarnation, which the Greek fathers brought so prominently forward. Theodoret asked himself how he, who is the author of life, could become mortal. He, who has suffered, is a man whom God took from our midst. Sufferings belong to man, who is passible. It was the form of the servant which sufered. Ibas, of Edessa, said:--

*I do not envy Christ, who has become God, for I may become what he has become.*
*And on Easter Day he ventured to express himself thus:*
*To-day, Jesus has become immortal.*

That is the pure Ebionite or Nazarene doctrine. Islamism says nothing more. Mahomet knew Christianity from those communities established beyond the Jordan which were opposed to the Council of Nicæa and to the councils which it developed. For him, Christians are Nazarenes. Mussulman Docetism has its roots in the same sects. If Islamism substitutes the Kibla of Mecca for that of Jerusalem, on the other hand it renders the greatest honour to the site of the Temple: the mosque of Omar rises from that ground which was defiled by the Christians. Omar himself worked to clear away the filth, and pure monotheism rebuilt its fortress on Mount Moriah. It is often said that Mahomet was an Arian: that is not exact. Mahomet was a Nazarene, a Judeo-Christian. Under him Semitic monotheism regained its rights, and avenged itself for those mythological and polytheistic complications which Greek genius had introduced into the theology of the first disciples of Jesus.

There was one direction in which the Hebrew Ebionites were important in the literary work of the Universal Church. The study of Biblical Hebrew, which was so neglected in Paul's Churches, continued to flourish amongst them. From their midst, or from the midst of neighbouring sects, there sprang the celebrated translators Symmachus and Theodosion. They are represented now as Ebionites now as

Samaritans, always as proselytes, deserters, Judaising heretics. The controversies with regard to the Messianic prophecies, especially with regard to the Alma, the alleged virgin mother of Isaiah, brought men back to the study of the text. The Hebrew Gospel and its slightly altered brother the Gospel of St Matthew, with its legends and genealogies at the beginning, were another object of polemics. Symmachus, above all, seems to have been a universally respected doctor in those distant Churches.

It was under conditions which differed but little from those that have been described that, apparently, the Syriac version of the Old Testament, called Peschito, was made. According to some, Greeks were its authors; according to others, Judeo-Christians; it is, however, certain that Jews collaborated in it, as it is produced directly from the Hebrew, and as it has some passages which are remarkably parallel with the Targums. According to all appearances, this version was produced at Edessa. Later, when Christianity dominated in those countries, the New Testament writings were translated into a dialect which is altogether analagous to that of the ancient Peschito.

That school of Hebraising Christians did not outlive the second century. The orthodoxy of the Hellenistic Churches was always suspicious of Hebraic truth; piety did not inspire men with any wish to consult it, and the study of Hebrew offered almost insurmountable obstacles to any one who was not a Jew. Origen, Dorotheus of Antioch, and St Jerome were exceptions. Even Jews who were living in Greek or Latin countries greatly neglected the ancient text. Rabbi Meir, obliged to go to Asia, could not find a Hebrew copy of the book of Esther amongst the inhabitants; he wrote it for them from memory, so that he might be able to read it in the synagogue on the day of Purim. It is certain that, but for the Jews of the East, the Hebrew text of the Bible would have been lost. By preserving that invaluable document of the old Semitic world for us, the Jews have rendered a service to the human race which is equal to that which the Brahmins have rendered it by preserving the Vedas.

# CHAPTER XV

### *ANTONINUS PIUS*

Hadrian returned to Rome, which he did not leave again, in 135. Roman civilisation had just exterminated one of its most dangerous enemies, Judaism. On all sides there was peace, the respect of peoples, the barbarians apparently submissive, and the mildest maxims of government introduced and carried out.

Trajan had been perfectly right in believing that men can be governed whilst they are treated with civility. The idea that the State was not only tutelary but also benevolent was taking deep root. Hadrian's private conduct gave rise to grave reproach; his character got worse as his health became worse, but the people did not notice it. Unexampled splendour and well-being which enveloped everything like a brilliant halo, hid the defective sides of the social organisation. To speak the truth, these defective sides were capable of being corrected. The door was open to any progress. Stoic philosophy was penetrating the legislature, and introducing into it the idea of the rights of man, of civil equality, and of the uniformity of provincial administration. The privileges of the Roman aristocracy were daily disappearing, and the chiefs of society believed in and were working for progress. They were philosophers who, without looking for Utopia, yet desired the greatest possible application of reason to human affairs. That was worth a great deal more than the fanatical and inapplicable Thora, which at best was only good for a very small nation. Men had reason to be satisfied with life, and behind that fine generation of statesmen one could perceive another wiser, more serious, more upright still.

Hadrian was amusing himself, and he had the right to do so. His curious and active mind dreamt of all sorts of chimeras at one and the same time, but his judgment was not sure enough to preserve him from faults of taste. At the foot of the hills of Tibur he had a villa built which was, as it were, the album of his journeys and the pandemonium of celebrity. It might have been called the noisy and somewhat bold fair of a dying world. Everything was there: false Egyptian, false Greek, the Lyceum, the Academy the Prytaneum, the Canous, the Alpheus, the vale of Tempe, the Elysian Fields, Tartarus; temples, libraries, theatres, a hippodrome, a naumachia, baths. It was a strange place, and yet attractive I For it was the last place in which men amused themselves, where men of intellect went to sleep to the empty noise of "greedy Acheron." At Rome the chief care of the fantastic emperor was that senseless tomb, that vast mausoleum, where Babylon was outdone, and which, stripped of its ornaments, has been the citadel of Papal Rome. His buildings covered the world; the atheneums that he founded, the encouragement that he gave to letters and fine arts, and the immunities that he granted to professors, rejoiced the hearts of all men of learning. Unhappily superstition, eccentricity, and cruelty more and more gained the upper hand over him as his physical forces left him. He had built himself an elysium, in order not to believe in it, and a hell, to laugh at it; a hall of philosophers, to make fun of them; a canopus, to point out the impostures of priests, and to recall to his mind the foolish festivals of Egypt, that had made him laugh so much. Now, everything seemed to him hollow and empty: nothing more supported him.

Perhaps some martyrdoms which took place during his reign, and for which there seems to have been no motive, are to be attributed to the caprices and disorders of his last months. Telesphorus was then the head of the Church at Rome; he died confessing Christ, and passed to the number of the glories of the faith.

The death of this amateur Cæsar was sad and without dignity, for no really lofty moral sentiment animated him. Nevertheless, in him the world lost a powerful support. The Jews alone triumphed over the agonies of his last moments. It was customary amongst them not to mention him except saying after his name, "May God smash his leg." He was sincerely attached to civilisation, and understood well what it would come to in time. With him ancient literature and art came to an end. He was the last emperor who believed in glory, just as Ælius Verus was the last man who knew how to enjoy delicate pleasures. Human affairs are so frivolous that brilliancy and splendour must take their share in them. A world will not hold together without that; Louis XIV. knew it, and men lived and live still in his sun of gilded copper. In his own fashion, Hadrian marked a summit, after which a rapid descent commenced. Certainly Antoninus and Marcus Aurelius were vastly his superiors in virtue, but under them the world was getting sad and losing its gaiety, was beginning to wear the monk's cowl and become Christian; superstition was on the increase. Hadrian's art, although it also had its gnawing worm, still holds to principles: it is a clever and wise art; afterwards the decadence set in with irresistible force. Ancient society perceives that all is in vain; now, the day when one makes that discovery, one is near death. The two accomplished sages who are going to reign are two ascetics, after their own fashion. Lucius Verus and Faustina will be the unclassed survivors of the ancient elegance. It really was from that time that the world bade farewell to joy, treated the muses as seductresses, will no longer listen to anything but what keeps up its melancholy, and becomes changed into a vast hospital.

Antoninus was a St Louis as far as heart and rectitude went, with much more judgment, and a wider range of intellect. He was the most perfect sovereign that ever reigned. He was even superior to Marcus Aurelius, as the reproaches of weakness which may be addressed to the latter cannot be applied to him. To enumerate his virtues would be to enumerate all the qualities of which a perfect man can command. In him all the world saluted an incarnation of the mythical Numa Pompilius. He was the most constitutional of sovereigns, and, of the same time, simple, economical, quite taken up with good deeds and public works, far from any excess, free from rhetoric and any affectation of mind. By his means philosophy really became a power; everywhere philosophers were richly pensioned; already he was surrounded by ascetics, and the general direction of the education of Marcus Aurelius was his work.

Thus the world's ideal seemed to have been attained, wisdom reigned, and for twenty-three years the world was governed by a father. Affectation, false taste in literature, fell to the ground; people became simple; public instruction became an object of lively solicitude. The condition of the whole world was ameliorated; excellent laws, especially in favour of slaves, were carried; the relief of those who suffered became the object of universal care. The preachers of moral philosophy even surpassed the successes of Dion Chrysostom; the seeking for frivolous applause was the rock which they had to avoid. A provincial aristocracy of upright people who wished to do right, had succeeded the cruel aristocracy of Rome. The force and the loftiness of the ancient world were being lost, and men were becoming good, gentle, patient, humane. As always happens, socialistic ideas profited by that largeness of views and made their appearance, but general good sense and the force of established order prevented them from becoming a public evil.

The similarity between these aspirations and those of Christianity was striking, but a profound difference separated the two schools, and was bound to make them hostile to each other. By its hope in the approaching end of the world, by its badly-concealed wishes for the ruin of ancient society, Christianity in the midst of the beneficent empire of the Antonines became a subverter that it was necessary to combat. Always pessimistic, inexhaustible in mournful prophecies, the Christian, far from being of service to national progress, showed that he disdained it. Nearly all the Catholic doctors looked upon war between the empire and the Church as necessary, as the last act in the strife between God and Satan; they boldly affirmed that persecution would last till the end of time. The idea of a Christian empire, though it sometimes presented itself to their mind, seemed to them a contradiction and an impossibility.

Whilst the world again began to live, the Jews and Christians wished more obstinately than ever that it should be approaching its last hour. We have seen the false Baruch exhaust himself in vague announcements. The Judeo-Christian Sibyl never ceased thundering the whole time. The ever-increasing splendour of Rome was a terrible insult to divine truth, to the prophets, to the saints, and so they boldly denied the happiness of the century. All the natural scourges, which continued to be tolerably numerous, were represented as signs of implacable anger. The past and present earthquakes in Asia were made the most of as signs of fearful terrors. According to the fanatics, the only cause of these calamities was the destruction of the Temple of Jerusalem. Rome, the harlot, had given herself up to a thousand lovers, who have intoxicated her; in her turn she shall be a slave. Italy, covered with blood from civil wars, had become the haunt of wild beasts. The new prophets, to express the ruin of Rome, employed nearly the same images which had served the Seer of 69 to depict his sombre rage.

It was difficult for a society to put up with such attacks, without replying. The Sibylline books which contained those which were attributed to the pretended Hystaspes, and which announced the destruction of the empire, were condemned by the Roman authorities, and those who possessed them or read them were condemned to death. The uneasy search into the future was a crime under the empire; in fact, such vain curiosity almost always served as a cloak or a wish for revolutions and incitements to murder.

It would certainly have been worthy of the wise emperor, so many humane reforms, if he had despised the intemperate imagination without a real object, and if he had abrogated the severe laws which, under Roman despotism, weighed on the liberty of worship and of meeting; but evidently no one about thought of it, any more than any one did who was about Marcus Aurelius. The unfettered thinker alone can be quite tolerant; now Antoninus observed and scrupulously maintained the ceremonies of the Roman worship. The policy of his predecessors had been unvarying in that respect. They saw in Christianity a secret anti-social sect which dreamt of the overthrow of the empire; like all the men who were attached to the old Roman principles, they believed it necessary to repress it. There was no necessity for special edicts: the laws against coetus illiciti and illicita collegia were numerous. The Christians came in a quite regular manner under the power of those laws. It must be observed, first of all, that the true spirit of liberty, as we understand it, was not understood by any one at that time; and that Christianity, when it became the master, did not practise it any more than the heathen emperors; in the second place, that the abrogation of the law of illicit societies would most likely in fact have been the ruin of the empire, founded essentially on this principle that the State cannot admit any society which differs from it into its midst. The idea was wrong, according to our ideas; however, it is quite certain that it was the corner-stone of the Roman constitution. The foundations of the empire would have been thought to be overthrown if those repressive laws which were looked upon as essential conditions to the stability of the State had been relaxed.

The Christians seemed to understand this. Far from finding fault with Antoninus personally, they rather looked upon him as having ameliorated their lot. A fact which does this sovereign infinite honour, is that the principal advocate of Christianity ventured to address him with full confidence, in order to obtain redress from a legal situation which he reasonably found unjust and unbecoming in such a fortunate reign. They went further, and there is no doubt that during the first years of Marcus Aurelius different rescripts were forged in the name of Antoninus, which, supposed to be addressed to the Lariseans, the Thessalonians, the Athenians, to all the Greeks, to the Asiatic States, were so favourable to the Church that if Antoninus had really countersigned them he would have been very inconsistent in not turning Christian. These documents only prove one thing,--the opinion which the Christians retained of the excellent emperor. He did not show himself less benevolent towards the Jews, who no longer menaced the empire. The laws forbidding circumcision, which had been the consequence of Bar-Coziba's revolt, were abrogated, as far as they were vexatious. The Jew was at perfect liberty to sacrifice his sun, but the penalty for practising the operation on a non-Jew was castration, that is, death. Civil jurisdiction within the community does not appear to have been restored to the Jews till later.

Such was the rigour of the established legal order, such was the popular effervescence against the Christians, that even 'during this reign one is sorry to find many martyrs. Polycarp and Justin are the most illustrious amongst them, but they were not the only ones. Asia Minor was stained with the blood of very many judicial murders, which were all provoked by riots; we shall see Montanism rise up like a hallucination of that intoxication for martyrdom. In Rome, the book of the false Hernias will appear to us as if it came out of a bath of blood. Prejudice for martyrdom, questions relating to renegades, or to those who had shown some weakness, fill up the whole book. Justin has described to us on every page Christians as victims who expect nothing but death; their very name, like in the time of Pliny, was a crime.

Jews and heathens persecute us on all sides; they rob us of our possessions, and only leave us our life when they cannot deprive us of it. They cut off our heads, nail us to the cross, expose us to wild beasts, torture us with chains, with fire, with the most horrible torments. But the more ills we have to endure, the more the number of the faithful increases. The vine-grower prunes his vines to make them shoot out anew; he cuts off the branches that have borne fruit, to make it throw out others more vigorous and fruitful; the same thing happens to God's people, which is like a fertile vine, planted by its band and that of our Lord Jesus Christ.

# CHAPTER XVI

### THE CHRISTIANS AND PUBLIC OPINION

In order to be just, one must picture to oneself the prejudices amongst which the public then lived. Christianity was very little known. The lower classes do not like distinctions, or for some to live apart by themselves, for others to be more Puritan than they are, and to abstain from feasts and their usages. When one hides oneself, they always suppose that there is something to hide. In all time secret religious rites have provoked certain calumnies, which are always the same. The mysteries by which they are surrounded cause others to believe in unnatural debaucheries, in infanticide, incest, even in anthropophagy. They are tempted to believe that it is a secret camorra, organised in opposition to the laws. Besides this, informing had in ancient law, in spite of the efforts of good emperors, an importance which fortunately it no longer possesses, and thence sprang a type of libel, drawn up, so to say, in advance, from which no Christian could escape.

Everything was certainly false in those popular rumours, but some badly-understood fact seemed to give some substance to them. Certain inquiries had turned out to the detriment of those who were inculpated. The apologists do not deny it: respect for the matter which had been judged stops them, but they charge the sectaries with the evil, and ask that the faults of some may not be laid to all. The nocturnal gatherings, the signs of recognition, certain eccentric symbols, everything that had anything to do with the mystery in the Eucharist, the sacramental phrases with regard to the body and blood of Christ, excited suspicion. That bread which the Christian woman ate in secret before every meal must have appeared to be a philtre. A number of practices seemed tokens of the crime of magic, which was punished with death. The custom of the faithful to call each other brother and sister, and above all the holy kiss, the kiss of peace, which was given without distinction of sex at the most solemn moment of the assemblage, would be sure to provoke the most unfavourable interpretations in the mind of a public that was incapable of understanding this golden age of purity. The idea of meetings where all familiarities and promiscuities were allowed, naturally arose from such facts, which were distorted by malice and sarcasm.

The accusation of atheism was even more redoubtable. It entailed the punishment of death as a parricide, and worked up all superstitions at once. The undissembled aversion of the Christians for the temples, statues, and altars was constantly productive of some incident. There was no scourge, no earthquake, for which they were not held responsible. Every act of sacrilege, every fire in a temple, was attributed to them. Christians and Epicureans were confounded in this respect, and their secret presence in any town caused consternation, which was worked upon to raise the mob. The lower classes were thus the centre of hatred for the Christians. What the authentic acts of the martyrs treat with the greatest contempt, and as the worst enemies of the saints, are the ruffians of the large towns. The faithful never looked upon themselves as belonging to the people; they seemed in the towns to form the respectable middle class, very respectful towards the authorities, and very much disposed to come to an understanding with them. To defend themselves before the people seemed to the bishops to be a disgrace; they would only argue with the authorities. How plain it is that the very day the government would relax its rigour, Christianity and it would soon come to an understanding! How clear it is that Christianity would be delighted to be the religion of the government. A singular thing is that the only portion of heathen society with which the Christians had any analogy of opinion was the group of Epicureans. The name of Atheists was equally assigned to the disciples of Jesus and those of Epicurus. They had, in fact, this feature in common, that they denied, though certainly from very different reasons, the puerilely supernatural and the ridiculous wonders in which the people believed. In them the Epicureans saw the impostures of the priests, the Christians the impostures of the devil. What aggravated the case of the Christians was that by their exorcisms they were supposed to be able to stop local wonders, and to impose silence on the oracles which made the fortune of a city or of a country. When Alexander of Abonotica saw that his frauds were discovered, he said,--"There is nothing surprising in that; Pontus is full of Atheists and Christians!" That frightened the people, and restored to the impostor a momentary popularity. He burnt the books of Epicurus, and ordered the partisans of both sects to be stoned. Amastris, a Christian and Epicurean town, was particularly hateful to him. At the beginning of his mysteries there was a cry: " If there is any Atheist, Christian, or Epicurean here, let him go out!" He himself said: "Put the Christians out!" and the mob replied: "Put the Epicureans out!" In that superstitious country the name Epicurean was synonymous with accursed. Like that of Christian, any one who bore it ran the risk of his life, or at least was put under the ban of society.

The Christians made use of the arguments of free-thinkers and of the incredulous to turn the popular beliefs into ridicule, and to fight against fatalism. The oracles were an object of mockery to all men of intellect and common sense; the Christians applauded this quizzing. One curious fact is that of OEnomaüs of Gadara, a Cynic philosopher, who having been deceived by a false oracle, lost his temper, and took his revenge in a book called The Deceits Unveiled, in which he wittily ridiculed as an imposture the superstition of which he had for a moment been the dupe. This book was eagerly received by Jews and Christians. Eusebius has inserted it entire in his Evangelical Preparations, and the Jews appear to have put the author on a footing with Balaam, in the class of involuntary apologists of Israel, and of the apostles amongst the heathen.

The Christians and Stoics, between whom there was really more resemblance than between the Christians and the Epicureans, never blended. The Stoics did not make a parade of contempt for public worship. The courage of the Christian martyrs seemed to them foolish obstinacy, an affectation of tragical heroism, a determination to die, which merited nothing but blame. These crowds of infatuated individuals of Asia irritated them. They confounded them with vain and proud Cynics who sought for theatrical deaths, and burnt themselves alive, in order that they might be spoken about.

There was certainly more than one point of resemblance between the Christian philosopher and the Cynic; austere dress, constant declamation against the century, an isolated life, open resistance to the authorities. The Cynics, besides a dress which was analogous to that of the begging friars in the Middle Ages, had a certain organisation, novices, superiors. They were the public professors of virtue, censors, bishops, "angels of the gods," in their own manner; a pastoral vocation was attributed to them, a mission from Heaven to preach and give advice, a mission that required celibacy and perfect renunciation. Christians and Cynics excited the same antipathy in moderate men, because of their common contempt for death. Celsus reproaches Jesus, like Lucian reproaches Peregrinus, with having spread abroad that fatal error. "What will become of society," men asked themselves, "if this spirit gets the upper hand, if criminals no longer fear death?" But the immorality, the coarse impudence of the Cynics, would not allow such a confusion, unless to very superficial observers. Nothing that is known of the Cynics authorises the belief that they were anything but attitudinarians and villainous fellows.

There is no doubt that in many cases the provocation came from the martyrs. But civil society is wrong to allow itself to be drawn into acts of rigour, even towards those who seem to ask for them. The atrocious cruelty of the Roman penal code creates a martyrology which is itself the source of a vast legendary literature, full of unlikelihoods and exaggeration. Criticism, in exposing what is untenable in the accounts of the acts of the martyrs, has sometimes gone to the opposite extreme. The documents which were at first represented as reports of the trials of the martyrs, have been mostly found to be apocryphal. As the texts of historians, properly so called, relating to persecutions are rare and short; as the collections of Roman laws contain next to nothing about the matter, it was natural that the greatest reserve should be imposed on it. One might be tempted to believe that the persecutions really were only a slight matter, that the number of martyrs was inconsiderable, and that the whole ecclesiastical system on this point is nothing but an artificial structure. By degrees light was thrown on the subject. Even freed from legendary exaggeration, the persecutions remain one of the darkest pages of history, and a disgrace to ancient civilisation.

Certainly if we were reduced to the acts of the martyrs to know about the persecutions, scepticism could have a free course. The composition of the acts of the martyrs became at a certain period a species of religious literature for which the imagination, and a certain pious enthusiasm, were much more consulted than authentic documents. With the exception of the letter relative to Polycarp's death, that which contains the account of the sufferings of the heroes of Lyons, the acts of the martyrs of Africa, and some other accounts which bear the stamp of being written in the most serious manner, one must allow that the documents of this character, which have been too easily accepted as sincere, are nothing but pious romances. We know also that the historians of the empire were singularly poor in detail on what refers to the Christians as well as on other matters. The true documents concerning the persecutions which the Church had to suffer, are the works that compose the primitive Christian literature. These works need not be by the authors to whom they are attributed, to have authority on such a question. There was such a widespread taste at that date for attributing documents, that a great number of those books which have been left to us by the first two centuries are by uncertain authors; but that does not prevent these books from being exact mirrors of the time at which they were written. The first Epistle attributed to St Peter, the Revelation of St John, the fragment that is called the Epistle of Barnabas, the Epistle of Clement Romanus, even though it be not by him, the totally or partially apocryphal Epistles of St Ignatius and Polycarp, the Sibylline poems that belong to the first or second century, all the original documents that Eusebius has preserved for us on the origin of Montanism, the controversies between the Gnostics and the Montanists about martyrdom, the Pastor of Hermas, the Apologies of Aristides and of Quadratus, of St Justin, Tatian, Athenagoras, show at each page a state of violence that weighs on the thoughts of the writer, besets him in a measure, and leaves him with no just appreciation of the situation.

From Nero to Commodus, except at short intervals, one might say that the Christian lived continually with the prospect of being put to death before his eyes. Martyrdom is the basis of Christian apology. To listen to the controversialists of the period, it is the sign of the truth of Christianity. The orthodox Church alone has martyrs; the dissenting sects, the Montanists, for example, made ardent efforts to prove that they were not deprived of that supreme criterion of truth. The Gnostics are put under the ban by all the Churches, above all because they declared martyrdom to be useless. In fact then, as Tertullian wishes, persecution was the natural state of the Christian. The details of the acts of the martyrs may be mostly wrong, but the terrible picture that they lay before us, was nevertheless a reality. One has often drawn a wrong picture to oneself of that terrible strife which has surrounded the origins of Christianity with a brilliant halo and impressed on the most beautiful centuries of the empire a hideous blot of blood: one has not exaggerated its gravity. The persecutions were an element of the first order in the formation of that great association of men which was the first to make its rights triumph over the tyrannical pretensions of the State.

As a matter of fact, men die for their opinions, not for certainties--for what they believe, and not for what they know. A scholar who has discovered a theorem has no need to die in order to attest the truth of that theorem; he proves his demonstration, and that is enough. On the other hand, as soon as it is a question of beliefs, the great sign and the most efficacious demonstration is to die for them. That is the explanation of the extraordinary success which some of the religious attempts of the East have obtained.

"You Europeans will never understand anything about religions," said to me the most intelligent of Asiatics, "for you have never had the opportunity of seeing them formed amongst yourselves; whereas we, on the contrary, see them formed every day. I was there whilst people who were cut to pieces and burnt, suffered the most horrible tortures for days, danced and jumped for joy because they were dying for a man whom they had never known (the Bab), and they were the greatest men of Persia. I, who am now speaking to you, was obliged to stop my legend, which in a manner preceded me, to prevent the people from getting killed for me."

Martyrdom does not at all prove the truth of a doctrine, but it proves the impression that it has made on men's minds, and that is all that is needed for success. The finest victories of Christianity, the conversion of a Justin, of a Tertullian, were brought about by the spectacle of the courage of the martyrs, of their joy under torments, and of the sort of infernal rage which urged the world on to persecute them.

# CHAPTER XVII

*THE SECTS AT ROME--THE CERYGMAS--THE ROMAN CHRISTIAN--DEFINITIVE RECONCILIATION OF PETER AND PAUL*

Rome was at the highest period of her grandeur: her sway over the world seemed uncontested; no cloud was visible on the horizon. Far from growing weaker, the movement that led the provincials, above all those of the East, to come there in crowds, increased in intensity. The Greek speaking population was more considerable than ever. The insinuating Græculus, who was good for every trade, was driving the Italian from the domesticity of great houses; Latin literature was daily losing ground, whilst Greek was becoming the literary, philosophical, and religious language of the enlightened classes, just as it was the language of the lower classes. The importance of the Church of Rome was measuring itself with that of the city itself. That Church, which was still quite Greek, had an uncontested superiority over the others. Hyginus, her chief, obtained the respect of the whole Christian world. Rome was then for the provinces what Paris is in its brilliant days, the city of all contacts, all fecundations. Whoever wished to find a place of mark aspired to go thither; nothing was consecrated but what had received its stamp at that universal exhibition of the productions of the entire universe.

Gnosticism, with its ambition of setting the fashion in Christian preaching, especially yielded to that tendency. None of the Gnostic schools sprang from Rome, but nearly all came to an end there. Valentinus was the first to try it. That daring sectary may even have had the idea of seating himself on the episcopal throne of the unrivalled city. He showed every appearance of Catholicism, and preached in the absurd style that he had invented. Its success was mediocre; that pretentious philosophy, that unquiet curiosity, scandalised the faithful. Hyginus drove the innovator from the Christian pulpit. From that time forward the Roman Church indicated the purely practical tendency which was always to distinguish her, and showed herself ready quickly to sacrifice science and talent to edification.

Another heterodox doctor, Cerdon, appeared at Rome about that time. He was a native of Syria, and introduced doctrines which differed but little from those of the Gnostics of that country. His manner of distinguishing God from the Creator; of placing another unknown god above God, the father of Jesus; of representing one of the gods as just, the other as good, sounds contrary to right. Cerdon found that this world was as imperfect a work as that Jehovah Himself to Whom it was attributed, and who was represented as subject to human passions. He rejected all the Jewish books in a mass, as well as all the passages in Christian writings, from which it might result that Christos had been able to take real flesh. It was quite simple: matter seemed to him to be a deterioration, an evil. The Resurrection was repugnant to him for the same reason. The Church censured him; he submitted, and retracted his opinions, then began to dogmatise afresh, either in public or private. Thence arose a most equivocal position. His life was spent in leaving the Church and joining it again, in doing penance for his errors, and in maintaining them afresh. The unity of the Church was too strong in Rome for Cerdon to be able to dream of forming a separate congregation there as he would certainly have done in Syria. He exercised his influence over a few isolated individuals, whom the apparent depth of his language and of doctrines which were then quite novel seduced. A certain Lucain or Lucian is particularly quoted amongst his disciples, without mentioning the celebrated Marcion, who, as we shall see, sprang from him.

The abstract Gnosticism of Alexandria and Antioch, appearing under the form of a bold philosophy, found little favour in the capital of the world. It was the Ebionites, the Nazarenes, the Elkasaites, the Essenes, which were all Gnostic heresies in a way, but of a moderate and Judeo-Christian Gnosticism in their affinities, it was those heresies, I say, that swarmed at Rome, which made the legend of Peter, and created the future of that great Church. The mysterious formulas of Elkasaism were usual in their midst, especially for the baptismal ceremony. The neophyte, presented on the edge of a river or a fountain of flowing water, took heaven and earth, air and water, to witness that it was his firm resolve to sin no more. For these sectaries, who sprang from Juda, Peter and James were the two corners of the Church of Jesus. We have often remarked that Rome was always the principal home of Judeo-Christianity. The new spirit, represented by the school of Paul, was checked there by a highly conservative one. In spite of the efforts of conciliatory men, the apostle of the Gentiles had here also obstinate adversaries. Peter and Paul fought their last battle before becoming definitely reconciled in the bosom of the Universal Church for eternity.

The life of the two apostles was beginning to be much forgotten. They had been dead about seventy-seven years; all who had seen them had disappeared, the greater portion without leaving any writings behind them. One was at perfect liberty to embroider on that still virgin canvas. A vast Ebionite legend had been formed in Rome and was settled at about the time at which we have arrived. St Peter's journeys and sermons were its principal object. In it the missionary journeys of the chief of the apostles, especially along the coasts of Phoenicia; the conversions which be had effected; his strifes, especially with the great Antichrist who at that time was the spectre of the Christian conscience, Simon Magus, were related. But often in hidden words, under that abhorred name was hidden another personage, the false Apostle Paul, the enemy of the Law, the destroyer of the true Church. The true Church was that of Jerusalem, over which James, the Lord's brother presided. No apostolate was valid which could not produce letters emanating from that central college. Paul had none, he was therefore an intruder. He was the "enemy" who came behind the real sower to sow the bad seed. With what force, too, Peter exposed his impostures, his false allegations of personal revelations, his ascension into the third heaven, his pretensions of knowing things about Jesus which those who had heard the Gospel had not heard, his disciples' exaggerated conceptions of the divinity of Jesus! At Antioch especially Peter's triumph was complete. Simon had succeeded in turning the people of that city away from the truth. By a series of clever manoeuvres Peter brought one of the victims of Simon's sorceries, to whom the magician had imparted his own form, to show himself to the people of Antioch. What was their astonishment on hearing him whom they took for the Samaritan magician, retract in these terms:--

I have lied about Peter he is the true apostle of the prophet who was sent by God for the salvation of the world. The angels beat me last night for having calumniated him. Do not listen to me if I speak against him in the future!

Naturally all Antioch returned to Peter and cursed his rival.

Thus the real apostle continued his journeys, following the traces of the Samaritan impostor, and arrived at the capital of the empire immediately after him. The impostor redoubled his artifices, invented a thousand spells, and gained Nero's mind. He even succeeded in passing off as God, and in being adored. His admirers raised altars to him, and, according to the author, these altars were still shown in his time. On the island of the Tiber, in fact, a college of the Sabine god Semo Sancus was established. There there were a number of votive columns, SEMONI DEO SANCO, on which it was easy to read, with a little goodwill, SIMONI DEO SANCTO.

The decisive struggle was to take place in the emperor's presence. Simon's programme was that he would raise himself into the air, and would hover there like a god. He did raise himself in fact, but on a sign from Peter the skin of his magic was burst, and he fell ignominiously, and was shattered to pieces. A similar accident had happened in the amphitheatre of the Campus Martius under Nero. An individual who had claimed to be able to raise himself into the air like Icarus, fell on to the angle of the emperor's box, and he was covered with blood. Perhaps some real facts in the life of the Samaritan charlatan served as a foundation for these stories. At any rate the discomfiture of the impostor was represented as Peter's greatest glory, and by it he really took possession of the eternal city. According to the legend his death followed very soon on his victory; Nero, irritated at the misadventure that had happened to his favourite juggler, put the apostle to death.

Such is the legend which, started about the year 125 by the passions and rancour of the Jewish party in the Church at Rome, was by degrees softened down, and produced, towards the end of Hadrian's reign, the work, in ten books, called "The Preaching of Peter," or "The Journeys of Peter." The legend had been cut into three parts for the purposes of publication. " The Preaching" contained the account of Peter's apostolate in Judea; the Periodi comprised Peter's journeys and his controversies with Simon in Syria and Phoenicia. His sojourn at Rome and his struggles before the Emperor were the subject of the "Acts of Peter," another composition which formed, in some sort, the sequel of the Cerygma and of the Periodi. Those accounts of his apostolical journeys, full of charm for the Christian imagination, gave rise to numerous compositions, which soon became romances. The narrative was interspersed with pious sermons; Peter was made the preacher of all good doctrines; the picture of chaste love vivified and imparted warmth to the painting; Christian romance was created, and no essential machinery has been added to it since.

All that first literature of the Cerygmas and of the Periodi was the work of Ebionite, Essenian, and Elkasaite sectaries. Peter, represented as the real apostle of the Gentiles, was always its hero; James appeared in it as the invisible president of a coenaculum filled with the divine spirit, having its seat at Jerusalem. Animosity against Paul was evident Like the Essenes and the Elkasaites of the East, those of Rome attached great importance to the possession of a secret literature which was reserved for the initiated, and the commonest frauds were employed to give to those later productions of Christian inspiration an authority which they did not merit.

The most ancient edition of the Cerygmas of Peter is lost, and we only possess two fragments which form a sort of introduction to the work. The first is a letter in which Peter addresses the book of his Cerygmas to James, "master and bishop of the Holy Church," and begs him not to communicate it to any heathen, nor even to any Jew with a preliminary test. Peter says that the admirable policy of the Jews ought to be imitated, who, in spite of the diversities of the interpretation to which the Scripture gives rise, have succeeded in keeping the unity of the faith and of hope. If the book of the Cerygmas were to be circulated indiscreetly, it would give rise to schisms. Peter adds,--

I do not know that as a prophet, but because I already see the beginning of the evil. Some of those who are of heathen origin have rejected my preaching, which is conformable to the Law, and have attached themselves to the frivolous teaching of the enemy, which is contrary to the Law. During my life people have tried, by different interpretations, to pervert my words, in the sense of destroying the Law. According to them, that is my idea, but I am not bold enough to declare it. God forbid! that would be to blaspheme the Law of God which Moses proclaimed, and whose eternal duration our Saviour attested when He said: "Heaven and earth shall pass away, but not one jot or tittle of the Law shall pass away." This is the truth, but there are some people who think themselves authorised, I do not know how, to expound my thoughts, and who claim to interpret the discourses that they have heard from me more pertinently than I do myself. They put before their catechumens as my true opinion matters of which I have never dreamt. If such lies are produced during my life, what will they not dare to do after my death?

James decided in fact that the book of the Cerygmas should only be communicated to circumcised men of mature age who aspired to the title of doctor, and who had been tested for at least six years. The initiation was to take place by degrees, in order that if the results of a first experience were bad it might be stopped. The communication was to be made mysteriously, on the very spot where baptism was administered, and with the formulas of baptismal promises according to the Essenean or Elkasaite rite. The person who was initiated was to promise to submit himself to him who gave the Cerygmas, not to pass them on to any one else, not to copy them or allow them to be copied. If some day the books which were given to him as Cerygmas should not appear to him any longer to be true, he was to give them back to him from whom he had received them. On setting out on a journey he was to give them up "to his bishop professing the same faith as himself, and starting from the same principles." When he was in danger of death he was to do the same thing, if his sons were not yet fit to be initiated. When they had become worthy of it the bishop would give them the books back, as a paternal deposit. The most singular thing is that the sectary is to foresee the case in which he may himself change his religion, and go over to the worship of some strange god. In that case, he must swear by his final god, and rob himself of the subterfuge of saying afterwards, to establish the nullity of his oath, that that God did not exist. "If I break my engagements," the neophyte was obliged to add, "may the universe be hostile to me, as well as the ether that penetrates everything, and the God who is over all, the best, the greatest of beings. And if I come to know any other god, I swear also by that god that I will keep the engagements that I have taken, whether that god exists or does not exist." Then, as a sign of secret partnership, the initiator and the initiated took bread and salt together.

The absurdities of the sectaries would have been without any consequence anywhere but in Rome, but everything that referred to Peter assumed considerable proportions in the capital of the world. In spite of its heresies, the book of the Cerygmas was of great interest for the orthodox. The primacy of Peter was proclaimed in it; St Paul was abused, but a few after touches might soften down anything offensive in such attacks. Thus several attempts were made to lessen the singularities of the new book and to adapt it to the wants of the Catholics. This fashion of altering books to suit the sect to which one belonged was quite usual. By degrees the force of circumstances made itself felt: all sensible men saw that there was no safety for the work of Jesus except in the perfect reconciliation of the two chiefs of Christian preaching. For a long time still Paul had bitter enemies in the Nazarenes, and he had also exaggerated disciples like Marcion. Outside this stubborn right and left, a fusion of the moderate parties took place, who, although they owed their Christianity to one of the schools and remained attached to it, yet fully recognised the right of the others to call themselves Christians. James, who was the partisan of an absolute Judaism, was sacrificed; although he had been the real chief of the Christians of the circumcision, Peter was preferred to him, as he had shown more regard for Paul's disciples, and James only retained his vehement partisans amongst the Judeo-Christians.

It is difficult to say who gained most by that reconciliation. The concessions chiefly came from Paul's side: all his disciples admitted Peter without difficulty, whilst most of the Christians of Peter rejected Paul. But concessions often come from the strongest. In reality, every day gave the victory to Paul, and every Gentile who was converted made the balance incline to his side. Out of Syria, the Judeo-Christians were, so to say, drowned by the waves of the newly converted. St Paul's churches prospered; they had sound sense, a sobriety of intellect, and pecuniary resources which the others did not possess. The Ebionite churches, on the other hand, were daily getting poorer. The money of Paul's churches was used for the support of poor saints who could not gain their own livelihood, but who possessed the living tradition of the primitive spirit. The communities of Christians of heathen origin admired, imitated, and assimilated to themselves the others' elevated piety and strictness of morals. Soon more distinction could be made as regarded the most eminent persons in the Church of Rome. The mild and conciliatory spirit that had already been represented by Clemens Romanus and St Luke prevailed, and the contract of peace was sealed. It was agreed, according to the system of the author of the Acts, that Peter had converted the first fruits of the Gentiles, and that he was the first to deliver them from the yoke of the Law. It was admitted that Peter and Paul had been the two chiefs, the two founders of the Church of Rome, and thus they became the two halves of an inseparable couple, two luminaries like the sun and the moon. What one taught, the other taught also; they were always agreed, they combated the same enemies, were both victims of the perfidies of Simon Magus; at Rome, they lived like two brothers, the Church of Rome was their common work. Thus the supremacy of that Church was founded for centuries.

So from the reconciliation of parties and the settlement of the earlier strifes there sprang a great unity, the Catholic Church, the Church at the same time of Peter and of Paul, a stranger to the rivalries which had marked the first century of Christianity. Paul's churches had shown the most conciliatory spirit, and they triumphed. The stubborn Ebionites remained Jewish, and shared the Jewish immovableness. Rome was the point where this great transformation took place. Already the high Christian destiny of that extraordinary city was being written in luminous characters. The transference of Easter to the day of the resurrection, which was in some measure the proclamation of the autonomy of Christianity, was accomplished there, at anyrate in the time of Hadrian.

The fusion that took place between the groups also took place with regard to their writings. Books were exchanged from one country to another. The writings passed from the Judeo-Christian school to that of Paul, with slight modifications. That Cerygma of Peter, which was, in its first shape, so offensive to Paul's disciples, became the Cerygma of Peter and Paul. They were supposed to have travelled together, sailed in company, preached the gospel everywhere in perfect harmony. The Church of Corinth, especially, claimed to have been founded at the same time by Peter and Paul. The person of Simon Magus, who in the first Ebionite editions of the Cerygma and of the Periodi of Peter, was Paul himself designated by an offensive epithet, was rather a formidable obstacle. In the Cerygma of Peter and Paul the name of Simon was preserved, and restored to its proper sense. As the symbolism of the Ebionite pamphlet was not evident, Simon for the future was the common adversary whom Peter and Paul had pursued together hand in hand.

The fundamental condition of the success of Christianity was now settled. Neither Peter nor Paul could succeed separately. Peter was preservation, Paul revolution: both were necessary. It is told in Brittany that when St Peter and St Paul went to preach Christianity in America, they reached a deep and narrow arm of the sea. Although they were agreed on essential points, they determined to establish themselves one on one side and one on the other, so that they might both teach the Gospel in their own fashion; for it seems that, in spite of their intimate fellowship, they could not live together very well. Each of them, according to the custom of the saints of Brittany, set to work to build his chapel. They had the materials, but only one hammer, so that every evening the saint who had worked during the daytime threw the hammer across the arm of the sea to his neighbour. Thanks to the alternative labour resulting from this arrangement, the work went on well, and the two chapels, which are yet to be seen, were built.

Above all, the death of the two apostles preoccupied the different parties, and gave rise to the most diverse combinations. A legendary tissue was woven with regard to this by an instinctive work which was almost as imperious as that which had presided over the formation of the legend of Jesus. The end of the life of Peter and Paul was ordered à priori. It was maintained that Christ had announced Peter's martyrdom just as he had foretold the death of the sons of Zebedee. A want was felt of associating two persons in death who had been forcibly reconciled. Men wished to prove, and perhaps in that they were not far wrong, that they were put to death at the same time, or at least in consequence of the same event. The spots which were looked upon as having been sanctified by this sanguinary drama were fixed upon at an early date, and consecrated by memoriæ. In such a case, what the people wants always gains the day in the end. There is no popular place in Italy where the portraits of Victor Emmanuel and Pius IX. are not seen side by side, and general belief will have it that those two men, representing principles whose reconciliation is, according to the most general sentiment, necessary to Italy, were really very good friends. If such ideas obtruded themselves into history in our time, one would read some day, in documents which are looked upon as serious, that Victor-Emmanuel, Pius IX. (most probably Garibaldi would be joined in with them) saw each other secretly, understood each other, and liked each other. The association of Voltaire and Rousseau was brought about by analogous necessities. The Middle Ages also tried several times, in order to appease the hatred between Dominicans and Franciscans, to prove that the founders of those two orders had been two brothers, living on the most affectionate terms together, that at first their rules were identical, that St Dominic wore the cord of St Francis, etc.

The Cerygma of Peter and Paul was all the more important as it filled up the unfortunate gaps which the Acts of the Apostles showed. In this latter book Peter's preaching was cut very short, and the circumstances of the apostles' deaths were passed over in silence. The success of a book that represented Peter and Paul going everywhere in company to convert the Gentiles,--going to Rome, preaching there, and both finding the crown of martyrdom there, was assured. The doctrine which they taught, according to this book, was equally removed from Judaism and Hellenism. The Jews were treated by them as enemies of Jesus and of the apostles. At Rome, Peter and Paul announced the destruction of their city, and their perpetual exile from Judea, because they had leaped with joy at the trials of the Son of God.

It seems at first sight as if such an important work ought to find a place in the canon of Scripture immediately after the Acts of the Apostles. But the wording of it was incoherent, and incapable of satisfying the whole Christian community in a permanent manner. The evangelical knowledge of the author was too incomplete. He admitted the most childish statements from the Gospel to the Hebrews. Jesus confessed his sins; his mother Mary forced him to be baptised, and at the moment of his baptism the water seemed to be covered with fire. In his discourses to the Gentiles, Paul cited the apocryphal Sibyl of the Jews of Alexandria and of Hystaspes, a heathen prophet who announced the league of the kings against Christ and the Christians, the patience of the martyrs, and the final appearance of Christ, as authorities that ought to convince them. Then, contrary to Paul's formal assertions in the Epistle to the Galatians, Peter and Paul are supposed to have met for the first time in Rome. Other singular opinions soon caused that old compilation to be condemned by the orthodox doctors. The Cerygma of Peter and Paul had only a very uncertain place amongst the canonical writings. The romance of Peter had, from the very beginning, contracted a sort of sectarian bust, which must prevent its being admitted, even after corrections, into the lists of the imposed dogmas.

Thus the account of the death of the two apostles, like that of their preaching and journeys, was a matter of caprice, at anyrate as far as regarded form. Simplicity of style, which assures the eternal fortune of a narrative text, something decided in the outline, which makes the reader believe that events could not have happened differently, all those qualities which constitute the beauty of the Gospels and of the Acts of the Apostles, are wanting in the legend of the death of Peter and Paul. Ancient compilations about it existed which have disappeared, but which were not very different from those which have been preserved, and which have fixed the tradition on this important subject. The effect of the legend was abundant and rapid. Rome and all its environs, above all the Via Ostia, were, so to say, filled with pretended recollections of the last days of the apostles. A number of touching circumstances--Peter's flight, the vision of Jesus bearing his cross, the iterum crucifigi, the last farewell of Peter and Paul, the meeting of Peter with his wife, St Paul at the fountain of Salvian, Plautilla sending the kerchief which kept up her hair to bandage Paul's eyes--all that made a beautiful whole that only required a clever and simple compiler. It was too late; the vein of the first Christian literature was exhausted; the serenity of the historian of the Acts was lost, and the tone never rose above the level of story or romance. No choice could be made amongst a number of compilations all of which were equally apocryphal; in vain was it sought to cover those feeble accounts with the most venerated names (pseudo-Linus, pseudo-Marcellus); the Roman legend of Peter and Paul always remained in a sporadic state, and was more frequently related by pious guides than seriously read. It was an altogether local affair; no text was consecrated to be read in churches, and none obtained any authority.

The creative vein with regard to Gospel literature also grew daily weaker, although it had not absolutely dried up. The Gospel of the Nazarenes, or of the Hebrews, or of the Ebionites, was almost as different in texts as it was in manuscripts. Egypt extracted from them its "Gospel of the Egyptians," in which the exaggeration of a sickly enthusiasm bordered so closely on immorality. A compilation which had a very great success for a long time was the Gospel of Peter, which was most likely composed at Rome. Justin and the author of the pseudo-Clementine romance seem to have made use of it. It differed little from the Ebionite Gospel, and already showed that prepossession in favour of many which is the feature of the apocryphal writings. Men reflected more and more on the part which would be suitable to the mother of Jesus. They sought to connect her with David's race; round her cradle miracles were created which were analogous to those which occurred at John Baptist's birth. A book that was later filled with absurdities by the Gnostics, but which perhaps, when it appeared, did not go beyond the main note of the Catholic Church, the Genna Marias, which differed but little from the writing that is called the Protovangelium of James, satisfied those wants of the imagination. Legends got more material every day. Men occupied themselves with the evidence of the midwife who attended Mary, and who vouched for her virginity. It did not suffice any longer that Jesus was born in a stable; men wished him, according to certain Jewish ideas which are to be found again in the Haggadic legend of Abraham, to be born in a cave. They tried to turn the journey to Egypt to some account, and as Egypt was the country in which there were the most idols, it was pretended that the mere view of the exiled child sufficed to make all the profane statues fall with their faces to the ground. It was known exactly what trade Jesus carried on. He made carts and other vehicles. They claimed to know the name of the woman who had the issue of blood (Berenice or Veronica), and the statues were shown which she had raised to Jesus in her gratitude.

74

The desire of finding arguments which the heathen could not challenge was the cause of some pious frauds whose success was rapid in that world, which was not hard to please, and which it was intended to impress. The monotheistic Sibyl of Alexandria, which for centuries had not ceased to anounce the ruin of idolatry, was becoming more and more Christian. The authority that was accorded to it was of the first order. The ancient Sibylline collections were continually increasing, by additions in which no trouble was taken to keep up an appearance of probability. The heathen were enraged at what they looked upon as interpolations into venerable books. The Christians answered them with more humour than justice: "Show us any old copies in which those passages are not to be found." Men of intellect made fun equally of the heathen and Christian Sibyls, and parodied them cleverly, so much so that Origen, for instance, never makes use of these depreciated arguments.

To these oracles were added those of a certain Hystaspes, under whose name some pretended books on the mysteries of Chaldea were current amongst the heathen. He was made to announce the coming of Christ, the Apocalyptic catastrophes, the end of the world by fire, with an amount of assurance that argued extreme credulity in those to whom they were addressed.

About the same time, the documents which were supposed to be official, of Pilate's administration relating to Jesus, may have been forged. In a controversy with the heathen and the Jews it was a great power to be able to appeal to pretended reports contained in the State archives. Such was the origin of those Acts of Pilate which St Justin, the Quartodecimans, and Tertullian had quoted, and which possessed sufficient importance for the Emperor Maximian II., at the beginning of the fourth century, to look upon it as an act of fair warfare to counterfeit them, in order to cast ridicule and contempt on the Christians. From the moment that it was admitted that Tiberius was officially informed of the death of Jesus, it was natural to suppose that this notification had some effect, and from that fact sprang the opinion that Tiberius had proposed to the Senate to place Jesus in the ranks of the gods.

Rome, as has been seen, continued to be the centre of an extraordinary movement. Heretics of all sorts met there, and were anathematised there. The centre of a future orthodoxy was evidently there. Pius had succeeded Hyginus, and was as firm as his predecessor had been in defending the purity of the faith. Pius is already a bishop in the proper sense of the word. Valentinus and Cerdon, although condemned by Hyginus, were always at Rome, trying to regain their lost ground, retracting at times, received as penitents, then returning to their dreams and continuing to have partisans. At length they were finally excommunicated. Valentinus would seem to have withdrawn to Cyprus; it is tot known what became of Cerdon. His name would have remained unknown if he had not left a disciple behind him who surpassed him in strength of intellect and in activity, and who became the greatest embarrassment for the Church that she had encountered hitherto, towards the middle of the second century.

# CHAPTER XVIII

### *EXAGGERATION OF ST PAUL'S IDEAS--MARCION*

The great peculiarity of Christianity, the fact of a new religion springing from another religion, and becoming by degrees the negation of the one that had preceded it, naturally gave rise to the most opposite phenomena, till the two forms of worship were completely separated. The reaction would be of two kinds amongst those who did not exactly keep their balance on the narrow edge of orthodoxy. Some, going beyond Paul's principles, fancied that the religion of Jesus had no connection with the religion of Moses. Others, Judeo-Christians, looked upon Christianity as a mere continuation of the Jewish religion. In general, it was the Gnostics who inclined to the former idea, but those dreamers seemed to be attacked by a sort of practical incapacity. An ardent, intelligent man was found to give the necessary cohesion to the divergent elements, and to form a lasting Church, side by side with that which already called itself--

The Universal Church, the great Church of Jesus.

Marcion was a native of Sinope, a city full of activity, which had already given the two Aquilas, and would later give Theodation, as participators in the religious disputes of the time. He was the son of the bishop of that city, and appears to have been a sailor. Although born a Christian, he had seriously examined his faith, and had devoted himself to the study of Greek philosophy, especially of Stoicism. To that he joined an ascetic appearance and great austerity. His father, as is alleged, was obliged to drive him from his Church, as he was dangerous to the orthodoxy of his faithful hearers.

We have already remarked several times on the sort of attraction which brought to Rome, under the pontificate of Hyginus and in the first years of Pius, all those whom the phosphorescent lights of growing Gnosticism seduced. Marcion arrived in the eternal city at the moment when Cerdon unsettled the most sincere believers by his brilliant metaphysics. Marcion, like all the sectaries, first of all showed himself a zealous Catholic. The Church of Rome possessed such great importance that all those who felt any ecclesiastical ambition aspired to govern her. The rich Sinopean apparently made the community a present of a large sum of money, but his hopes were disappointed. He had not that spirit which the Church of Rome has always required in her clergy. Intellectual superiority was but little valued there. His ardent curiosity, his vivacity of thought, and his learning, all appeared dangerous. It could easily be seen that they would not allow him to remain quietly within the narrow limits of orthodoxy. Cerdon, like he did, expiated his pretensions to dogmatic originality in isolation. Marcion became his disciple. The transcendent theories of Gnosticism, taught by that master, must have appeared to be the highest form of Christianity to a mind imbued with philosophical doctrines. Moreover, Christian dogma was so little settled as yet that every one of strong individuality aspired to impress it with his own seal. That is enough to explain the intricate roads in which this great man lost himself, without it being necessary to put any faith in the everyday calumnies by which ecclesiastical writers strive to show that the leader of every sect, when he separates himself from the majority of the faithful, obeys the lowest motives.

Marcion's theology only differed from that of the Gnostics of Syria and Egypt by its simplicity. The distinction between the good God and the just God, between the invisible God and the demiurge, between the God of the Jews and the God of the Christians, formed the basis of his system. Matter was the eternal evil. The ancient Law, Jehovah's work, which was essentially material, interested, severe, cruel and loveless, had only one object: to subject the other peoples, Egyptians, Canaanites, etc., to Jehovah's people, and it did not even succeed in procuring their happiness, as Jehovah was continually obliged to console them by the promise of sending them his Son. It would have been vain to have expected that salvation from Jehovah if the Supreme God, who was good and invisible and unknown to the world till then, had not sent his Son Jesus, that is to say meekness itself under the apparent form of a man, to combat the influence of the demiurge and to introduce the law of love. The Jews will have their Messiah, son of their God, that is to say, of the demiurge. Jesus is by no means that Messiah; his mission, on the contrary, was to abolish the Law, the prophets, and the works of that demiurge generally; but his disciples understood him wrongly: Paul was the only true apostle. Marcion imposed the task upon himself of finding the ideas of Jesus again which had been obliterated and maladroitly brought back to Judaism by those who succeeded him.

That was already Manichæism, with its dangerous antithesis, making its appearance in the field of Christian beliefs. Marcion supposes that there are two Gods, one of whom is good and gentle, the other who is severe and cruel. The absolute condemnation of the flesh led him to look upon the continuation of the human race as only serving to prolong the reign of the evil demiurge; he objected to marriage, and would not admit married people to baptism. No sect sought for martyrdom more, nor reckoned, proportionately, more confessors of the faith. According to the Marcionites, martyrdom was the highest Christian liberation, the most beautiful form of deliverance from this world, which is an evil. Bodies do not rise, only the souls of true Christians are brought back to existence. Besides, all souls are not equal, and only arrive at perfection by a series of transmigrations.

It will be seen that the doctrine of the Epistles to the Colossians and Ephesians, and that of the fourth Gospel, was far exceeded. Everything Jewish in the Church became mere dross which must be eliminated. Marcion looked upon Christianity as an entirely new religion, and one without precedent. In that he was a disciple of Paul who had lost his way. Paul believed that Jesus had abolished Judaism, but he did not mistake the divine character of the ancient Law. Marcion, on the contrary, declared that there was no appearance of God in history till Jesus. The Law of Moses was the work of a particular demiurge (Jehovah) whom the Jews adored, and who, to keep them in the fetters of theocracy, gave them priests, and sought to retain them by promises and threats. Such a Law, without any superior character, was powerless against evil. It represented justice but not kindness. The appearance of Christ was the manifestation of a complete God who was kind and just at the same time. The Old Testament was not only different from Christianity, it was contrary to it. Marcion wrote a work called Antithesis, in which the two Testaments were put in flagrant contradiction. Apelles, his disciple, wrote a book to show that Moses had written nothing concerning God but what was false and unbecoming.

A chief objection to that theory arose from the different Gospels which were then in circulation, and which more or less agreed with what we call the synoptic type. The fourth Gospel had as yet but very little circulation, and Marcion did not know it, otherwise he would have preferred it to the others. In the generally admitted accounts about Jesus, the Jewish impress can be seen on every page; Jesus speaks as a Jew and acts as a Jew. Marcion imposed the difficult task upon himself of changing all that. He composed a Gospel in which Jesus was no longer a Jew, or rather, was no longer a man; he wanted a life of Jesus which should be that of a pure won. Taking St Luke's Gospel as his basis, which may be called Paul's Gospel up to a certain point, he remodelled it according to his own ideas, and was not satisfied till Jesus had no more ancestors, parents, forerunners, or masters. If Jesus had only been known to us from texts of that nature, one might doubt whether he had really existed, or whether he were not an à priori fiction, detached from any tie with reality. In such a system, Christ was not born (for Marcion, birth was a stain), did not suffer, did not die. All the Gospel passages in which Jesus recognised the Creator as his father, were suppressed. After his descent into hell he took to heaven with him those persons who were cursed in the Old Testament--Cain, the Sodomites, etc. These poor wanderers, interesting, like all those who have revolted under an ancient fallen régime, came to meet him and were saved. On the other hand, Jesus left Abel, Noah, Abraham, who were servants of the demiurge, that is to say, of the God of the Old Testament, in the dark places of oblivion, as their only merit consisted in having obeyed a tyrant's laws. It was that God of the Old Testament who caused Jesus to be put to death, and thus worthily crowned an era which had been the reign of evil.

It would be impossible to take up a position more utterly opposed to the ideas of Peter, James, and Mark. The last conclusions had been drawn from St Paul's principles. Marcion put no author's name to his Gospel, but he certainly looked upon it as "the Gospel according to Paul." Jesus is no more a man at all, he is the first ideal appearance of a good God, nearly like Schleiermacher understood it sixteen centuries later. A very fine system of morality, summed up in a striving after good, resulted from this spiritualistic and rationalist philosophy. Marcion was the most original of the Christian masters of the second century after the author of the pseudo-Johannistic writings. But the belief in two gods, which was the foundation of his system, and the colossal historical error which it contained in representing a religion which sprang from Judaism as contrary to Judaism, were profound blemishes which must prevent such a doctrine from becoming those of the Catholicity.

Its success was extraordinary at first: Marcion's doctrines spread very quickly over the whole Christian world, but they met with strenuous opposition. Justin, who was then in Rome, combated the innovator in writings which we have not got any longer. Polycarpus received the new ideas with the most lively indignation. It appears that Meliton wrote against them. Several anonymous priests attacked them, and furnished Irenæus with the weapons that he was to use later. Marcion's position in the Church was a very false one. Like Valentinus and Cerdon, he wished to be part of the Church, and doubtless to preach in it; now the Church of Rome much preferred docility and mediocrity to originality and vigorous logic. Like Valentinus, Marcion made semi-retractations, and retreated; all was useless: the incompatibility was too strong. After being condemned twice, a definite excommunication drove him from the Church. The sum of money which he had given in the first warmth of his faith was refunded to him, and he returned to Asia Minor, where he continued to display immense activity in the propagation of error. It seems that in his latter years he instituted fresh negotiations to attach himself to the Church again, but death prevented their success. Often a certain timidity of character is associated with great speculative boldness, and Marcion seems often to have contradicted himself. On the other hand, such an end answered so perfectly to the wants of orthodox polemics that one must suspect it of having been invented. Apelles restored the Marcionite school to an almost orthodox deism.

In any case, Marcion remains the boldest innovator whom Christianity has known, not even excepting St Paul. He never denied the connection between the two Testaments; Marcion opposed them to each other as two antitheses. He even went so far as to claim the right of re-making the life of Jesus according to his own fashion, and of systematically altering the Gospels. Even St Paul's Epistles, which he adopted, were arranged and mutilated by him in order to efface the quotations from the Old Testament, and Abraham's name, which he hated.

This was the third attempt to make the life of Jesus the life of an abstract being instead of a Galilean reality. The results of different tendencies, which were all equally necessary,--of the wish to idealise a life which became that of a God,--of the desire of denying that that God had a family lineage or country upon earth,--of the impossibility for the Greek Christian to admit that Christianity had anything in common with Judaism, which he despised, these three attempts had very different successes. The author of the pseudo-Johannistic writings set to work in an inconsistent and incoherent manner, but which possessed the advantage of letting an historical biography of Jesus subsist side by side with the theology of the Logos. His attempt was the only one that succeeded, for, whilst looking upon modern Judaism as an evil, and imagining that Truth had descended from heaven with the Logos, he admits that the true Israel has had its mission, and that the world, far from being the work of a demiurge who was hostile to God, was created by the Logos. The Gnostics drowned the Gospel in metaphysics, eliminated every Jewish element, dissatisfied even the Deists, and so destroyed their future. Marcion's speculations were of a more sober kind; but Christianity was already too much formed, its texts were too settled, its Gospels too much valued, for Catholic opinion to be shaken. Marcion then was nothing but the mere head of a sect, though it is true it was by far the most numerous before that of Arius. The rage with which orthodoxy pursued him is the best proof of the profound impression that he made on the minds of his contemporaries.

# CHAPTER XIX

## THE CATHOLIC APOLOGY--ST JUSTIN

A principal fact which may clearly be seen developing from this time forward, is that in the midst of these agitated waves there is a sort of immovable rock, a doctrine between the two extremes, which resists the most diverse attacks, Judeo-Christian and Gnostic exaggerations, and constitutes a central orthodoxy which is destined to triumph over all sects. That universal doctrine which laid claim to priority over all particular doctrines, and to go as far back as the apostles, constitutes the Catholic Church in opposition to heresies. Gnosticism, especially an invincible obstacle in that sort of ecclesiastical tribunal, this was a question of life or death for the Christian religion. The extravagant tendencies of the innovators would have been the annihilation of all unity. Now, as nearly always happens, anarchy created authority, and thus it may be said that in the formation of the Catholic Church Gnosticism and Marcionism played the principal part by antithesis.

A man who is very highly esteemed for his profane studies, and his knowledge of the Scriptures-- Justin of Neapolis, in Samaria, who had been residing in Rome for several years--taught Christian philosophy and fought energetically for the orthodox majority. He was used to and fond of polemics. Valentinians, Marcionites, Samaritan Jews, heathen philosophers, were in turn the object of his attacks. Justin was not a man of great intellect; he did not know much of philosophy and criticism, and, above all, his exegesis would be looked upon as very defective in our time; but he gives proof of general good sense; he had that sort of mediocre credulity which allows a man to reason sensibly from puerile premisses, and to stop in time so as only to be half ridiculous. His general treatise against heresies, his particular writings against the Valentinians and Marcionites, have been lost, but his works for the general defence of Christianity had an extraordinary success amongst the faithful, and they were copied and imitated; thus, Justin was, in a manner, the first Christian doctor, in the classic sense of the word, whose works have been preserved to no in a relatively complete state.

Justin, as we have said, had not a strong intellect, but he had a noble and good heart. His great demonstration of Christianity was the persecution of which that doctrine, which was so beneficial in his eyes, was the ceaseless object. The fact that the other sects, the Jews especially, were not persecuted, the joy that the Christians evinced under torture, the calumnies that were spread abroad with regard to the faithful, the number of informers, the peculiar hatred which the princes of this world showed towards the religion of Jesus, a hatred that Justin could only explain to himself by the hatred of evil spirits, all that seemed to him to be a glorious sign of divine truth in favour of the Church. This idea inspired him to take a bold step, to do which he must have been encouraged by the earlier example of Quadratus and Aristides. This was to address himself to the Emperor Antoninus and his two associates, Marcus Aurelius and Lucius Verus, in order to obtain redress for a position which he rightly looked upon as unjust and in contradiction to the liberal principles of the government. The Emperor's great wisdom, the philosophical tastes of one at least of his associates, Marcus Aurelius, who was then twenty-nine years old, inspired him with the hope that such a great injustice would be made good. Such was the occasion of that eloquent petition which begins thus:--

To the Emperor Titus Ælius Hadrianus Antoninus Pius Augustus Cæsar; and to his son Verissimus, a philosopher; and to Lucius, a philosopher, son of Cæsar according to nature, and of Pius by adoption, the friend of knowledge; and to the sacred senate; and to the whole Roman people, for a group of men of every race who are hated and persecuted unjustly, I, one of them, Justin, son of Prixus, grandson of Bacchius, citizens of Flavia Neapolis of Syria, Palestine, I have made this pleading and this request.

The two titles of Pius and Philosophus obliged those who bear them only to love what is true, and to renounce ancient opinions if they find them bad. The Christians are victims of inveterate prejudice, of calumnies that have been circulated by a united league of all superstitions. They must be punished if they are found guilty of ordinary crimes, but no attention ought to be paid to malevolent rumours. A name in itself is no crime, it only becomes so by the acts that are attached to it. Now the Christians are punished on account of the name they bear, a name that only indicates upright ideas. He who declares that he is not a Christian when he is persecuted, is acquitted without inquiry; he who declares that he is one, is put to death. What is more unreasonable? The life of the confessor and of the renegade ought to be inquired into, to see what good or evil they have done.

The reason for this hatred of the Christians is quite simple: it comes from demons. Polytheism was nothing more than the reign of demons. Socrates was the first who wished to overthrow their worship; the demons succeeded in having him condemned as an atheist and an impious man. What Socrates did amongst the Greeks in the name of reason, Reason itself, clothed in a form become man and called Jesus Christ, did amongst the barbarians. This is why the Christians are called Atheists. They are, if by Atheism is understood the denial of the false gods in which men believe, but they are not so in a true sense, since their religion is the pure religion of the Creator, admitting, in the second rank, the worship of Jesus, the Son of God, and in the third rank the worship of the Prophetic Spirit. They do not expect an earthly kingdom, but a divine one. How is it that the authorities do not see that such a faith is a great aid to them in maintaining order in the world? What stronger barrier can there be against crime than the Christian doctrine?

Here Justin draws a picture of the morality inculcated by Christ according to the texts of Matthew, Mark, and Luke, and especially according to Matthew. He shows how harmless it is, and how useful to the State. There was no school of philosophy which had not taught one or other of the Christian dogmas, and yet those schools had not been persecuted on that account. The title of Son of God was not so unusual as it appears. A crucified God, born of a virgin, was not unheard of before. Greek mythologies, the thousand religions of the world, have said much stronger things. Was there not a personage called Simon, of the little town of Gitton in Samaria, known to have passed for God at Rome, in the reign of Claudius, on account of his miracles, which he performed by the power of demons? Was not a statue erected to him on the island of the Tiber, between the two bridges, with this Latin inscription: SIMONI DEO SANCTO? Nearly all the Samaritans and some other nations adore him as the chief God, and look upon a certain Helen, who was a prostitute in her time, and who followed him everywhere, as his chief Ennoia. Menander, one of his disciples, seduced many in an extraordinary manner at Antioch by demons' arts. Marcion, a native of Pontus, who is alive still, another agent of demons, teaches a large number of disciples to rob the Father of the title of Creator and to transfer it to another pretended God. All those people call themselves Christians, as persons who profess different doctrines are called philosophers. Do they practise the monstrous deeds with which Christians are reproached, overturned lamps, nocturnal embraces, promiscuous intercourse, feasts of human flesh? We do not know, is Justin's answer; in any case, they are not persecuted for the mere fact of their opinions.

The purity of Christian morals contrasts admirably with the general corruption of the century. The faithful who prohibit marriage live in perfect chastity. A striking example of this was seen at Alexandria. A young Christian, as he wished to give a decisive denial to the calumnies that were spread abroad about the alleged obscene mysteries of their nocturnal reunions, requested Felix, Prefect of Egypt, that a physician, whom he should nominate, might be allowed to castrate him. Felix refused; the young man persisted in his virginity, satisfied with the testimony of his own conscience and the esteem of his brethren. What a contrast to the good Antoninus!

The picture of the Christian reunions is chaste and beautiful. First the introduction of those who have just received baptism, that is to say, the "illuminated," to their place amongst the brethren takes place. Then long prayers are offered up for the whole human race.

When prayers are over we mutually kiss each other. Then the bread, a cup of water, and some wine, is brought to the president. He, taking them into his hands, gives praise and glory to the Father of all things, in the name of his Son and of the Holy Ghost; then he thanks God at some length for those gifts which he has bestowed on us. The people show their assent by saying Amen. Then those who are called deacons amongst or give the bread, the wine, and water over which the prayers have been pronounced, to all those who are present, and take them to those who are absent.

"This food we call the Eucharist. Only those who believe in the truth of our doctrines, and who have been washed in the laver of regeneration for the remission of sins, and who live according to Christ's precepts, are allowed to participate in it. For we do not take this food as ordinary bread and wine; but as Jesus Christ, our incarnate Saviour, assumed flesh and blood for our salvation by the word of God, no we are taught that the nourishment over which the prayer composed from the words of Jesus has been pronounced with thanksgiving,--we are taught, I say, that this nourishment, by which our blood and our flesh are nourished by assimilation, are the flesh and blood of Christ Incarnate. For the Apostles, in the memoirs which they have written, and which are called Gospels, tell us that Jesus bade them do this. Taking the bread, he gave thanks, and said: "Do this in remembrance of me; This is my body;" likewise taking the cup he gave thanks, and said: "This is my blood; " and he reserved that dogma for them alone. If the same thing takes place in the mysteries of Mithra, it is because evil demons, imitating Christ's institution, have taught how it is to be done; for you know, or can know, that the bread and the cup full of water, with certain words pronounced over it, form a part of the ceremonies of initiation.

During the days that follow the meetings, we continually remind each other of what has taken place, and those who are able supply the wants of the poor, and we habitually live together. In our oblations we bless the Creator of all things through his Son Jesus Christ and the Holy Spirit. And on the day which is called the Day of the Sun all those who live in towns or in the country assemble in the same place, and the memorials of the apostles and the writings of the prophets are read, as far as time allows. When the reader has finished, the president addresses words of exhortation and admonition to those who are present, to induce them to conform to such beautiful teaching. Then we all rise together, and send up our prayers to heaven, and, as we have already said, when the prayer is ended the bread and the wine and water is distributed, and he who presides prays and gives thanks with all his night, and the people show their assent by saying "Amen." Then the offerings over which thanksgivings have been pronounced are distributed; each one receives his share, and that of the absent is sent to them by the deacons. Those who are well off and who wish to give, give what they please, each one as he is disposed. The amount of the collection is handed over to the president; he succours the widows and orphans and those who are m distress through sickness or any other reason, those who are in prison, and strangers who may come; in short, he takes care of all those who are in want. We have this general meeting on the day of the Sun, in the first place, because it is the first day, the day on which God, having metamorphosed darkness and matter, made the world; in the second place, because our Saviour Jesus Christ rose from the dead on that day. They crucified him, in fact, on the day which precedes that of Saturn, and, the day that follows that of Saturn--that is to say, the day of the Sun--having appeared to his apostles and disciples, he taught them those things which we have just submitted to your judgment.

Justin finished his pleading by quoting a letter of Hadrian to Minicius Fundanus. Believer as he was, he was naturally astonished that men would not yield to such clear arguments, and his manner proves that he thought he should have converted the Cæsars. Certainly the frivolous Lucius Verus did not touch this solemn writing with the tip of his fingers. Perhaps Antoninus and Marcus Aurelius read it; but were they as culpable as Justin believed in not being converted? We cannot pretend to say. Justin had fair game with the immoral fables of Paganism; he demonstrated without difficulty that the Greek and Roman religions were scarcely aught but a tissue of shameful superstitions. But was the unbridled demonology which formed the foundation of all these systems much more reasonable? His confidence in the argument drawn from the prophecies is very artless. Antoninus and Marcus Aurelius did not know the Hebrew literature; if they had known it, they would certainly have found good Justin's exegesis very trifling. They would have observed, for example, that the 22d Psalm (21) only includes the nails of the Passion by taking the puerile interpretation, contrary to reason, of the Septuagint. The assertion that the Greeks have borrowed all their philosophy from the Jews would have been incredible to them. They would, at best, have found that passage strange, where the pious writer, wishing to prove that the cross is the key to everything, finds this mysterious form in the masts of ships, in the plough and mattock of the labourer, in the workman's tool, in the human body when the arms are stretched out, in the ensigns and trophies of the Romans, in the attitude of the dead emperors consecrated by apotheosis. The direction in which Herod and Ptolemy Philadelphus are thought to have been contemporaries would also, doubtless, have inspired in them some doubts as to the precision of the statement relating to the Septuagint version, the version which serves as the base for all the Messianic reasonings of Justin. If they had been asked to search in the archives of the Empire for the registers of Zuirinius, the acts of Pilate relating to Jesus, they would have had difficulty in finding them. Indeed, the writings of the Sibyl and Hystaspes would have seemed to them of weak authority. They would have been amazed to learn that demons, afraid of the annoyance which these books were going to cause them, had pronounced the penalty of death on these who would read them.

It appears that Justin joined to his pleading some illustrations from these apocryphal apologies, and imagined that they would exercise a decisive influence on the minds of the Cæsars. His hopes went beyond that; he demanded that his request should be communicated to the Senate and the Roman people, especially that the falsity of the divinity of Simon the magician should be acknowledged, and that the statue he had at Rome (a certain half column of Semo Sancus) should be officially cast down.

Justin's ardent convictions would allow him no rest. He imagined himself responsible for all the errors he did not combat. The Jews who persisted in not becoming Christians, were the perpetual object of his pre-occupations. He wrote against them in dialogue form, perhaps in imitation of Aristo of Pella, a polemical work which may be reckoned among the most curious literary monuments of budding Christianity.

Justin supposes that, in his journey from Syria to Rome, about the time of the war of Bar-Coziba, kept back by an accident in navigation at Ephesus, he walked into the alleys of the Xystus, when an unknown person, surrounded by a group of disciples, was struck by the dress he wore, and, approaching him, said, "Hail, philosopher!" He told him, at the same time, that a Socratic sage, whose lessons he had learned at Argos, had instructed him always to respect the philosopher's mantle, and to seek to have himself instructed by those who wore it. The conversation took a very literary turn, and he found that the unknown was no other than the Rabbi Tryphon or Tarphon, who had fled from Judea to escape the fury of Bar-Coziba's war, had taken refuge in Greece, and lived oftenest at Corinth. They spoke of God, of Providence, of the immortality of the soul. Justin records how, after having tried all the schools and systems, he has found nothing better than to adhere to Christ. The controversy then becomes lively. Justin accumulates against the Jews the most disdainful reproaches. Not content with having killed Jesus, they would not cease to persecute the Christians. If they did not kill them, it was because power prevented them; but they overwhelmed them with curses, chasing them from the synagogues, and, as often as they could, maltreating, assassinating, and punishing them. The prejudices which the Pagans had against Christianity were inspired by the Jews: they were more guilty of persecutions than even the Pagans who ordered them. They had sent from Jerusalem certain men chosen to spread abroad over the whole world the calumnies with which they sought to crush the Christians. They did worse than that; they mutilated the Bible by cutting out the passages which proved the Messiahship and divinity of Jesus. They repelled the LXX. translation, only because that contained the proofs of that very divinity. In controversies they threw out loud cries against the cavils, and the little details they did not comprehend, and refused to see the force of the whole.

Impartiality compels us to say that if Justin was in those oral disputes such as we see him to be in his book (and unfortunately what we know of his controversies with Cresceus leads us to believe so), the Jews had thoroughly good reason to complain of his inexactness. There never had been a weaker interpreter of the Old Testament. Not only did Justin not know Hebrew, but he had no critical talent; he admitted the most manifest interpretations. His Messianic applications of the texts of the Bible are of the most arbitrary description, and are founded on the errors of the Septuagint. His book certainly did not convert a single Jew, but in the bosom of Catholicism he founded the apologetic exegesis. Almost all the arguments of this order have been invented by St Justin, scarcely any have been added since his time.

It is useless to say that the gulf between Judaism and Christianity appears as absolute in this book. Judaism and Christianity are two enemies occupied in doing each other all the evil possible. The Law is abrogated--it has always been powerless to produce justification. Circumcision and the Sabbath not only are abolished things, they were never good things. Circumcision had been imposed by God on the Jews, in foresight of their crimes against Christ and the Christians. "This sign has been given you that you may be separated from other nations and ourselves, and that you should suffer alone that which you now justly suffer, that your country may be rendered desert, your towns delivered to the flames, that strangers may eat your fruits before your eyes, and that no one among you may be able to go up to Jerusalem." This pretended mark of honour is thus become for the Jews a punishment, a visible sign which marks them out for punishment. The law of the Mosaic precepts has only been instituted because of the iniquities and the hardness of the heart of the people. The Sabbath and the sacrifices have had no other cause. The impossibility which there was for a Jew holding to his old Scriptures, to admit that God had been born and become man, is not even comprehended by Justin. Tarphon would truly have been a most tractable man, if after such controversy he had left his adversary confessing, as Justin pretends, that he had profited much by the discussion.

Conversions, moreover, became more and more rare. Sides were taken. The moment when dispute is organised is usually that in which already each is hardened in his own view. Transfers have been numerous, so that Christianity had been a badly defined colony, scarcely separate from Judaism. When it is a complete place, guarded by its fortifications, in face of its metropolis, one can no longer pass from one side to another. The Jew, like the Mussulman, will be the most unconvertible of human beings, the most Anti-Christian.

Justin still lived for some years disputing always against the Jews, the heretics, and the Pagans, writing polemical works without end. An act of juridic severity on the part of Q. Lollius Urbicus, prefect of Rome, will place again the advocate's pen in his band in the last years of Antoninus' reign. Like nearly all the apologists, he was not a member of the hierarchy. This position without responsibility suits the volunteers of the faith better, and at a pinch allows the Church to disavow them. Justin was always dear to the Catholics. His distance from the sects preserved him from the aberrations which Tatian and Tertullian could not escape. His theology is far from being the orthodox theology of the following ages, but the sincerity of the author made that to be easily shown on his behalf. The Trinity, according to St Justin, was in a state of badly formed embryo; his angels and his demons were conceived in a prodigiously materialistic and infantine fashion; his millenarianism is naive as that of Papias; he systematically grieved St Paul. He believed that Jesus was born in a supernatural fashion, but he knew some Christians who did not admit it. His Gospel differed considerably from some texts held sacred to-day; he made no use of the Gospel called that of John; and the writing that he quotes although approaching most frequently Matthew, sometimes Luke, is not precisely any of the three synoptists. It was probably the Gospel of the Hebrews, called "the Gospel of the Twelve Apostles," or of Peter, not without analogy with the Gemma Marias, or Protevangel of James, and perhaps identical with the Gospel of the Ebionites. Fables, in any case, abounded in these: they were only a few steps from the puerilities which filled the apocryphal Gospels. But a certain correct sense made Justin avoid these extreme errors. His pagan erudition, all adulterated as it was, struck under-educated people. In fact, he was a splendid pleader. All the apologists who followed him were inspired by him.

His admiration for the Greek philosophy could not be to the taste of everyone, but it appeared to be good policy. The time had not yet arrived when insults were hurled against the sages of antiquity: people took the good where they found it; they saw in Socrates a forerunner of Jesus, and in Platonic idealism or sort of pre-Christianity. Justin was as much a disciple of Plato and Philo as he was of Moses and Christ; Moses was older than the Greek sages, and they had borrowed from him their dogmas of natural religion, hence its whole superiority. No theologian had ever opened so widely as Justin the portals of salvation. Revelation, according to him, is a permanent fact in humanity; it is the eternal fruit of the Logos spermaticos, who enlightens naturally the human understanding. All that philosophers and legislators--the Stoics, for instance--ever discovered of good, they owed to the contemplation of the Logos. The Logos is nothing else than reason universally diffused; all who, in whatever country or time they may be, have loved and cultivated reason, have been Christians. Socrates shines in the first rank in this phalanx of the Christians before Jesus. He knew Christ partly. He did not perceive the whole truth, but what he saw was a fraction of Christianity; the combated polytheism, as the Christians do, and be had the honour, like them, to give up his life in the conflict. The Logos descended and resided absolutely in Jesus. He is disseminated among the human souls who have loved the truth and practised good; in Jesus, the Logos is absolutely concentrated.

With such an idea of reason, it was natural to admit philosophy as an element in the composition of the Christian dogmas. The traces of Greek philosophy are still weak in St Paul and in the pseudo-Johannic writings. In the gnosis, on the contrary, according to Marcion, according to the author of the psuedo-Clementine romance, according to Justin, the Greek philosophy runs with full stream. It was found quite natural to mingle in the Jewish theory of the Logos ideas of the same kind as were believed to be met in Stoicism. Far from renouncing reason, they pretended to give it its share. They held sound philosophy to be the surest ally for Christianity; the great men of the past were considered as the anticipative disciples of Christ, who had come not to overthrow but to purify, complete, and accomplish their work. They admired Socrates and Plato; they were proud of the courage of their great contemporaries, such as Musonius. They said, with a just and large sentiment of truth: "What has been thought or felt before among the Greeks and barbarians, belongs to us."

A sort of eclecticism, founded on a mystical rationalism, was the character of this first Christian philosophy. The apologist applied himself to show that the fundamental points of Christianity had not been strange to Pagan antiquity,--that the dogmas on the divine essence, on the Logos, the divine spirit, special providence, prayer, angels, demons, the future life, and the end of the world, might be established by certain profane texts. Even the teaching, most specially Christian, on the birth, the life, death, and resurrection of Jesus Christ, had analogues in the religions of antiquity. It was maintained that Plato had expressed in the Timæus the doctrine of the Son of God. It was remarked that, in all religions, the ceremonies resembled each other--that the morale is the same throughout all. Far from finding in that an objection, they concluded from this universality the existence of a permanent revelation, of which Christianity had been the most brilliant act.

# CHAPTER XX

### *ABUSES AND PENITENCE--NEW PROPHECIES*

The Church was like the pious Israel at the time when it built its new temple; with the one hand they fought, with the other they built. The philosophic prepossessions were the act of a very small number. The great Christian work was moral and popular. The Church of Rome especially showed Itself more and more indifferent to these extravagant speculations which delighted minds full of the intellectual activity of the Greeks, but corrupted by the reveries of the East. The disciplinary organisation was the principal work at Rome; that extra-ordinary city applied to that its thoroughly practical genius and its strong energy.

Penitence had always been a fundamental institution of Christianity. The elect of the future city of God should be absolutely pure. To avoid sin was impossible; it was therefore necessary that means should be found for recovering lost grace. The Church accordingly at an early period erected itself into a tribunal, and transformed repentance into public penitence, imposed by authority and accepted by the delinquent. A mass of questions which were to trouble the Church for a century and a half date from that time. How could people, after having fallen often, become penitent again? Do those means of reconciliation apply to all time? The hypothesis of murder was scarcely thought of; the gentle and timid manners of the sect forbade the idea of a Christian assassin; but adultery in a little congregation of brethren and sisters was common enough. Apostacy, indeed, seeing the bitterness of the persecutions, was not rare. Some, to avoid punishment, went even so far as to curse Christ; some became the denouncers of their brethren; while others contented themselves with a simple denial, "I am not a Christian." They were ashamed of Christ without exactly blaspheming him.

It was this last category of persons who caused the greatest embarrassment. The Church was a source of such gentleness, that the day after their fall, the apostates, the denouncers of their brethren, experienced cruel remorse. They would have desired to re-enter the assembly they had betrayed. The situation of those unfortunates was distressing. Despairing of their salvation, they became the prey of frightful terrors. They could be seen prowling around the Church where they had tasted so many spiritual joys. There was no connection between them and the faithful. With a severity which Jesus would not have approved, but which the gravity of the circumstances excused, they were treated as people infected by the itch, and were called by a cruel pleasantry "the savages, the solitary ones." Many went to see the confessors in prison and found a sort of austere joy in the hard words which those addressed to them. The larger portion of the faithful considered them as totally dead to the Church, and would not admit that there could be any place of penitence for them there. Some, less harsh, distinguished between those who had blasphemed Christ or denounced their brethren and those who had simply denied their faith; these latter could be admitted to repentance. Others, more indulgent still, accorded penitence to those who had denied with the mouth and not with the heart. There was a danger of pushing rigour too far, for the Jews sought to gain to the synagogue those the Church had thus expelled.

Besides those great culprits, there were the weak, the uncertain, the worldly--Christians in some sense ashamed, and who dissembled as to their faith, and were thus led unceasingly into semi-apostacies. The Christian profession was something so strict that, if the Christian did not live in the society of his brethren, he was exposed to continual mockery. As he existed only with the end of the world before his mind, the Christian of that time was quite sequestered from public life. Those who were obliged to mix themselves in temporal affairs were led more and more to forsake the society of the saints, and soon to disdain them, to blush for them as brethren, to hear them laughed at without replying. Half-dead to the spiritual life, they fell into doubt. They became rich; they made a separate company, in virtue of the principle that man is led almost necessarily to cultivate the society of persons who have the same fortune as himself. They shunned meeting with the servants of God, fearing that they would ask for alms. The company of the faithful appeared humble; those quitted it in order to lead a more brilliant life with the Gentiles. These worldlings did not abandon God, but they deserted the Church; they kept the faith, but ceased to practise it. Some became repentant, and gave themselves up to works of charity; others, brought into the society of the Pagans, became like them, and abandoned themselves to pleasure.

This equivocal middle course did not dispose them to martyrdom. At the least sound of persecution they made an appearance of returning to idols, to escape being disturbed.

In the very bosom of the Church what imperfection! Such were constantly associated with the congregation, and did not cease to be slanderous, envious, blundering, bold, and presumptuous. The administration of the funds of the Church gave place to such abuses; certain deacons took the supplies of the widows and orphans for themselves. Then the teachers of strange doctrines abounded and seduced the faithful. Placed as judges in the midst of all these troubles, the saints inclined sometimes to indulgence and sometimes to severity. What was serious was that certain sectarian doctors flattered those who had sinned, in the view of personal interest. They sold them indulgence, after a fashion; and in the hope of being recompensed for their casuistry, they told them that they had no need of penitence, and that the pastors were people of an exaggerated severity.

The fact is that, in such an assembly of saints, there was scarcely room for lukewarmness. An enthusiastic piety made them believe everything. Prophecy and revelations flourished as in the palmiest days. There resulted serious abuses from this. The individual prophets became the plague of the Church. People went to interrogate them as to the future, even as to temporal affairs. These men received money, and gave the replies which were desired of them. The orthodox admitted that the devils sometimes revealed certain things to impostors, the better to try the righteous; but they maintained that they could always distinguish the prophets of God from frivolous prophets. Naturally this caused serious embarrassment, for he whom one called frivolous the other believed guided by "the angel of the prophetic spirit."

The orthodox scrupled no more than the heterodox to provide as food for the pious public the most audaciously fabricated revelations, and these revelations were greedily received. Such especially was a prophecy whose title alone marked sufficiently its tendency of spirit. It is related in the book of Numbers that Eldad and Modad, clothed with a portion of the prophetic power of Moses, prophesied out of the ranks and in their entirely individual capacity. Joshua wished them to be silenced. Moses stopped him. "Are you jealous for me?" he asked. "Would to God that all the people of Jehovah were prophets, and that Jehovah sent his spirit upon all!" Eldad and Modad were thus the representatives, among the ancient people, of the individual prophet. They were credited with a book which made much impression on many, and was quoted as inspired Scripture.

The symbolism of these new prophets appears sometimes strange and in bad taste. The exhaustion of their species was visible. All these used-up machines produce on us nothing but a result of fatigue and disgust. But for the simple the effect was great; such prophecies fortified the hesitating and warmed the cool. They believed they heard admonitions directly from God.

An apocalypse attributed to Peter was a very great success; it was admitted into the canon, beside that of John, and read in the greater number of the Churches. Like all apocalypses, it told the faithful of terrors and future calamities; like the Shepherd, of which we shall soon speak, it insisted on the punishment of different sins; like the apocalypse of Esdras, it treated, it would seem, of the state of souls after death. A particular idea of the author is that abortions are entrusted to a guardian angel, who charges himself with their education and development. They suffer the share of sufferings they would have endured if they had lived, and they are saved. The milk that women lose, and which coagulates, is changed into little animalculæ, which devour them at once. From the beginning, the bizarre aspects of the book provoked a strong opposition, and many wished it not to be read in public. This opposition only increased with time. The gloomy images which were to be found in it, however, made them keep it for the readings of the holy week. Then the antipathy of the Greek orthodox Church against apocalypses--an antipathy which was powerless against the apocalypse of John--succeeded in expelling this, and even in destroying it altogether.

The habit of public reading of the apostolical and prophetical readings in the Churches consumed, if one may so express it, many books: the circle of received writings was quickly run through, and the readers were thrown with earnestness on the new books which appeared, even when their titles to theopneusty were not very correct. There resulted from this a certain style of habit which went on for ten or twenty years. Sometimes, when the book was out of vogue, they limited its reading to one fixed day yearly.

This may be seen clearly in a curious little writing of that time, which has been preserved to us. It is a sort of homily, evidently for the use of the Roman Church, which the anagnost read after the large readings drawn from the sacred pages. This homily is itself a tissue of quotations taken from the Gospels, the ancient prophecies, and writings which it is now impossible to determine. The most compromising passages of the Gospel of the Egyptians are there quoted side by side with Matthew and Luke, and framed in a style of language destined to excite the piety of the "brethren and sisters." The writing was attached, as a Roman document, to the epistle of Clement, and, with it, was copied accordingly into a great number of Bibles.

# CHAPTER XXI

### ROMAN PIETISM--THE SHEPHERD OF HERMAS

One book had in this fashion a durable success, and served during several centuries for the nourishment of Christian piety. It had as its author a brother of Pius, the bishop of Rome. This personage, who doubtless occupied a considerable place in the Church, conceived the project of striking a great blow, sufficient to awaken the saints. He pretended that, fifty or sixty years before, in the time of the persecution of Domitian, a certain Hermas, an elder of the Church of Rome, had had a revelation. Clement, the guarantee for all the pious frauds of Roman Ebionism, covered the book with his authority, and was believed to have it addressed to the churches of the whole world.

Hermas, a foundling born in slavery, had been sold, by the proprietor of slaves who had brought him up, to a Roman lady named Rhoda. He had doubtless succeeded in buying his liberty, and setting himself up in life; for at the opening of the work, he is under the blow of annoyances which his wife, his children, and his affairs have caused him, as these last, in consequence of the disagreement of his family, proceed very badly. His sons had even committed the greatest crime of which a Christian could be culpable; they had blasphemed Christ to escape persecution, and had denounced their parents. In the midst of these sorrows, poor Hermas found out Rhoda, whom he had not seen for many years. The small consolation he had in her household rendered his heart sensitive, it would appear; he began to love his old mistress like a sister. One day, seeing her bathe in the Tiber, he presented his hand to her to help her out of the river, and said to her, "How happy should I be if I had a wife as beautiful and accomplished!" His thought did not go further, and such a reflection was all the more excusable that his wife was bitter, disagreeable, and full of defects. But the severity of Christian morals was so great that the quiet Platonic love of Hermas was remarked in heaven by the jealous watcher of pure souls; and he was to be convicted of it as of a crime.

Some time after--in fact, as he was going to his country house, situated at Cuma, ten stadia from the Campanian Way, and while he admired the beauty of God's works, he slept when travelling. In spirit he traversed rivers, ravines, mountain crevasses, and, returning to the plain, began to pray to the Lord and to confess his sin.

Now, while he prayed, the heaven was opened, and he saw the woman he had desired saying to him, "Good day, Hermas." Having looked at her, "Mistress, what are you doing here?" asked he. And she replied, "I have been brought here to accuse you of your sins before the Lord." "What! are you my accuser?" "No; but listen to the words I am speaking to you. God, who dwells in heaven, who has created all things that exist out of nothing, and has made them great for the holy Church, is angry with you, because you have sinned in regard to me." "I have sinned in regard to you!" replied Hermas; "and in what way? Have I ever said an improper word to you? Have I not always treated you as my mistress? Have I not always respected you as my sister? Why do you represent me falsely, oh, woman, for wicked and impure acts?" And then, smiling, she said to him, "For a righteous man like you desire alone is a great sin; but pray to God and he will pardon your sins and those of all your household and those of all the saints." After she had said these words, the heavens were closed, and Hermas was afraid. "If this is to be looked on as sin, how is it possible to be saved?"

As he was plunged in these reflections, he saw before him a great armchair covered with white cloth. An aged female, richly dressed, having a book in her hand, came and sat down in it. Having saluted Hermas by name, "Why are you sad, Hermas--you who are usually so patient, equable, and always smiling?" "I am," said Hermas, "under the stroke of reproaches from a very virtuous woman, who has told me that I have sinned regarding her." "Ah, fie!" said she to me, "that this evil should be on the part of one of God's servants--a man respectable and well tried, the chaste, simple, and innocent Hermas! Perhaps, indeed, there has some sentiment taken possession of your heart on the subject. But that is not the reason God is angry with you." The good Hermas breathed hard while the old woman informed him that the true cause of God's anger was his weakness as the father of a family. He did not restrain his wife and children with sufficient severity; this was the cause of the ruin of his temporal affairs. The old woman then read out of her book some terrible words which Hernias did not remember, and finished by some good words which he recollected.

The following year, at the same period, as he went to his country house at Cuma, Hermas saw the same old woman walking and reading a little book. She explained to him the object of the book, which was to exhort all men to repentance, for the times of persecution were drawing very near. A handsome young man appeared. "Who, do you think, is that old woman from whom you have received the book?" "The sibyl perhaps," answered Hermas, his mind pre-occupied by the neighbourhood of Cuma. "No; she is the Church." "Why then is she old?" "Because she has been first created, and the world has been made for her." The old woman enjoined Hermas to send two copies of the book--the one to Clement, the other to the Deaconess Grapte. "Clement," said she, "will address the book to the cities without, for there is in that his special work. Grapte will send it to the widows and orphans, and you will read it in the city for the elders who preside over the Church. This little book is naturally the work of the pretended Hermas. The heavenly origin of it is thus attested."

The third vision is more mysterious. The old woman appeared again to Hermas, after some fasts and prayers. They arranged to meet in the country. Hermas arrived first; to his great astonishment he found himself in front of an ivory bench; on the bench was placed a linen pillow, covered with very fine gauze. He began to pray and confess his sins. The old woman arrived with six young people. She made Hermas sit at her left (the right being reserved for those who have suffered for God the lash, the prison, tortures, the cross, the wild beasts). Hermas then saw the six young men build a square tower, emerging from the bosom of the water. Some thousands of men served them, and brought the stones to them. Among the stones, those drawn from the channel of the water were hewn. Those were the most perfect; they joined so well that the tower appeared a monolith. Among the others, the young men made a selection. Around the tower was a pile of rubbishy materials, either because they had defects, or because they were not cut as they should have been.

"The tower," said the old woman, "is the Church--that is, I, who have appeared to you, and who shall appear to you again. . . The six young men are the angels created first, to whom the Lord has entrusted the care of developing and governing his creation; those who carry the stones are the inferior angels. The beautiful white stones, which are dressed no finely, are the apostles, bishops, doctors, deacons, living or dead, who have been chaste, and who have lived on a good understanding with the faithful. The stones which are drawn from the channel of the water, represent those who have suffered death for the name of the Lord. Those which have been rejected, and remain near the tower, represent those who have sinned, and who wish to repent. If they did this while the building was going on they might be employed in it; but once the building is completed, they are of no more use. The stones which are broken and rejected are the wicked there is no more place for them. Those which are thrown to a distance from the tower, which roll into the road, and from thence into the wilderness, are the unsteady, who, after they have believed, have quitted the true path. Those which fall near the water and cannot enter it, are the souls who desire baptism, but recoil before the holiness of religion and the necessity of renouncing their lusts. As to the beautiful white but round stones, and which cannot in consequence be used in a square building, these are the rich who have embraced the faith. When persecution comes, their riches and business make them renounce the Lord. They will be useless to the building except when their riches are curtailed, just as to make a round stone enter into a square construction, it would be necessary to cut off a large portion. Judge this by yourself, Hermas; when you were rich you were useless, now that you are ruined, you are useful and fit to live."

Hermas asks his informant as to the proximity more or less of the consummation of the times. "Fool," replies the old woman, "do you not see that the tower is yet being built? When it shall be finished, the end will be; now it advances towards completion. Ask no more!"

The fourth vision is again on the Campanian Way. The Church, which has appeared up till now throwing aside all the signs of old age, and with all the marks of rejuvenation, now appears in the style of a girl wonderfully arrayed. A frightful monster (perhaps Nero) would have devoured her, but for the help of the angel Thegri, who presides over the fierce beasts. This monster is the herald of a fearful persecution which is at hand. Some tortures shall be passed through which nothing but purity of heart can enable one to escape. The world shall perish in fire and blood.

There is here only the mise en scene, in some sense preliminary. The essential part of the book commences with the appearance of a venerable personage in shepherd dress, clothed with a white beast's skin, with a scrip hung on his shoulders, and a crook in his hand. It is the guardian angel of Hermas, clothed as the angel of penitence, who is sent by the venerable angel to be his companion all the rest of his life. This shepherd, who now takes speech till the end of the book, recites a little treatise on Christian morals, embellished with symbols and apologues. Chastity is the favourite virtue of the author. To think of another woman than one's own wife is a crime. A man ought to take back his wife after her first act of adultery, expiated by repentance, but not after her second. Second marriages are permissible, but it is better not to involve oneself in them. The good conscience of Hermas shows in his taste for gaiety. Gaiety is a virtue, sadness distresses the Holy Spirit, and chases him from a soul, for the spirit is given joyfully to man. The continually sad prayer of a man does not go up to God. Sadness is like the drop of vinegar, which spoils the good wine. God is good, and the commandments impossible without him are easy with him. The devil is powerful, but he has no power over the true believer.

An affecting asceticism filled up the entire life of the Christian. The cares of business hindered from the service of God: it was necessary to withdraw from these. Fasting is recommended: now fasting consists in withdrawing every morning to one's retreat; in purifying one's thoughts from the remembrances of the world; in not eating all day anything but bread and water; in saving what you might have spent, and giving it to the widows and orphans, who will pray for you. Repentance is necessary even to the righteous for their venial sins. Certain severe angels are charged with over-looking them, and with punishing not only their sins but even those of their family. All the misfortunes of life were held to be chastisements inflicted by these angels on "penitenital pastors." The penitent should afflict himself voluntarily, should humble himself, seek adversities and sorrows, or at least accept those which come upon him, as expiations. It would seem, according to this view, that penitence imposes on God--forces his hand. No, penitence is a gift of God. To those whom God foresees to be going to sin still, he does not accord the favour.

In the weighty questions relating to public penitence, Hermas avoids exaggerated severity; he has comparisons which shall irritate Tertullian, and give him, on the part of that fanatic, the name of "the friend of adulterers." He explains the delay in the appearing of Christ by a decree of the mercy of God which allows sinners the chance of a last and definitive appeal. He who has blasphemed Christ to escape punishment, those who have denounced their brethren, are dead for ever: they resemble dry branches into which the sap can no longer ascend; but yet is their lot irrevocable? In certain cases, mercy is brought into the author's mind; for the sons of Hermas, who were blasphemers of Christ and traitors to the Church, were admitted to pardon, for their father's sake. Those who have simply denied Jesus can repent. "As to him who has denied from the heart," says Hermas, "I do not know if he can live." It is necessary also to distinguish the past from the future. To those who henceforth would deny Christ, there is no pardon; but those who had this misfortune before may be admitted to penitence. Sinners who have not blasphemed God nor betrayed his servants may return to penitence; but they hasten onwards; death threatens; the tower is about to be finished, and then the stones which have not been employed would be irrevocably rejected. For great crimes, there is but one repentance; for the lesser faults, it is allowable to repent more than once; but he who is constantly falling is a suspected penitent, and penitence will serve him in no wise.

A perfume of chastity, somewhat unhealthy, is breathed from the vision of the mountain of Arcadia, and the twelve virgins. The fêtes which are given in the dream, one would say, were the imagination of a poor faster. Twelve beautiful girls, fine and strong as caryatides, stand at the gate of the future temple, and pass the stones for the construction with their open arms.

"Thy shepherd will not come to-night," they said "if he does not come thou wilt remain with us." "No," said I to them; "if he does not come, I shall return home, and to-morrow I will come back." "Thou shouldst confide in us," they replied; "thou canst not leave as!" "Where would you have me remain?" "Thou shalt sleep with us like a brother, and not as a man," they answered; "for thou art our brother henceforth; we shall remain with you, for we love you very much" I blushed to remain in their company, but, lo! she who seemed to be their leader, began to embrace me; seeing which, the others imitated, causing me to make the tour of the building, and to play with me. And, as I was young, I began also to play with them. Some executed choruses, some danced, and others sang. As for me, I walked silently with them round the building, and was joyful with them. As it was late, I wished to return to the house, but they would not allow me, and I remained with them over night, sleeping by the side of the tower. The virgins had stretched out their linen tunics on the ground, and did nothing but pray. I prayed also with them incessantly, and the virgins rejoiced to see me pray thus: and I remained there till next morning at the second hour with the virgins. Then the shepherd arrived, and he addressed himself to them, "You have not done him any harm?" asked he, looking at them. "My lord," I said to him, "I have only had the pleasure of abiding with them." "Of what have you eaten? said he. "My lord," said I to him; "I have lived all the night on the words of the Lord." "Did they receive you well?" asked he. "Yes, my lord," said I to him.

Those virgins are the "holy spirits," the gifts of the Holy Ghost, the spiritual powers of the Son of God, and also the fundamental virtues of the Christian. A man cannot be saved except through these. The guardian angel of Hermas giving good testimony to the purity of his house--the twelve virgins who wish to have extreme propriety around them, and are repelled by the slightest defilement, consent to dwell there. Hermas promises that they shall always have with him a residence suited to their tastes.

The author of Hermas is a pure Ebionite. The only good use of a fortune is to redeem slaves--captives. The Christian, as to himself, is essentially a poor man; to practise hospitality towards the power, the servants of God, that washes out even great crimes. "One does not imagine," says he, "what torment is in the punishment; it is worse than prison; so that we even see people committing suicide to escape it. When such a misfortune occurs, he who, knowing the unfortunate one, does not save him, is guilty of his death." The antipathy of Hermas to people of the world is extreme. He is not pleased except when in a circle of simple people, not knowing what wickedness is, without differences among themselves, and looking on one another's affairs, and mingling with each other; rejoicing in each other's virtues, always ready to share with him who has nothing the result of their labours. God, seeing the simplicity of the holy child-likeness of these good workers, is pleased with their little charities. Childlikeness is that which, to Hermas as to Jesus, takes the first place in God's sight.

The Christianity of the author of Hermas suggests Gnosticism. He never names Jesus in any other way than as Christ. He always calls him the Son of God, and makes him a being before the creatures, a counsellor of the plans on which God made his creation. At the same time as this Divine assessor has created all things, he maintains all things. His name is beyond comparison with every other name. Sometimes, in the style of the Elkasaites, Hermas would conceive Christ as a giant. Oftener still he identifies him with the Holy Spirit, the source of all the gifts. Like the Gnostics, Hermas plays with abstractions. At other times, the Son of God is the law preached throughout all the earth. The dead will receive the seal of the Son of God, baptism, when the apostles and the Christian preachers, after their death, descend into hell and baptise the dead.

A parable explains this singular Christology, and gives it much analogy with that which, later on, constituted Arianism. A master (God) plants in a certain corner of his property (the world) a vine (the circle of the Elect). Leaving for a journey, he has entrusted it to a servant (Jesus), who attends to it with wonderful care, roots out the weeds (blots out the sin of believers), and endures extreme pain (an allusion to the sufferings of Jesus). The master filled with joy at his return (on the day of judgment), calls his only Son and his friends (the Holy Spirit and the angels) and communicates to them the idea he has of associating this servant as an adopted son in the privileges of the only Son (the Holy Spirit). All consent to this by acclamation. Jesus is introduced by the resurrection into the divine circle; God sends him a part of the feast, and he, remembering his old fellow-servants, shares with them his heavenly gifts (the charisma). The divine rôle of Jesus is thus conceived as a sort of adoption and co-optation which places him beside a former Son of God. Moreover, Hermas sets forth a theology analogous to that which we have found among the Ebionites. The Holy Spirit pre-existed before all, and has created all. God chose him a body in which he could dwell in all purity, and realises for him a completed humanity: it is the life of Jesus. God takes counsel of his Son and of his angels, so that this flesh which has served the Spirit without reproach should have a place of rest, that this body without stain, in which the Holy Spirit dwells, would appear not to remain without reward.

All the chimeras of the times came into collision with each other, we can see, without succeeding in coming into agreement in the head of poor Hermas. Some grotesque theories, such as the descent of the apostles into hell, are peculiar to him. He was an Ebionite in his fashion of comprehending the kingdom of God and the position of Jesus. He was a Gnostic in his tendency to multiply beings and to give angels even to one who has never existed. A guardian angel is not enough for him; each man has two angels--the one to care for his well-being, the other to seek his hurt. Indeed, in many points of view, he is a Montanist in advance. He has no trace of episcopacy about him. The elders of the Church are, in his eyes, all equal; he appears to have been of the number of those who made opposition to the growing institution which reversed the equality of the presbyteri. Hermas is an experienced pneumatist; he is an anchorite, an abstainer. He shows himself severe on the clergy. He complains of the general laxity. The name of Christian, according to him, is not enough to save one; a man is saved above all by the spiritual gifts. The Church is a body of saints, and it must be disembarrassed of all impure alliance. Martyrdom completes the Christian. Prophecy is a personal gift, free, and not subjected to the Church; those who receive it, communicate its revelation to the leaders; but they do not require their permission. Eldad and Modad were two prophets without mission, and beyond the authority of superiors. The great objection which the orthodox have to the Shepherd, as to the Montanist revelations, is that it comes too late,--"that the number of the prophets is complete already."

The intention of the pseudo-Hermas has been, in fact, simply and well to introduce a new book into the body of the sacred writings. Perhaps his brother Pius lent himself as his support in this. The attempt of the pseudo-Hermas was very nearly the last of this kind; it did not succeed, for the author was known; the origin of the book was too clear. The writing pleased by what was edifying in it; the better minds advised that it should be specially read, but not permitted to be read in the Church, nor as an apostolic writing (it was too modern), nor as a prophetic writing (the number of these scriptures was closed). Rome especially never admitted it; the East was more easy, Alexandria especially. Many Churches held it to be canonical, and did it the honour of having it read from the pulpit. Some eminent men--Irenæus, Clement of Alexandria--gave it a place in their Bible, after the apostolic writings. The more reserved conceded to it an angelic revelation and an ecclesiastical authority of the first order. There had always been some doubts and protestations; some even went as far as scorn. At the beginning of the fourth century, the Shepherd was no longer looked on but as a book for edification, very useful for elementary instruction. Piety and art made considerable borrowings from it. The Roman council of 494, under Gelasus, placed it among the Apocrypha, but did not take it out of the hands of the believers, who found in it a help for their piety.

The work has in some parts a charm; but a certain want of taste and talent are to be felt in it. The symbolism so energetic and so just in the old apocalypses, is here feeble, ill-adjusted, and without precise adaptation. The vein of Christian prophecy is altogether weakened. The language, simple, and in some sense flat, is nearly that of modern Greek as to the syntax; the choice of expression, on the contrary, is happy enough. It is the eloquence of a country curé, simple and grumbling, mingled with the cares of a sacristan concerned as to gauzes, cushions, and everything which serves to ornament his church. Hermas, in spite of his temptations and his pecadilloes, is certainly chastity itself, although the way he insists on this point makes us smile a little. To the terrible images of the old apocalypses, to the gloomy visions of John, and the pseudo-Esdras, succeed the gentle imaginations of a little pious romance, at once affecting and simple, and whose childish style is not free from insipidity.

The prophetic attempt of pseudo-Hermas was not, moreover, an isolated fact; it belonged to the general state of the Christian conscience. In fifteen years the same causes will produce facts of the same order in the most remote districts of Asia Minor, against which the episcopacy will employ much greater severity.

# CHAPTER XXII

## ORTHODOX ASIA--POLYCARPUS

Although Asia was already disturbed by the sectarian spirit, it nevertheless continued to be, next to Rome, the province in which Christianity flourished the most. It was the most pious country in the world; the country in which credulity offered to the inventors of new religions the most fertile field. To become a god was a very easy matter; incarnations, the terrestrial alternations of the immortals, were looked upon as ordinary events: every kind of imposture succeeded. People were still full of the recollection of Apollonius of Tyana--the legend regarding him increased day by day. An author, who took the name of Moeragenes, wrote the most marvellous stories about him; then a certain Maximus of Æges composed a book exclusively devoted to the extraordinary things which Apollonius had done at ages in Cilicia. In spite of the railleries of Lucian, "the tragedy," as he calls it, succeeded astonishingly. Later, about the year 200, Philostratus wrote at the request of the Syrian lady, Julia Domna, that insipid romance which passed for an exquisite hook, and which, according to a very serious Pagan writer, should have been entitled, "Sojourn of a God among Men." Its success was immense. Because of it, Apollonius came to be considered as the first of sages, a veritable friend of the gods, as a god himself. His image was to be seen in the sanctuaries; temples were even dedicated to him. His miracles, his beautiful speeches, afforded edification for all classes. He was a sort of Christ of Paganism; and undoubtedly the intention of opposing an ideal of beneficent holiness to that of the Christians was not foreign to his apotheosis. In the last days of the struggle between Christianity and Paganism he was compared only to Jesus, and his life, as revealed in his letters, was preferred to the Gospels, the work of grosser minds. A Paphlagonian charlatan, Alexander of Abonoticus, attained through his assurance a success no less prodigious. He was a very handsome man. He had a superb presence, a most melodious voice, hair of enormous length, which it was pretended he had inherited from Perseus, and passed as one who predicted the future with the frantic enthusiasm of the ancient soothsayers. He enclosed a small serpent in a goose's egg, broke the egg before the multitude, and made believe that it was an incarnation of Esculapius, who had chosen for his abode the city of Abonoticus. The god attained maturity in a few days. The people of Abonoticus were astonished soon to see on a canopy an enormous serpent with a human head, splendidly clothed, opening and closing its mouth and brandishing its sting. It was Alexander himself who was thus decked out, he having coiled round his chest and about his neck a tame serpent, whose tail hung down in front. He had made himself a head of linen, which he had besmeared artistically enough; and by means of horse hair he made the jaws and the sting move. The new god was called Glycon, and people came from every part of the empire to consult it. Abonoticus became the centre of unbridled thaumaturgy. The result was an abundant manufacture of painted images, talismans, idols of silver and of bronze, which had an extraordinary popularity. Alexander was powerful enough to raise in his district a genuine persecution against the Christians and the Epicureans who refused to believe in him. He established a cult which, in spite of its wholly charlatanistic and even obscene character, had much vogue, and attracted a multitude of religious people. But the most singular thing of all was that Romans of high standing, such as Severian, legate of Cappadocia, and Rutilianus, a man of consular dignity, one of the first men of his time, were his dupes, and that the impostor succeeded in having the name of Abonoticus changed to Ionopolis. He required also that the coinage of that city should bear henceforth on the one side the effigy of Glycon, on the other his own, with the arms of Perseus and of Esculapius. Actually the coins of Abonoticus, at the time of Antonine and Marcus Aurelius, bore the figure of a serpent with the head of a man with long hair and beard, and on the obverse the word ΓΛΥΚΟΝ. The coins of the same city, with the medal of Lucius Verus, bore the serpent and the name ΙΩΝΟΠΟΛΕΙΤΩΝ. Under Marcus Aurelius we shall see this ridiculous religion assume an incredible importance. It lasted until the second half of the third century.

Nerullinus, at Troas, succeeded in a fraudulent enterprise of the same kind. His statue uttered oracles, cured maladies; sacrifices were offered to it, and it was crowned with flowers. It was especially the absurd ideas about medicine, the belief in medical dreams, in the oracles of Esculapius, etc., which kept the minds of people in that state of superstition. We are dumfounded at seeing Galian himself addicted to similar follies. More incredible still is the career of that Ælius Aristides, religious sophist, devout Pagan, a sort of bishop or saint, pressing pious materialism and credulity to its utmost limits; yet this did not prevent him from being one of the most admired and most honoured men of his age. The Epicureans alone repudiated these follies unreservedly. There were still some men of intellect, such as Celsus, Lucian, Demonax, who could laugh at it. Soon, however, there shall be no more such, and credulity will reign mistress over a debased world. The name of Atheist was dangerous, for it put him to whom it was attributed without the pale of the law, and exposed him even to the scaffold; yet one was an Atheist because he denied the local superstitions and stood up against charlatans. We can conceive how such devices must have been favourable to the propagation of Christianity. We do not perhaps exaggerate much when we admit that nearly the half of the population had avowed Christianity. In certain cities, such as Hierapolis, Christianity was publicly professed. Some inscriptions, still decipherable, attest beneficent foundations which were to be distributed at Easter and at Pentecost. Co-operative associations of workmen, societies for mutual succour, were there skilfully organised. These manufacturing cities, which contained for a long time colonies of Jews, who perhaps had carried with them thence the industries of the East, were ready to receive every social idea of the age. Works of charity were wonderfully developed. Nursing institutions and establishments for foundlings were there. The labourer, so depised in ancient times, attained, through association, to dignity of existence and to happiness. That interior life, all the more active because it was not disturbed by politics, made of Asia Minor a field closed to all the religious strifes of the times. The directions in which the Church was divided there were singularly visible; for nowhere else was the Church in such a state of fermentation, or showed its internal labour more distinctly. Conservatives and Progressists, Judeo-Christians and enemies of Judaism, Millenarians and Spiritualists, were there opposed as two armies, who, after having fought, finished by breaking their ranks and fraternising together. There had lived, or was still living, a whole Christian world which did not know St Paul. Papias, the most narrow-minded of the Fathers of his times; Melito, almost as materialistic as he; the ultra-conservative Polycarpus; the presbyteri who taught Irenæus his unpolished Millenarianism; the chiefs of the Montanist movement, who pretended to have witnessed again the scenes of the first supper at Jerusalem. There too were to be found, or had come thence, the men who had most boldly launched themselves into innovations--the author of the fourth Gospel, Cerdo, Marcion, Praxeas, Noetus, Apollinarius of Hierapolis, the Aloges, who, full of aversion for the Apocalypse, Millenarianism, Montanism, gave the hand to Gnosticism and to philosophy. Spiritual exercises which had disappeared elsewhere, continued to flourish in Asia. They had prophets there--a certain Quadratus, and one Amnia of Philadelphia.

People gloried especially over the considerable number of martyrs and confessors. Asia Minor witnessed numerous executions, in particular crucifixions. The different Churches made a boast of this, alleging that persecution was the privilege of truth; a matter that is debateable, seeing that all those sects had martyrs; at times, the Marcionites and Montanists had more than the orthodox. No calumny then was spared by the latter in order to depreciate the martyrs of their rivals. These enmities endured to the death. We see the confessors, while expiring for the same Christ, turning their backs on one another, in order to avoid all that might resemble a mark of communion. Two martyrs, born at Eumenia, namely, Caine and Alexander, who were executed at Apamea Kibotos, went the length of taking the most minute precautions in order that it might not be thought that they adhered to the inspirations of Montanus and of his wives. Such conduct shocks us, but we must not forget that, according to the opinions of the times, the last words and the last acts of martyrs possessed a high importance. Martyrs were consulted on questions of orthodoxy; from the depths of their dungeons they reconciled dissentients, and gave certificates of absolution. They were regarded as being charged by the Church with the rôle of pacificators, and with a sort of doctrinal mission.

Far from being hurtful to propagandism, these divisions were serviceable to it. The churches were rich and numerous. Nowhere else did the episcopate contain so many capable, moderate, and courageous men. We may cite Thraseas, Bishop of Eumenia; Sagaris, Bishop of Laodicea; Papirius, whose birthplace is not known; Apollinaris of Hierapolis, who was destined to play a considerable part in the capital controversies which were soon to divide the Churches of Asia; Polycrates, the future Bishop of Ephesus, the descendant of a family seven members of which before him had been bishops. Sardis possessed a real treasure, the learned Bishop Melito, who already had prepared himself for the vast labours which, later on, rendered his name celebrated. Like Origen, at a subsequent date, he was anxious that his chastity should be distinctly attested. His erudition resembled much that of Justin and of Tatian. His theology had also a little of the materialistic dulness which was a characteristic of these two doctors; for he thought that God had a body. He appears to have been reproached by Papias for his apocalyptic ideas. Miltiades, on his part, was a laborious author, a zealous polemic, who struggled against the heathen, the Jews, the Montanists, the ecstatic prophets, and made an apology for Christian philosophy, which he addressed to the Roman authorities.

The aged Polycarpus, in particular, enjoyed high authority at Smyrna. He was more than an octogenarian, and it would seem that he was believed to have inherited his longevity from the Apostle John. He was accredited with the gift of prophecy: it was alleged that each word that he uttered would come to pass. He himself lived in the belief that the world was full of visions and of presages. Night and day he prayed, including in his prayers the wants of the entire world. As everybody admitted that he had lived several years with the Apostle John, people believed that they still possessed in him the last witness of the apostolic age. People surrounded him; everybody sought to please him; a mark of his esteem was regarded as a high favour. His person was charming in the extreme. The docile Christians adored him; a band of disciples and of admirers pressed around him, eager to render him every service. But he was not popular in the city. His intolerance, the pride of orthodoxy, which he did not pretend to dissimulate, and which he communicated to his disciples, wounded deeply both the Jews and the heathen; the latter knew but too well that the disdainful old man looked upon them as wretches.

Polycarpus had all the peculiarities of an old man; he had a certain manner of acting and speaking which made a vivid impression on young auditors. His conversation was fluent, and when he went to sit down on the place which he affected--doubtless one of the terraces of the slopes of Mount Pagus, whence one could see the sparkling gulf, and its beautiful surrounding of mountains, it was known beforehand what he was going to say. "John and others who have seen the Lord;" this was the way in which he always commenced. He would tell about the intimacy he had had with them, what he had heard them say about Jesus, and about his preaching. An echo of Galilee was thus made to resound, at a distance of a hundred and twenty years, upon the shores of another sea. He repeated constantly that those men had been ocular witnesses, and that he had seen them. He made no more difficulty than did the Evangelists in regard to borrowing from the presbyteri the maxims best adapted to the second century, at the epoch in which they were reputed to have lived. To so many other obscure traditions in regard to the origins of Christianity, a new source, more troublesome than the others, was now about to be added.

The impression which Polycarpus produced was not less profound. A long time after, his disciples would remind one another of the bench on which he sat, his gait, his habits, his bodily peculiarities, his manner of speaking. Every one of his words were graven on their hearts. Now in the circle which surrounded him there was a young Greek, of about fifteen years of age, who was destined to play one of the leading parts in ecclesiastical history. His name was Irenæus, who afterwards transmitted to us the image--doubtless often false, yet, at the same time, in many respects very vivid--of the last days of the apostolic world, whose setting sun he had, in a sort of way, been a witness of. Irenæus was born a Christian, which did not prevent him from frequenting the schools of Asia, where he acquired an extensive knowledge of the poets, and of the profane philosophers, especially of Homer and of Plato. He had for a young friend and co-disciple, if one may so express oneself, near the old man, a certain Florinus, who held a somewhat important posit on at court, and who, subsequently, embraced at Rome the Gnostic ideas of Valentinus.

Polycarpus, in the eyes of every one, was regarded as the perfect type of orthodoxy. His doctrine was the materialistic Millenarianism of the old apostolic school. Far from having broken with Judaism, he conformed to the practices of the moderate Judeo-Christians. He resented the foolish embellishments which the Gnostics had introduced into the Christian teaching, and appears to have ignored the Gospel which in his time already circulated under the name of John. He held to the simple and unctuous manner of the apostolic catechesis, and would not have anything at all added to it. Everything that had the resemblance of a new idea put him beside himself. His hatred of heretics was intense, and some of the anecdotes which he delighted to tell about John were destined to make the violent intolerance which, in his opinion, formed the basis of the apostle's character, appear in a strong light. When any one dared to give vent in his presence to some doctrine analogous to that of the Gnostics, some theory calculated to introduce a little of rationalism into the Christian theology, he would get up, stop his ears, and take to flight, exclaiming, "Oh, good God, to what times hast thou reserved me, that I should have to put up with such language!" Irenæus was permeated to a large extent with the same spirit, but the sweetness of his character served to correct it in practice. The idea of holding fast to the apostolic teaching became the basis of orthodoxy, in opposition to the presumption of the Gnostics and Montanists, who pretended to have re-discovered the actual doctrine of Jesus, which, in their opinion, had been corrupted by his immediate disciples.

Following the example of Paul, Ignatius, and other celebrated pastors, Polycarpus wrote many letters to the neighbouring Churches and to individuals, in order to instruct and exhort them. Only one of these letters has been preserved to us. It is addressed to the faithful at Philippi, as touching some confessors who were destined to martyrdom, who chanced to be with them on their way from Asia to Rome. Like all the apostolic or pseudo-apostolic writings, it is a short treatise addressed to each of the classes of the faithful which composed the Church. Some serious doubts might be raised against the authenticity of this epistle if it were not certain that Irenæus had known it, and held it to be a work of Polycarpus. Without this authority, we should rank this short treatise with the epistles of St Ignatius, in that class of writings of the end of the second century by which it was sought to cover, by the most revered names, the anti-Agnostic doctrines, and those which were favourable to the episcopate. The document, which is somewhat commonplace, possesses nothing that is specially befitting the character of Polycarpus. The imitation of the apostolic writings, particularly the false Epistles to Titus and Timothy, the first of Peter, and the Epistles of John, makes itself fully felt in it. The author makes no distinction between the authentic writings of the apostles and those which have been attributed to them. He evidently knew the Epistle of St Clement by heart. The way in which lie reminds the Philippians that they have an epistle from Paul, is suspicious. What singular things all those hypotheses are! The Gospel attributed to John is not cited, whilst a phrase of the pseudo-Johannine epistle is brought in. Docility, submission to the bishop, enthusiasm for martyrdom, after the example of Ignatius, horror of heresies, which, like Docetism, overthrew the faith in the reality of Jesus; such were the dominant ideas of the author. If Polycarpus is not the author, we can at least say that if he had been resuscitated a few years after his death, and had seen the compositions which were read as his, he would not have protested, and would have even found that people had correctly enough interpreted his thoughts. Irenæus at Lyons may have been deceived in this matter like every one else. If it was an error, he recognised in this fragment the perfect character of the faith and the teaching of his master.

Polycarpus, in those years of extreme old age, was regarded as the President of the Church of Asia. Some grave questions, which at first had barely been stated, began to agitate these Churches. With his ideas of hierarchy and of ecclesiastical unity, Polycarpus naturally thought of turning towards the Bishop of Rome, to whom almost the whole world about that time acknowledged a certain authority in composing the divisions in Churches. The controversial points were numerous; it appears, moreover, that the two heads of the Churches--Polycarpus and Anicetus--had some petty grievances against one another. One of the questions in controversy was in regard to the celebration of Easter. In the early days, all the Christians continued to make Easter their principal feast. They celebrated that feast on the same day as the Jews, the 14th Nisan, no matter on what day of the week that day fell. Persuaded, according to the allegations of all the ancient Gospels, that Jesus, on the eve of his death, had eaten the Passover with his disciples, they regarded such a solemnity rather as a commemoration of the supper than as a memorial of the resurrection. When Christianity became separated more and more from Judaism, such a manner of viewing it was found to be much out of place. First, a new tradition was circulated, according to which Jesus before his death had not eaten the Passover; but died on the same day as the Jewish Passover, thus substituting himself for the Paschal Lamb. Besides this, that purely Jewish feast wounded the Christian conscience, especially in the Churches of St Paul. The great feast of the Christians was the resurrection of Jesus, which occurred, in any case, the Sunday after the Jewish Passover. According to this idea, the feast was celebrated on the Sunday which followed the Friday next after the 14th of Nisan.

At Rome this practice prevailed, at least from the pontificates of Xystus and Telesphoros (about 120). In Asia, people were much divided. Conservatives like Polycarpus, Melito, and all the old school, held to the ancient Jewish practice, in conformity with the first Gospels and with the usage of the Apostles John and Philip. It hence happened that people did not pray or fast on the same days. It was not till about twenty years after that this controversy attained in Asia the proportions of a schism. At the epoch in which we now are, it had only just had its birth, and was no doubt one of the least important among the questions about which Polycarpus felt himself obliged to go to Rome to have an interview with Pope Anicetus. Perhaps Irenæus and Florinus accompanied the old man on that journey, which being undertaken during the summer, according to the customs of navigation of the age, had nothing fatiguing about it. The interview between Polycarpus and Anicetus was very cordial. The discussion upon certain points appears to have been somewhat lively; but they understood one another. The question of Easter had not yet reached maturity. For a long time before this, the Church of Rome had acted upon the principle of exhibiting in this matter great tolerance. Conservatives of the Jewish order, when they came to Rome, practised their rites without anybody finding fault with them, or without causing any one to cease fraternising with them. The Bishops of Rome sent the Eucharist to some of the bishops who followed in this particular another rule. Polycarpus and Anicetus observed between them the same rule. Polycarpus could not persuade Anicetus to renounce a practice which the Bishops of Rome had followed before him. Anicetus, on his part, forebore when Polycarpus said to him that he held by the rule of John and the other apostles with whom he had lived upon a footing of familiarity. The two religious chiefs continued in full communion with one another, and Anicetus even bestowed on Polycarpus an honour almost unexampled. He was willing, in fact, that Polycarpus should, in the assembly of the faithful at Rome, pronounce instead of him, and in his presence, the words of the eucharistic consecration. These ardent men were full of too passionate a sentiment to rest the unity of souls upon the uniformity of rites and exterior observances. Later, Rome will display the greatest pertinacity to make her rites prevail To speak the truth, the point at issue, in this matter of Easter, was not merely a simple difference of calendar. The Roman rite, in choosing for its base the grand Christian festival the anniversaries of the death and the resurrection of Jesus, created the holy week--that is to say, a whole cycle of consecrated days, to the mysterious commemorations during which fasting was continued. In the Asiatic rite, on the contrary, the fast terminated on the evening of the 14th Nisan: Good Friday was no longer a day of sadness. If that usage had prevailed, the scheme of the Christian festivals would have been arrested in its development.

The orthodox bishops had still too many common enemies for them to pay attention to pitiful liturgic rivalries. The Gnostic and Marcionite sects inundated Rome, and threatened to put the orthodox Church in a minority. Polycarpus was the declared adversary of such ideas. Like Justin, with whom he was probably in accord, he inveighed fiercely against the sectaries. The rare privilege which he possessed of having seen the immediate disciples of Jesus, gave him an immense authority. He pleaded, as was his custom, the teaching of the apostles, of which he alleged he was the only living auditor, and maintained as a simple rule of faith the tradition which ascended by an unbroken chain to Jesus himself. Nor was he free from rudeness. One day he encountered in a public place a man who, for a thousand reasons, should have commanded his respect--Marcion himself. "Do you not recognise me? " said the latter to him. "Yes," responded the passionate old man; "I recognise the first-born of Satan." Irenæus cannot enough admire this response, which shows how very narrow the Christian mind had already become. Jesus had much more wisely remarked: "He who is not for you is against you." Is one always quite sure of not being oneself the first-born of Satan? How much more wise it is, instead of anathematising at first him who chooses a different path from oneself, to apply oneself to discover in what points one may be right, what method he employs in looking at things, and if there is not in his manner of observing some grain of truth that one ought to assimilate.

But that tone of assurance exercises a great efficacy upon semi-cultured men. Many Valentinians and Marcionites saw Polycarpus at Rome, and returned to the orthodox Church. Polycarpus hence left in the capital of the world a venerated name. Irenæus and Florinus in all probability remained at Rome after the departure of their master; these two minds, so different from one another, were destined to pursue paths the most opposite.

An immense result was accomplished. The rule of prescription was laid down. The true doctrine will henceforth be that which is generally professed by the apostolic Churches, which it has always been. Quod semper quod ubique. Between Polycarpus and Valentin the matter is quite clear. Polycarpus held to the apostolic tradition; Valentin, whatever he may say himself, has not got it. Individual Churches formed by their union the Catholic Church, the absolute depository of the truth. He who prefers his own ideas to those of this universal authority is a sectary, a heretic.

# CHAPTER XXIII

### MARTYRDOM OF POLYCARPUS

Polycarpus returned to Symrna, as far as we can make out, in the autumn of 154. A death worthy of him awaited him there. Polycarpus had always professed the doctrine that one ought not to court martyrdom; but many people who were not possessed of his virtue were not so prudent as he. To be in the vicinage of the sombre enthusiasts of Phrygia was dangerous. A Phrygian named Quintus, a Montanist formerly, came to Smyrna and attracted a few enthusiasts, who followed his example of self-denunciation, and provoked penal condemnation. Sensible men blamed them, and said, with good reason, that the Gospel did not demand such a sacrifice. Besides these fanatics, several Smyrniote Christians were also imprisoned. Amongst them were found some Philadelphians, whom either accident had conducted to Smyrna or whom the authorities, after arresting them, had caused to be transferred to Smyrna--a city of very considerable importance, in which were celebrated great games. The number of those so detained was about a dozen. According to the hideous usage of the Romans, it was in the stadium, in default of an amphitheatre, that their execution took place.

The tortures endured by these unfortunates were of the most horribly atrocious character. Some were so lacerated by whips that their veins, their arteries, and the whole of their intestines were exposed. Onlookers wept over them, but they could not extort from them either a murmur or a plaint. The idea was hence spread abroad that the martyrs of Christ, during the torture, were separated from the body, and that Christ himself assisted them, and spoke with them. Fire produced on them the effect of a delicious coolness. Exposed to wild beasts, dragged over sand full of jagged shells, they appeared insensible to pain.

One only succumbed, and that was rightly the one who had compromised the others. The Phrygian was punished for his boasting. In sight of the wild beasts he began to tremble. The men of the pro-consul who surrounded him urged him to give in; he consented to take the oath and the sacrifice. In that the faithful saw a sign from heaven, and the condemnation of those who of their own accord sought for death. Such conduct, arising from pride, was considered as a sort of defiance of God. It was admitted that the courage to endure martyrdom came from on high, and that God, in order to demonstrate that he was the source of all strength, was pleased sometimes to show the greatest examples of heroism in those who, put to the proof, had been, distrustful of themselves, almost cowards.

People admired especially a young man named Germanicus. He gave to his companions in agony an example of superhuman courage. His struggle with the wild beasts was admirable. The pro-consul, Titus Statius Quadratus, a philosophic and moderate man, a friend of Ælius Aristides, exhorted him to take pity on his own youth. He thereupon set himself to excite the wild beasts, to call to them, to tease them, in order that they might despatch him more quickly from a perverse world. Such heroism, far from touching the multitude, only irritated it. "Death to Atheists! Let Polycarpus be brought!" was the general cry.

Polycarpus, although blaming the foolish act of Quintus, had not at first any desire to flee. Yielding to eager solicitations, he consented, however, to withdraw into a small country house, situated at no great distance from the city, where he passed several days. They came thither to arrest him. He quitted the house precipitately and took refuge in another; but a young slave, when put to the torture, betrayed him. A detachment of mounted police came to take him. It was a Friday evening, the 22d February, at dinner-hour, the old man was at table in an upper room of the villa; he might still have escaped, but he said, "Let God's will be done!" He quietly came downstairs, spoke with the police, gave them something to eat, and asked only an hour in which to pray unmolested. He made then one of those long prayers to which he was accustomed, in which he included the whole Catholic Church. The night was passed in this manner. The following morning, Saturday, 23d February, he was placed upon an ass, and they departed with him.

Before reaching the city, Herod, the Irenach, and his father Nicetas, appeared in a carriage. They had had some relations with the Christians. Alces, sister of Nicetas, appears to have been affiliated with the Church. They, it is said, placed the old man in the carriage between them, and attempted to gain him over. "What harm can it be," said they, "in order to save one's life, to say Kyrios Kesar, to make sacrifice, and the rest?" Polycarpus was inflexible. It seems that the two magistrates then flew into a passion, said hard words to him, and ejected him so rudely from the carriage as to peel the skin off his leg.

He was taken to the stadium, which was situated about midway up Mount Pagus. The people were already assembled there; there was a tumultuous noise. At the moment the old man was brought in, the noise redoubled; the Christians alone heard a voice from heaven saying: "Be strong, be manly, Polycarpus!" The bishop was led to the pro-consul, who employed the ordinary phrases in such circumstances.

"From the respect that thou owest to thy age, etc., aware by the fortune of Cæsar, cry as every one does, Death to Atheists'"

Polycarpus thereupon cast a severe look upon the multitude which covered the steps, and pointed to them with his hand.

"Yes, certainly," said he, "no more Atheists," and he raised his eyes to heaven with a deep sigh. "Insult Christ," said Statius Quadratus.

"It is now eighty-six years that I have served him, and he has never done me any injury," said Polycarpus. "I am a Christian. If thou wishest to know what it is to be a Christian," added he, "grant me a day's delay, and give me thy attention."

"Persuade, then, the people to that," responded Quadratus.

"With thee it is worth one's while to discuss," responded Polycarpus. "We hold it as a principle to render to the powers and to the established authorities, through God, the honours which are their due, provided that these marks of respect do no injury to our faith. As for these people there, I will never deign to condescend to make my apology to them."

The pro-consul threatened him in vain with wild beasts and with fire. It was necessary to announce to the people that Polycarpus held obstinately to his faith. Jews and Pagans cried out for his blood.

"Look at him, the doctor of Asia--the father of the Christians," said the former.

"Behold him, the destroyer of our gods, he who teaches not to sacrifice, not to adore," said the latter. At the same time they demanded of Philippe of Tralles, asiarch and high priest of Asia, to let loose a lion upon Polycarpus. Philippe drew attention of the multitude to the fact that the games with the wild beasts were at an end.

"To the fire, then!" So was the shout which went up from all sides. The people dispersed themselves amongst the shops and the baths to search for wood and fagots. The Jews, who were numerous at Smyrna, and always strongly incensed against the Christians, exhibited in this work, as usual, a zeal wholly peculiar to them.

While the funeral pile was being made ready, Polycarpus took off his girdle, divested himself of all his garments, and attempted also to take off his shoes. This was not accomplished without some difficulty; for in ordinary times the faithful who surrounded him were in the habit of insisting on relieving him from that trouble, as they were jealous of the privilege of touching him. He was placed in the centre of the apparatus which was used for fixing the victim, and they were about to begin to nail him to it.

"Leave me thus," said he; "He who gives me the fortitude to endure the fire will bestow on me also the strength to remain immovable on the pile, without its being necessary for you to nail me to it."

They did not nail him, they simply bound him. So, with his hands tied behind his back, he had the look of a victim; and the Christians who watched him from afar saw in him a ram chosen from amongst the whole flock to be offered up to God as a burnt-offering. During this time he prayed and thanked God for having included him in the number of the martyrs.

The flames then began to rise. The exaltation of the faithful witnesses of this spectacle was at its height. As they were some distance from the pile, they might indulge in the most singular illusions. The fire seemed to them to round itself into a vault above the body of the martyr, and to present the aspect of a ship's sail filled with the wind. The old man, placed amidst that chapelle ardent, appeared to them not as flesh which burned, but as bread being baked, or as a mass of gold and silver in the furnace. They imagined that they felt a delicious odour like that of incense, or of the most precious perfumes (probably the vine branches, and the light wood of the pile had something to do with this). They even declared afterwards that Polycarpus had not been burned, that the confector was obliged to give him a thrust with a poignard, and that there flowed from the wound so much blood that the fire was extinguished by it.

The Christians naturally attached the greatest value to their possessing the body of the martyr. But the authorities hesitated to give it to them, fearing that the martyr would become the object of a new worship. "They might be capable," said they, laughing, "of abandoning the Crucified One for him." The Jews mounted guard near to the funeral pile, to watch what they were going to do. The centurion on duty showed himself favourable to the Christians, and allowed them to take these bones, "more precious than the most precious stones, and than the purest gold." They were calcined. In order to reconcile this fact with the marvellous recital, they pretended that it was the centurion who had burned the body. They put the ashes into a consecrated place, where people resorted every year to celebrate the anniversary of the martyrdom, and to incite one another to walk in the steps of the holy old man.

The fortitude of Polycarpus made a deep impression on the Pagans themselves. The authorities, not wishing a renewal of similar scenes, put an end to executions. The name of Polycarpus continued to be celebrated at Smyrna, whilst people soon forgot the eleven or twelve Smyrniotes or Philadelphians who had suffered before him. The Churches of Asia and of Galatia, at the news of the death of their great pastor, asked the Smyrniotes for the details of what had taken place. Those of Philomelium, in Phrigian Parorea, exhibited, in particular, a touching zeal. The Church of Smyrna caused one of the elders to write down the account of the martyrdom, in the form of a circular epistle, which was addressed to the different Churches. The faithful of Philomelium, who were not far off, were charged with transmitting the letter to the brethren at a distance.

The copy of the Philomelians, copied by a certain Evarestur, and carried by one named Marcion, served subsequently as the basis of the original edition. As happens frequently in the publication of circular letters, the finales of the different copies were made to dovetail the one into the other. This rare fragment constitutes the most ancient example known of the Acts of Martyrdom. It was the model which people imitated, and which furnished the form and the essential parts of those kinds of compositions. Only the imitations had not the naturalness and simplicity of the original. It seems that the author of the false Ignatian letters had read the Smyrniote epistle. There is the closest connection between these writings, and a great similarity of thought. After Ignatius, Polycarpus was the person who copied the most of the thoughts of the false letters and it is in the true or supposed epistle of Polycarpus that he seeks his point d'appui. The idea that martyrdom is the supreme favour that one ought to seek after, and to request of Heaven, found in the Smyrniote encyclical its first and perfect expression. But the enthusiasm for martyrdom is there kept within the limits of moderation. The author of this remarkable writing loses no occasion to show that true martyrdom, the martyrdom conformable with the Gospel, is that which one does not seek after, but which one expects. The provocation appeared to him so blameable, that he experiences a certain satisfaction in showing that the Phrygian fanatic yielded to the entreaties of the pro-consul, and became an apostate.

Frivolous, light-headed, prone to whimsicalities, Asia turned these tragedies into stories, and made a caricature of martyrdom. About that time there lived a certain Peregrinus, a cynic philosopher of Parium, upon the Hellespont, who called himself Protéus, and in regard to whom people boasted of the facility with which he could assume any character, and undertake any adventure. Among these adventures was that of posing as a bishop and a martyr. Having begun life by committing the most frightful crimes, parricide even, he became a Christian, then a priest, a scribe, a prophet, a thiasarch, and chief of the synagogue. He interpreted the sacred books, as composed by himself; he passed for an oracle, for a supreme authority, in fact, on ecclesiastical rules. He was arrested for that offence, and put in chains. This was the commencement of his apotheosis. From that hour he was adored; people raised heaven and earth to affect his escape, and manifested the greatest anxiety in regard to him. In the mornings, at the prison gate, the widows and orphans gathered to see him. The notables obtained, by means of money, the privilege of passing the night in his society. It was a constant succession of dinners and of sacred feasts; people celebrated the Mysteries in close proximity to him; he was called only "the excellent Peregrinus," and was looked upon as a new Socrates.

All this took place in Syria. These public scandals delighted the Christians; they spared no effort in such a case to render the manifestation a brilliant affair. Envoys arrived from every town in Asia for the purpose of rendering service to the confessor, and of condoling with him. Money flowed in upon him. But it was found that the governor of Syria was a philosopher; he penetrated the secret of our subject, saw that he had but one idea, that of dying in order to render his name celebrated, and he set him free without punishment. Everywhere in his travels Peregrinus revelled in abundance, the Christians surrounded him, and gave him an escort of honour.

"These imbeciles," adds Lucian, "were persuaded that they were absolutely immortal, that they would live eternally, which was the reason that they held death in contempt, and that many amongst them offered themselves up as sacrifices. Their first legislator had persuaded them that they were all brothers, from the moment that, denying the Hellenistic gods, they adored the Crucified One, their sophist, and lived according to his laws. They had, then, nothing but disdain for things terrestrial, and they held the latter as belonging to all in common But it were useless to say that they had not a serious reason for believing all this. If, then, some impostor, some crafty man, capable of making use of the situation, came to them, they immediately laid their riches at his feet, while he laughed in his sleeve at the silly fools."

Peregrinus having exhausted his resources, sought, by means of a theatrical death at the Olympian Games, to satisfy the insatiable desire that he had, to wit: to make people speak of him. Pompous and voluntary suicide was, it is well known, the great reproach which the sage philosophers brought against the Christians.

# CHAPTER XXIV

### CHRISTIANITY AMONGST THE GAULS--THE CHURCH OF LYONS

For a short time it was believed that the death of Polycarpus had put an end to persecution, and it would seem that there was in fact an interval of calm. The zeal of the Smyrniotes was but redoubled; and it is about this time that must be placed the departure of a Christian colony, which, setting out probably from Smyrna, carried the Gospel with a bound into distant countries, where the name of Jesus had not yet penetrated. Pothinus, an old man of seventy, probably a Smyrniote and a disciple of Polycarpus, was, it seems, the chief of this new departure.

For a long time a course of reciprocal communication had been established between the ports of Asia Minor and the shores of the Mediterranean of Gaul. The ancient traces of the Phoenicians were not yet wholly effaced. These populations of Asia and Syria, for whom emigration to the East possessed a great attraction, were fond of ascending the Rhone and the Saone, carrying with them a portable bazaar of divers merchandise, or else stopping on the banks of these great rivers, at spots which held out to them the hope of making a living. Vienne and Lyons, the two principal towns of the country, were mostly the points aimed at by the emigrants, who went into Gaul as merchants, servants, workmen, and even as physicians, whom the peasants amongst the Allobroges and Segusiavii did not possess to the same extent. The laborious and industrial population of the great towns on the banks of the Rhone was in a great part composed of those Orientals, who are more gentle, more intelligent, less superstitious than the indigenous population, and, by reason of their insinuating and amiable manners, capable of exercising upon the former a profound influence. The Roman Empire had broken down the barriers of national sentiment, which prevented different peoples from coming into contact. Certain propaganda which the ancient Gaulish institutions, for example, had laid down from the beginning, had become possible. Rome persecuted, but did not use preventive means, so that, far from being hurtful to the development of an opinion aspiring to be universal, she aided it. These Syrians and Asiatics arrived in the East not knowing any tongue except the Greek. Among themselves they did not cast aside that language; they made use of it in their writings, and in all their personal relations; but they quickly acquired Latin, and even Celtic. Greek, moreover, which continued to be spoken in the region of the lower Rhone, was known to a great extent in Vienne and in Lyons.

These Christians of Lyons and Vienne, in setting out from a very limited region, Asia and Phrygia, being almost all compatriots, and having been instructed by the same books and by the same teachings, afford an instance of rare unity. Their intercourse with the Churches of Asia and Phrygia was frequent: in grave circumstances it was to these Churches that they wrote. Like Phrygians generally, they were ardent pietists; but they had not that sectarian tinge which soon made the Montanists a danger, almost a plague, in the Church. Pothinus, who was at first recognised as the head of the Church of Lyons, was a respectable old man, and moderate even in his enthusiasm.

Attains of Pergamos, who like him was a very old man, appears to have been, after the former, the pillar of the Church and the principal authority. He was a Roman citizen and a rather important personage: he knew Latin, and was recognised in every city as the principal representative of the little community. A Phrygian named Alexander, practising the medical profession, was loved and known by all. Initiated into the pious secrets of the saints of Phrygia, he possessed some of the graces, that is to say, the supernatural gifts, of the apostolic age, which had been revived in his native land. Like Polycarpus, he had reached the highest state of the internal spiritual communion. It was, as we see, a corner of Phrygia which chance had transported bodily into Gaul. The continual accessions coming from Asia maintained that first hold and conserved there the spirit of mysticism which had been its primitive character. As soon as he was able, Irenæus, wearied out perhaps by his struggles with Florimus and Blastus, quitted Rome for this Church, composed entirely of the countrymen, disciples, and the friends of Polycarpus.

Communication between Lyons and Vienne was constant: the two Churches, in reality, were but one, and in both the Greek dominated; but in both likewise there existed between the emigrants of Asia and the indigenous population, who spoke Latin or Celtic, the closest relations. The effect of this familiar preaching in the house and in the workshop was rapid and profound. The women especially felt themselves vehemently carried away by it. The Gaulish nature, naturally sympathetic and religious, promptly embraced the new ideas brought by the strangers. Their religion, at once most idealistic and most materialistic, their belief in perpetual visions, their habit of transforming lively and delicate sensations into supernatural intuitions, suited those races very well which were carried away by religious dreams, and which the insufficient worships of Gaul and Rome could not satisfy. The evangelic ministry was sometimes exercised in the Celtic tongue. It is remarkable that amongst the new converts a great number were Roman citizens.

One of the most important conquests was that of a certain Vettius Epagathus, a young noble Lyonese, who, when he had hardly been affiliated to the Church, excelled everybody in piety and in charity, and became one of the most distinguished amongst them. He led so chaste and so austere a life that he was, in spite of his youth, compared to the aged Zacharias, an ascetic who was constantly visited by the Holy Spirit. Devoted to works of mercy, he became the servant of all, and employed his life to the succour of his neighbours with admirable zeal and fervour. It was believed that the Paraclete dwelt in him, and that he acted in all circumstances under the inspiration of the Holy Spirit. The recollection left by the virtues of Vettius became a popular tradition, which pretended to ascribe to his family the evangelisation of the neighbouring countries. He was in truth the first-fruits of Christ in Gaul. Sanctus, the deacon of Vienne, and especially the maid-servant Blandina, who was much inferior to him in social dignity, equalled him in earnestness. Blandina, above all, worked miracles. She was so slender of body that it was feared she had not the physical strength sufficient to confess Christ. She displayed, on the contrary, the day when the struggle came, an unexampled nervous force; she wearied out the torturers for a whole day; and it might be said that at each torment she experienced a recrudescence of faith and of life.

Such was this Church, which in a bound attained to the highest privileges of the Christian Churches of Asia, and stood out in the centre of a still semi-barbarous country, like a shining beacon. The Christians of Lyons and Vienne, entrusted with the Gospel of John and of the Apocalypse, without having need of the stammering schools through which Christianity had passed, were carried at the very first to the summit of perfection. Nowhere was life more austere, enthusiasm more serious, the desire to create the kingdom of God more intense. Chilasmus, which had its home in Asia Minor, was not less loudly proclaimed in Lyons. Gaul hence entered the Church of Jesus through a triumph hitherto unequalled. Lyons was designated as the religious capital of that country. Fourvieres and Ainai are the two sacred points of our Christian origins. Fourvieres, at the time of the ecclesiastical annals of which we now speak, was still a city wholly Pagan; as for Ainai (Athanacum) it is allowable to suppose that the Christian souvenirs have some reason for attaching themselves to it. This suburb, situated on the islands at the confluence of the rivers, down the river from the Gaulish and Roman city, came to be the lower part of the town, the place where the Orientals disembarked, and where probably they made some sojourn before settling down. But this was undoubtedly the first Christian quarter, and the very ancient church which is to be seen there, is perhaps of all the edifices in France the one which those who love antique souvenirs ought to visit with the most respect. The Lyonese character from this time forth was sketched with all the features which distinguish it--need of the supernatural, fervour of soul, a taste for the irrational, perversity of judgment, ardent imagination, and a profound and sensual mysticism. With this passionate race, high moral instincts do not spring from reason, but from the heart and the bowels. The origin of the Lyonese school in art and literature was already fully traced in that admirable letter upon the frightful drama of 177. It is beautiful, odd touching, sickly. There is mixed up in it a slight aberration of the senses, a something resembling the nervous quivering of the saints of Pepuza.

The relations of Epagathus with the Paraclete savoured already of the city of spiritualism, the city in which, towards the end of the last century, Cagliostro had a temple. The anæstheses of Blandina, her familiar conversations with Christ, whilst the bull is tossing her into the air; the hallucination of the martyrs, believing that they saw Jesus in their sister, at the end of the arena bound naked to a stake--the whole of this legend which on the one hand transports you away from stoicism and where on the other one approaches the cataleptic state, and to the experiences of Salpetriere, seems a subject invented for those poets, painters, thinkers, wholly original and idealistic, who imagine themselves to paint only the soul, but in reality only dupes of the body. Epictetus deports himself better; he has shown in the battle of life as much heroism as Attalus and as Sanctus, but there is no legend concerning him. The hegemonikon alone says nothing to humanity. Man is a very complex being. One can never charm or arouse the multitude with pure truth: one has never made a great man out of a eunuch, nor a great romance without love.

We shall soon witness the most dangerous chimeras of Gnosticism Ending at Lyons a prompt reception, and almost by the side of Blandina the victims of the seductions of Marcus flee from the Church, or come there to confess their sin, in habits of mourning. The charm of the Lyonese, living in a sort of tender decency and of voluptuous chastity; her seductive reserve, implying the secret idea that beauty is a holy thing; her strange facility for letting herself be captivated by the appearances of mysticism and of pity, produced under Marcus Aurelius scenes which might lead one to think they had taken place in our own times. Marseilles, Arles, and the immediate environs received alike under Antonius a first Christian preaching; Nîmes, on the contrary, appeared to have resisted as long as possible the cult which came from the East.

It was about the same time that Africa witnessed the formation of stable Churches which were soon to constitute one of the most original parties of the new religion. Amongst the first founders of African Christianity, the mystic tinge which in a few years was denominated Montanist was no less strong than amongst the Christians of Lyons. It is probable, nevertheless, that the teaching of the kingdom of God was in this case brought from Rome and not from Asia. The Acts of St Perpetua, and in general the Acts of the Martyrs of Africa--Tertullian, and the other types of African Christianity--have an air of fraternity with Pastor Hermas. Assuredly the first bearers of the good news spoke Greek at Carthage, as they did everywhere else. Greek was almost as widespread in that city as Latin; the Christian community at first made use of both languages; soon, however, the language of Rome predominated. Africa thus gave the first example of a Latin Church. In a few years a brilliant Christian literature was produced in that eccentric idiom which the rude Punic genius had drawn, by the twofold influence of barbarism and rhetoric, from the language of Cicero and of Tacitus. A translation of the works of the Old and New Testaments in that energetic dialect responded to the requirements of the new converts, and was for a long time the Bible of the West.

# CHAPTER XXV

### THE STRIFE AT ROME--MARTYRDOM OF ST JUSTIN--FRONTON

Distressing scenes, the consequence of a vicious legislation, under the reign of one of the best of sovereigns, were taking place everywhere. Sentences of death and the denial of justice multiplied. The Christians were often in the wrong. Severity, and the ardent love of the good, by which they were animated, carried them sometimes beyond the bounds of moderation, and rendered them odious to those whom they censured. The father, the son, the husband, the wife, the neighbour, irritated by these prying spies, revenged themselves by denouncing them. Atrocious calumnies were the consequence of these accumulated hatreds. It was about this time that rumours, which up till then had no particular force, assumed a definite form, and became a rooted opinion. The mystery attaching to the Christian reunions, the mutual affection which reigned in the Church, gave birth to the most foolish notions. They were supposed to form a secret society, to have secrets known only to the initiated, to be guilty of shameful promiscuity, and of loves contrary to nature. Some spoke of the adoration of a god with the head of an ass, others of the ignoble homage rendered to the priest. One story which received general currency was this: They presented to the person who was being initiated an infant covered over with paste, in order to train his hand by degrees to murder. The novice struck, the blood poured forth, all drank eagerly, they divided the trembling limbs, and cemented thus their alliance through complicity, and bound themselves to absolute silence. Then they became drunk, lights were extinguished, and in the darkness they all gave themselves up to the most hideous embracements. Rome was a city much given to slander: a multitude of newsmongers and gossips were on the watch for bizarre tales. Those silly tales were repeated, passed off as being of public notoriety, were transformed into outrages and into caricatures. The serious part about it was this, that in the legal processes to which those accusations gave rise they put to the question slaves belonging to Christian houses--women, young boys--who, overcome by the tortures, said all that was wished of them, and afforded a judicial basis for many odious inventions.

The calumnies, moreover, were reciprocal, the Christians retorting on their adversaries the lies invented against themselves. These sanguinary feasts, these orgies, were practised only by the Pagans. Had not their god set them the example in every kind of vice? In some of the most solemn rites of the Roman worship, in the sacrifices to Jupiter Latiaris, did they not indulge in the shedding of human blood? The accusation was inaccurate, but, for all that, it became one of the bases of apologetic Christianity. The immorality of the gods of ancient Olympus afforded the controversialists an easy triumph. When Jupiter himself was only the pure blue sky, he was immoral like nature herself, and this immorality had no results. But morals had now become the essence of religion; people required of the gods examples of citizen-like integrity; examples like those of which mythology is full yielded only scandalous and irrefutable objections.

Above all things it was the public discussions between the philosophers and the apologist which embittered the minds of people, and led to the gravest disturbances. In those discussions people insulted one another, and, unhappily, the parties were not equal. The philosophers had a sort of official position and state function; they received emoluments for making profession of a wisdom which they did not always teach by their example. They ran no risks, and they were wrong in making their adversaries feel that by saying a word they could extinguish them. The Christians, on their side, jeered at the philosophers for accepting emoluments. Those were insipid pleasantries, analogous to those which we have seen exhibited in our times against salaried philosophers. "Could they not," said people to one another, "wear their beards gratis!" People affected to believe that they rolled in gold, treated them as sordid wretches, as parasites; people objected to their doctrine, on the ground that they knew how to do without men of their manner of life--a life which appeared as one of opulence to some people even poorer than themselves were.

The ardent Justin was at the head of these noisy altercations, where we see him, towards the end of his life, seconded by a disciple more violent yet than himself, we mean the Assyrian Latianus, a man of a gloomy disposition, and filled with hatred against Hellenism. Born a Pagan, he studied literature extensively, and kept a public school of philosophy, not without obtaining a certain reputation as a teacher. Endowed with a melancholy imagination, Latianus was anxious to possess clear ideas upon things which human destiny interdicted him from acquiring. He had traversed, like his master Justin, the whole circle of existing religions and philosophies, had travelled, wished to be initiated into all the pretended religious secrets, and attended the different schools. Hellenism offended him by its apparent levity of morals. Destitute of all literary sentiment, he was incapable of appreciating their divine beauty. The Scriptures of the Hebrews had alone the privilege of satisfying him. They pleased him by their severe morality, their simple style and assurance, by their monotheistic character, and by the peremptory manner in which they put to one side, by means of the creation dogma, the restless curiosities of physics and metaphysics. His contracted and dull mind had found in them that which it wanted. He became a Christian, and met in St Justin the doctor best fitted to comprehend his passionate philosophy; he attached him closely to him, and was in a manner his second in the contests which he sustained against the sophists and the rhetoricians.

Their usual antagonist was a cynic philosopher named Crescentius, a personage, it seems, contemptible enough, who had made a position at Rome by his ascetic appearance and by his long beard. His declamations against the fear of death did not impede him from often menacing Justin and Tatian, and of denouncing them: "Ah, you own, then, that death is an evil!" said they to him in turn, wittily enough. Certainly Crescentius was wrong in abusing thus the protection of the State to his adversaries. But it must be confessed that Justin did not in that case show him all the consideration he deserved. He treated his adversaries as gourmands and impostors; he was right, nevertheless, in reproaching them with the emoluments they accepted. One can be a pensioner without being, for all that, a niggardly and covetous person. A circumstance which occurred about that time in Rome, showed how dangerous it is to oppose persecution to fanaticism, even where fanaticism is aggressive and tantalising.

There was in Rome a very wicked household, in which the husband and the wife seemed to be rivals in infamy. The wife was converted to Christianity by one Ptolemy, abandoned her evils ways, made every effort to convert her husband, and not succeeding in this, thought of a divorce. She was afraid at being accomplice in the impieties of him with whom she lived united by society, sitting at the same table, and sharing the same couch. In spite of the counsels of her family, she sent to him the notifications required by law, and quitted the conjugal abode. The husband protested, entered an action, pleading that his wife was a Christian. The wife obtained several delays. The husband, irritated, directed, as was natural, all his anger against Ptolemy.

He succeeded through a centurion, a friend of his, in having Ptolemy arrested, and whom he persuaded to ask simply of Ptolemy whether he were a Christian. Ptolemy confessed that he was, and was put in prison. After a very cruel detention he was taken before Quintus Lollius Urbicus, prefect of Rome. He was questioned afresh, and made fresh avowals. Ptolemy was condemned to death. A Christian, named Lucius, present at the hearing, interpellated Urbicus. "How can you condemn a man who is neither adulterer, thief, nor murderer, who is guilty of no other crime than of avowing himself a Christian? Your judgment is indeed little in accord with the piety of our Emperor, and with the sentiments of the philosopher son of Cæsar" (Marcus Aurelius) Lucius having avowed himself a Christian, Urbicus condemned him likewise to death. "Thank you," responded Lucius; "I am obliged to you; I am about to exchange wicked masters for a father who is king of heaven." A third auditor was seized with the same contagious fury for martyrdom. He proclaimed himself a Christian, and was ordered to be executed with the two others, Justin was moved extremely by this sanguinary drama. As long as Lollius Urbicus was perfect of Rome, he could not protest; but as soon as that function passed to another, Justin addressed to the senate a fresh apology. His own position became precarious. He felt the danger of having for an enemy a man like Crescentius, who by a word could put him out of the way. It was with the presentiment of a near death that he committed to writing that eloquent defence against the exceptional situation to which the Christians were reduced.

There is something bold in the attitude which an obscure philosopher takes before the powerful body which the provincials never designated otherwise than hiera syncletos, "the holy assembly." Justin brings back these arrogant people to a sentiment of justice and of truth. The éclat of their pretended dignity may create an illusion in them; but whether they like it or like it not they are the brothers and the fellow-creatures of those whom they prosecute. This persecution is the proof of the truth of Christianity. The best among the Pagans have in like manner been persecuted--Musonius, for example--but what a difference! Whilst Socrates has not had a single disciple who has been put to death for him, Jesus has a multitude of witnesses--artisans, common people, as well as philosophers, men of letters--who have offered up their lives for him.

It is to be regretted that some of the enlightened men of which the senate was then composed did not study these beautiful pages. Perhaps they were turned from them by other passages less philosophic, in particular by the absurd demonomania which bristled in each page. Justin challenges his readers to prove a notorious fact, which was, that people brought to the Christians the possessed whom the Pagan exorcists were unable to heal. He held that to be a decisive proof of the eternal fires in which demons shall one day be punished along with the men who have adored them. One page which ought to shock wholly those whom Justin wished to convert, is the one in which, after having established that the violent measures of Roman legislation against Christianity were the work of demons, he announces that God will soon avenge the blood of his servants, in annihilating the power of the genii of evil, and in consuming all the world by fire (an idea that the worst wretches made use of for the purpose of disorder and pillage). If God differs, said he, it is only to wait until the number of the elect be complete. Till then, he will allow demons and wicked men to do all the evil that they wish.

That which shows indeed what an amount of simplicity of mind Justin combined with his rare sincerity, is the petition by which he finishes his apology. He requests that there should be given to his writing an official approbation, in order to correct the opinion as to what concerns the Christians. "At least," says he, "such a publicity would be less objectionable than that which is given every day to foolish farces, obscene writings, ballets, Epicurean books, and other compositions of the same sort, which are represented or are read with entire freedom. We see already how much Christianity shows itself favourable to the most immoderate exercise of authority, when this authority shall have been acquired by it"

Justin touches us more, when he regards death with impassability:--

I fully expect, says be, to see myself denounced some day, and put into the stocks by the people whom I have mentioned, at least by this Crescentius, more worthy of being called the friend of noise and of vain show than the friend of wisdom, who goes about every day affirming of as things of which he knows nothing, accusing us in public of atheism and of impiety, in order to gain the favour of an abused multitude. He must have a very wicked soul to decry us thus, since even the man of ordinary morality makes a point of not passing judgment upon things of which he is ignorant. If he pretends that he is perfectly instructed in our doctrine, it must be that the baseness of his mind has prevented him from comprehending its majesty. If he understood it thoroughly, there is nothing which obliges him to decry it, if it be not the fear of being himself regarded as a Christian. Understand, in fact, that I, having proposed some questions to him on the subject, have clearly perceived, and I have even convinced him that he knows nothing about them. And to demonstrate to the whole world that what I say is the truth, I declare that if you are still ignorant of this dispute I am ready to renew it in your presence. The latter would indeed be a truly royal work. For, if you were to see the questions which I proposed to him and the responses he made to them, you could not doubt his ignorance, nor his little love for the truth.

The forecasts of St Justin were but too well justified. Crescentius denounced him when he ought to have contented himself by refuting him, and the courageous doctor was put to death. Tatian escaped the snares of the Cynic. We cannot enough regret, for the sake of the memory of Antonine (or, if it is wished, of Marcus Aurelius), that the courageous advocate of a cause which was then that of liberty of conscience should have suffered martyrdom under his reign. If Justin called his rival "impostor," or "shark," as Tatian informs us, he deserved the full penalty which attached to the crime of proffering insults in public. But Crescentius may have been no less offensive, and he escaped punishment. Justin was therefore punished for being a Christian. The law was formal, and the conservators of the Roman common weal hesitated to abrogate it. How many precursors of the future suffered similarly under the reign of the just and pious St Louis!

The attacks of Crescentius were but an isolated circumstance. In the first century, some of the most enlightened men were wholly ignorant of Christianity; but this is no longer possible. Everybody has an opinion on the subject. The first rhetorician of the times, L. Cornelius Fronton, certainly wrote an invective against the Christians. That discourse is lost; we do not know in what circumstances it was composed, but we can form some idea of it from that which Municius Felix puts into the mouth of his Cæcilius. The work was not like that of Celsus, consecrated to exegetical discussion; it was nothing more than a philosophical treatise. It consisted of several considerations on the man of the world, and on politics. Fronton accepted without examination the most calumnious rumours against the Christians. He believed or affected to believe what was told of their nocturnal mysteries and of their sanguinary repasts. A very honest man, but an official man, he had a horror of a sect of men of no social standing. Satisfied with a sort of vague belief in Providence, which he capriciously associated with a polytheistic devotion, he held to the established religion, not because he alleged it was true, but because it was the ancient religion, and formed part of the prejudices of a true Roman. There is no doubt that in his declamation he only took up a patriotic point of view, so as to preach the respect that was due to national institutions, and that be only stood up in his conservative zeal against the foolish pretension of illiterate people of mean condition aspiring to reform beliefs. Perhaps he wound up ironically in regard to the impotence of that unique God who, too much occupied to be able to govern everything well, abandoned his worshippers to death, and with a few railleries upon the resurrection of the flesh.

The discourse of Fronton appealed only to the lettered. Fronton rendered a very bad service to Christianity in inculcating his ideas on the illustrious pupil whom he educated with so much care, and who came to be called Marcus Aurelius.

# CHAPTER XXVI

### THE APOCRYPHAL GOSPELS

If we accept the apologists, such as Aristides, Quadratus, and Justin, who addressed themselves to the Pagans, and the pure traditionists, such as Papias and Hegesippus, who regarded the new revelation as essentially consisting in the words of Jesus, almost all the Christian writers of the age we have just left had the idea of augmenting the list of sacred writings susceptible of being read in the Church. Despairing of succeeding in this through their private authority, they assumed the name of some apostle or of some apostolic personage, and made no scruple in attributing to themselves the inspiration which was indiscriminately enjoyed by the immediate disciples of Jesus. This vein of apocryphal literature was now exhausted. Pseudo-Hermas only half succeeded. We shall see the Reconnaissances of pseudo-Clementine and the pretended Constitutions of the twelve apostles equally stamped with suspicion in respect of canonicity. The numerous Acts of Apostles which were produced everywhere had only a partial success. No Apocalypse appeared again to disturb seriously the masses. The success of public readings had, up to this point, been the criterions of canonicity. A Church admitted such a writing imputed to an apostle or to an apostolic personage to the public reading. The faithful were edified. The rumour was spread in the neighbouring Churches that a very beautiful communication had been made in such a community, on such a day; people wished to see the new writing, and thus, little by little, this writing came to be accepted, provided that it did not contain some stumbling-block. But as time went on people became critical, and successes such as those which the Epistles to Titus and to Timothy, the Second Epistle to Peter, obtained, were no longer renewed.

The fertility of evangelical invention was in reality exhausted; the age of great legendary creation was past; people no longer invented anything of importance; the success of psuedo-John was the last. But the liberty of remodelling was sufficiently extensive, at least outside the Churches of St Paul. Although the four texts which became subsequently canonical, had already a certain vogue, they were far from excluding similar texts. The Gospel of the Hebrews retained all its authority. Justin and Tatian probably made use of it. The author of the Epistles of St Ignatius (second half of the second century) cites it as a canonical and accepted text. No text, in fact, destroyed the tradition or suppressed its rivals. Books were rare, and badly preserved. Dionysius of Corinth, at the end of the second century, speaks of the falsifiers of the "Scriptures of the Lord," which induces the belief that the retouching continued for more than a hundred years after the compilation of our Mathew. Hence the indecisive form in the sayings of Jesus which is to be remarked in the apostolic fathers. The source is always vaguely indicated; great variations are produced in the citations up to the time of St Irenæus. Sometimes the words of Isaiah and Enoch are put forth for the words of Jesus. There is no longer any distinction between the Bible and the Gospel, and some words of Luke are cited with this heading, "God says."

The Gospels thus were until about the year 160 and even beyond that, private writings designed for small circles. Each of the latter had its own, and for a long time individuals did not scruple to complete and to continue already accepted texts. The compilation had not taken a definite form. The texts were added to, they were abridged; such and such a passage was discussed, and the Gospels in circulation were amalgamated, so as to form a single and more portable work. The oral transmission, on the other hand, continued to play a part. A multitude of sayings were not written down: it would have been necessary to determine the whole tradition. Many of the evangelical elements were yet sporadic. It was thus that the beautiful anecdote of the woman taken in adultery circulated. It was made use of as best it might in the fourth Gospel. The phrase, "Be good money changers," which is cited as being "in the Gospel," and as "scripture," did not find a corner anywhere in it.

Certain abridgements which were threatened to be made were much more serious. Every detail which represented Christ as a man, appeared scandalous. The fine verse of Luke, where Jesus weeps over Jerusalem, was condemned by the uncultured sectaries who pretended that weeping was a token of weakness. The consoling angel and the bloody sweat on the Mount of Olives provoked objections and analogous mutilations. But orthodoxy, already dominant, prevented these individual conceits from seriously compromising the integrity of the texts already sacred.

In truth, amidst all this chaos, order was established. In like manner, between opposing doctrines an orthodoxy was designed, just as from amongst a multitude of Gospels four texts tended to become more and more canonical, to the exclusion of others. Mark, pseudo-Matthew, Luke, and pseudo-John, tended towards an official consecration. The Gospels of the Hebrews, which at first equalled them in value, but of which the Nazarenes and the Ebionites made a dangerous use, began to be discarded. The Gospels of Peter and the twelve apostles appeared to have various defects, and were suppressed by the bishops. How was it that people did not go still further, and were not tempted to reduce the four Gospels to one only, either by suppressing three, or in making a unity of the four, after the manner of the Diatesseron of Tatian, or in constructing a sort of Gospel a priori, like Marcion? The honesty of the Church never appears to greater advantage than in this circumstance. With a light heart she placed herself in the most embarrassing situation. It was impossible that some of these contradictions of the Gospels should have escaped observation. Celsus was already keenly alive to them. People preferred for the future to be exposed to the most terrible objections, than that the writings regarded by so many persons as inspired should be condemned. Each of the four great Gospels had its clientèle, if one may thus express oneself. To wrench them out of the hands of those who admired them would have been an impossibility. Besides, it might have resulted in condemning to oblivion a multitude of beautiful details in which we recognise Jesus, although the order of the narration was different. The tetractys gained the day, except in imposing upon ecclesiastical criticism the strangest of tortures--that of making a text accord with four texts discordant.

In any case, the Catholic Church no longer now accords to any person the right to revise from top to bottom the anterior texts, like as has been done by Luke and pseudo-John. We have passed from the age of living tradition to the age of moribund tradition. The book, which until now had been nothing, became everything for the people, who were already removed from the ocular witnesses by two or three generations. Towards the year 180, the revolution will be complete. The Catholic Church will declare the last of the Gospels rigorously closed. There are four Gospels. Irenæus tells us it is necessary to have four, and it is impossible there can be more than four; for there are four climates, four winds, four corners of the world, calling each for a defender; four revelations, that of Adam, of Noah, of Moses, and of Jesus; four animals in the cherub, and four mystic beasts in the Apocalypse. Each of these monsters who for the prophet of the year 69 were simple animated ornaments of the throne of God, became the emblem of one of the four accepted texts. It was admitted that the Gospel was like the cherub, tetramorphous. To put the four texts in accord, to harmonise the one with the other, was the difficult task which shall henceforth be pursued by those who attempt to form to themselves a conception, be it ever so little reasonable, of the life of Jesus.

The most original endeavour to get out of this confusion was certainly that of Tatian, the disciple of Justin. His Diatesseron was the first essay at harmonising the Gospels. The Synoptics, together with the Gospel of the Hebrews and the Gospels of Peter, were the basis of his labour. The text which resulted from it resembled closely enough the Gospel of the Hebrews; the genealogies, as well as everything which connected Jesus with the race of David, were wanting in it. The success of the book of Tatian was at first very considerable; many of the Churches adopted it as a convenient résumé of evangelical history, but the heresies of the author rendered the orthodoxy suspicious; in the end, the book was withdrawn from circulation, and the diversity of texts finally gained the day in the Church Catholic.

It was not thus with the numerous sects which sprang up everywhere. It did not please the latter that evangelical productions had in a manner become crystalised, and that there was no longer any reason for writing new lives of Jesus. The Gnostic sects desired to renew continually the texts, in order to satisfy their ardent fantasy. Almost all the heads of sects had Gospels bearing their names, after the example set by Basilides, or after the manner of Marcion, according to their good pleasure. That of Apelles was drawn, like so many others, from the Gospel of the Hebrews. Markos drew from every source the authentic and the apocryphal. Valentinus, as we have seen, pretended to ascend to the apostles through personal traditions given to him. People quoted a Gospel according to Philip, which was greatly prized by certain sects, and another that they called "The Gospel of Perfection." The names of the apostles furnished a sufficient guarantee for all these frauds. There was hardly one of the twelve who had not a Gospel imputed to him. No more Gospels were invented, it is true, but people wanted to know the details which had been omitted in the four inspired ones. The infancy of Christ, in particular, excited the liveliest curiosity. People would not admit that he, whose life had been a prodigy, had lived for some years as an obscure Nazarene.

Such was the origin of that which is called "Apocryphal Gospels," a long series of feeble productions, the commencement of which may be safely placed about the middle of the second century. It would be doing an injury to Christian literature to place those insipid compositions on the same footing with the masterpieces of Mark, Luke, and Matthew. The apocryphal Gospels are the Pouranas of Christianity; they have for their basis the canonical Gospels. The author takes these Gospels as a theme from which he never deviates; he seeks simply to elucidate and perfect by the ordinary processes of the Hebraic legend. Luke already had followed the same course. In his deductions in regard to the infancy of Jesus, and the birth of John the Baptist, he uses processes of amplification; his pious mechanism of mise en scene is the prelude to the apocryphal Gospels. The authors of the latter make the utmost use of the sacred rhetoric, which, however, was employed by Luke with discretion. Their innovations were few, imitated, and exaggerated. They did for the canonical Gospels what the authors of the Post-Homerica have done for Homer, what the comparatively modern authors of Dionysiacso or Argonautics have done for the Greek epopee. They dealt with those parts which the canonists, for good reasons, neglected; they added that which might have happened, that which appeared probable; they developed the situations by means of artificial reconciliations borrowed from the sacred texts. Finally, they sometimes proceeded by monographs, and sought to construct legend out of all the evangelical personages in the scattered details which had reference to them. They thus limited themselves in everything to embroidering on a given canvas. This was so different from the assurance of the old evangelists, who spoke as if inspired from on high, and pushed boldly forward, each in his way, the details of their narratives, without troubling themselves whether they contradicted one another. The fabricators of the apocryphal Gospels were timid. They cited their authorities; they were restricted by the canonists. The faculty for creating the myth was altogether wanting; they could no longer even invent a miracle. As for details, it is impossible to conceive anything more contemptible, more pitiful. It is the tiresome verbiage of an old gossip, the vulgar and familiar style of a literature of wet nurses and nursery maids. Like the degenerate Catholicism of modern times, the authors of the apocryphal Gospels on their part descended to the puerile side of Christianity--the infant Jesus, the Virgin Mary, Saint Joseph. The veritable Jesus, the Jesus of public life, was beyond them, and frightened them.

The real cause of this sad debasement was a total change in the manner of comprehending the supernatural. The canonical Gospels maintained themselves with a rare dexterity on the verge of a false situation, which, however, was full of charm. Their Jesus is not God, since his whole life is that of a man. He weeps, and allows himself to be moved by pity: he is filled with deity: his attitude is compatible with art, with imagination, and with moral sense. His thaumaturgy, in particular, is that which is becoming to a divine envoy. In the apocryphal Gospels, on the contrary, Jesus is a supernatural spectre, without bodily corporeity. In him humanity is a lie. In his cradle you would take him for an infant: but wait a little: miracles start up round about him; this infant calls out to you, "I am the Logos." The thaumaturgy of this new Christ is material, mechanical, immoral; it is the juggleries of a magician. Wherever he passes, he acts as a magnetic force. Nature is unhinged, and beside itself by the effect of his vicinage. Each word of his is followed by miraculous effects, "for good as well as for evil." Doubtless the canonical Gospels were sometimes not free from this defect; the episodes of the swine of the Gergesenes, of the fig-tree that was cursed, could have only inspired in contemporaries a rather barren moral reflection: "The author of such acts must indeed be powerful." But these cases are rare, whilst in the apocryphal the true notion of Jesus, at once human and divine, is perfectly obliterated. In becoming a pure déva, Jesus lost all which had rendered him amiable and affecting. People were constrained, logically enough, to deny his personal identity, to make of him an intermittent spectre, which showed itself to his disciples now young, now old, now an infant, now an old man, now tall, now short, and sometimes so tall that its head touched the sky.

The oldest and the least objectionable of these insipid rhapsodies is the narrative of the birth of Mary, of her marriage, of the birth of Jesus, reputed to be written by a certain James, a narrative to which has been given the erroneous title of Protevangel of James. A Gnostic book, the Genna Marias, which appears to have been known to St Justin, may have served as the first foundation of it. No book has had so much importance as the latter as regards the history of the Christian festivals and Christian art. The parents of the Virgin, Anne and Joachim; the Presentation of the Virgin in the Temple, and the idea that she had been brought up as if in a convent; the marriage of the Virgin; the meeting of the widowers, the circumstance of the miraculous wands, the picture of which, in certain parts, has been sketched so admirably. The whole of this comes from this curious writing. The Greek Church regarded it as semi-inspired, and admitted it in the public readings in the churches, at the feasts of St Joachim, of St Anne, of the Conception, of the Nativity, of the Presentation of the Virgin. Its Hebrew colouring is still sufficiently distinct. Some pictures of the manners of the Jews recall at times the Book of Tobias. There are distinct traces of Ebionite Judeo-Christianity and of Docetism; in it marriage is almost reprobated.

Many passages of that singular book are not destitute of grace, nor even of a certain naïveté. The author applies to the birth of Mary, and to all the circumstances of the infancy of Jesus, the methods of narration the germ of which was already to be found in Luke and Matthew. The anecdotes in regard to the infancy of Jesus in Luke and in Matthew are ingenious imitations of what is recounted in the ancient books and in the modern agadas about the birth of Samuel, Samson, Moses, Abraham, and Isaac. In this class of writings there was an habitual introduction giving the history of all the great men, several species of commonplaces, always the same, and topics of pious invention. The infant destined to play an extraordinary part must be born of aged parents for long sterile, "so as to demonstrate that the child was a favour bestowed by God, and not the fruit of an unbridled passion." It was held that the Divine power shone out to more advantage when human agency was absent. The result of long expectation and of assiduous prayers, the future great man was announced by an angel, at some solemn moment. It was thus in the case of Samson and of Samuel. According to Luke, the birth of John the Baptist occurred under such conditions. It is believed that it was the same in the case of Mary. Her birth, like that of John and of Jesus, was preceded by an annunciation, accompanied with prayers and with canticles. Anne and Joachim are the exact counterparts of Elizabeth and Zacharias. Some go even beyond that, and embellish the infancy of Anne. This retrospective application of the methods of evangelical legend becomes a fruitful source of fables responding to the requirements, constantly springing up, of Christian piety. People could no longer consider Mary, Joseph, and their ancestors as ordinary personages. The cult of the Virgin, which later on attained so enormous proportions, had already made invasions in every quarter.

A multitude of details, sometimes puerile yet always conforming to the sentiment of the times, or susceptible of removing the difficulties which the ancient Gospels presented, were disseminated by means of these compositions, at first not avowed, or even condemned, but which finished soon in being right. The case of the nativity was completed; the ox and the ass take definitely their places in it. Joseph is depicted as a widower four score years old, the simple protector of Mary. We could have wished that the latter had remained a virgin after as well as before the birth of Jesus. She was made to be of a royal and sacerdotal race, being descended at once from David and from Levi. People cannot represent to themselves that she died like a simple woman. They already speak of her ascension to heaven. The assumption was created, like so many other festivals, by the cycle of apocryphas.

An accent of lively piety distinguishes all the compositions of which we have just been speaking, whilst one cannot read without being disgusted the Gospel of Thomas--an insipid work, which does as little honour as possible to the Christian family, very old though it be, which produced it. It is the point of departure of these flat merveilles in regard to the infancy of Jesus which, by reason of their very dullness had a success so disastrous in the East. In them Jesus figures as an enfant terrible, wicked, rancorous, the dread of his parents and of everybody. He kills his companions, transforms them into he-goats, blinds their parents, confounds his masters, demonstrates to them that they know nothing about the mysteries of the alphabet, and forces them to ask pardon of him. People flee from him as from a pestilence. Joseph in vain beseeches him to remain quiet. This grotesque image of an omnipotent and omniscient gamin is one of the greatest caricatures that was ever invented, and certainly those who wrote it had too little wit for one to credit them with the intention of having meant it as a piece of irony. It was not without a theological design, that, contrary to the perfect system of tact of the old evangelists as regards the thirty years of obscure life, it was desired to be shown that the divine nature in Jesus was never idle, and that he continually performed miracles. Everything which made the life of Jesus a human life was vexatious. "This infant was not a terrestrial being," says Zachæus of him; he can subdue fire; perhaps he existed before the creation of the world. He is either something great, or a god, or an angel, or one I don't know what. This deplorable Gospel appears to be the work of the Marcosians. The Nessenes and the Manicheans appropriated it to themselves, and spread it over the whole of Asia. The inept Oriental Gospel, known by the name of the Gospel of the Infancy, brought into vogue especially by the Nestorians of Persia, is only, in act, an amplification of the Gospel according to Thomas. It passes in all the East as the work of Peter, and as the Gospel par excellence. If India knew any Gospel, it was this one. If Krechnaism embraced any Christian element, it is from this source that it came. The Jesus of whom Mahomet heard speak, is that of the puerile Gospels, a fantastic Jesus, a spectre proving his superhuman nature by means of an extravagant thaumaturgy.

The passion of Jesus owed likewise its development to a cycle of legends. The pretended Acts of Pilate were the framework which was made use of in which to group this order of ideas, with which were readily associated the better polemics against the Jews. It is only in the fourth century that the episodes, of an almost epic character, which were supposed to have taken place in the descent of Jesus to Hades, were put into writing. Later, these legends in regard to the subterranean life of Jesus were joined to the false Acts of Pilate, and formed the celebrated work called the Gospel of Nicodemus.

This base Christian literature, borrowed from a wholly popular state of mind, was in general the work of the Judaising and Gnostic sects. The disciples of St Paul had no part in them. It was created, to all appearances, in Syria. The apocryphal of Egyptian origin, The History of Joseph the Carpenter, for example, are more recent. Although of humble origin, and tainted with an ignorance truly sordid, the apocryphal Gospels assumed very early an importance of the first order. They pleased the multitude, offered rich themes for preaching on, enlarged considerably the circle of the evangelic personnel--St Anne, St Joachim, the Veronica, St Longinus--from that somewhat tainted source. The most beautiful Christian festivals--the Assumption, the Presentation of the Virgin--have no basis in the canonical Gospels; but they have in the apocryphas. The rich chasing of the legends which have made Christmas the jewel of the Christian year, is drawn for the most part from the apocryphas. The same literature has created the infant Jesus. The devotion to the Virgin finds there almost all its arguments. The importance of St Joseph proceeds entirely from them. Christian art finally owes to these compositions--very feeble, from a literary point of view, but singularly simple and plastic--some of its finest subjects. Christian iconography, whether Byzantine or Latin, has all its roots there. The Peregrine school would not have had any Sposalizio; the Venetian school no assumption, no presentation; the Byzantine school no descent of Jesus into limbo, without the apocryphas. The crib of Jesus without them would have lacked its most beautiful details. Their recommendation was their very inferiority. The canonical Gospels were too strong a literature for the people. Some vulgar narratives, often base, were nearer the level of the multitude than the Sermon on the Mount, or the discourses of the fourth Gospel.

So the success of these fraudulent writings was immense. From the fourth century the most instructed Greek fathers--Epiphanes, Gregory of Nyssa--adopted them without reserve. The Latin Church hesitated, even put forth efforts to take them out of the hands of the faithful, but did not succeed. The Golden Legend draws largely upon it. In the Middle Ages the apocryphal Gospels enjoyed an extraordinary popularity; they have even an advantage over the canonical Gospels, which is this: not being a sacred Scripture, they can be translated into the vulgar tongue. Whilst the Bible is in a manner put under lock and key, the apocryphas are in everybody's hands. The Miniaturists were ardently attached to them; the Rhymers seized upon them; the Mystics represented them dramatically in the porches of the Churches. The first modern author of a life of Jesus--Ludolphe le Chartreux--made them his principal document. Without theological pretension these popular Gospels have succeeded in suppressing, in a certain measure, the canonical Gospels; Protestantism also has declared war against them, and devotes itself to proving that they are the work of the devil.

# CHAPTER XXVII

### APOCRYPHAL ACTS AND APOCALYPSES

The literature of the false Acts pursues a line quite different from that of the false Gospels. The Acts of the Apostles, the individual work of Luke, were not produced, like the narrative of the life of Jesus, from the diversities of parallel compilations. Whilst the canonical Gospels served as a basis for the amplifications of the apocryphal Gospels, the apocryphal Acts have little connection with the Acts of Luke. The narratives of the preaching and of the death of Peter and Paul never received a final revision. Pseudo-Clement has used them as a literary pretext rather than a direct subject of narrative. The apostolic history was thus the roof of a romantic tissue which never assumed a definite literary form, and which people never cease revising. A sort of résumé of these fables, tainted with a strong Gnostic and Manichean colour, appeared under the name of a pretended Leucius or Lucius, a disciple of the apostles. The Catholics, who regretted that they could not make use of the book, sought to amend it. The final result of that successive emendation was the compilation made in the fifth or sixth centuries under the name of the false Abdias.

Almost all those who compiled this sort of works were heretics; but the orthodox, after subjecting them to corrections, soon adopted them. These heretics were very pious people, and at the same time highly imaginative. After they had been anathematised, their books were found to be edifying, and the Churches did their very best to have them introduced into their religious readings. It is in this way that many of the books, many of the saints, many of the festivals of the orthodox Church are the productions of heretics. The fourth Gospel was in this respect one of the most striking examples. This singular book made its way amazingly. It was read more and more, and, apart from the Churches of Asia, which were too well acquainted with its origin, it was accepted on all hands with admiration, and as being the work of the Apostle John.

The false Acts of the Apostles have no more originality than the apocryphal Gospels. In this order, similarly, the individual fancy did not succeed much better in making itself felt. This was plainly visible in that which concerned the legend of Paul. A priest of Asia, a greet admirer of the apostle, thought to satisfy his piety by constructing a short charming romance in which Paul converted a beautiful young girl of Iconium, named Hecla, who was drawn to him by an invincible attraction, and made of her a martyr of virginity. The priest did not conceal his game well; he was questioned, nonplussed, and finished by avowing that he had done all this out of love for Paul. The book succeeded none the lees for this, and it was only banished from the Canon with the other apocryphal writings about the fifth or sixth centuries.

St Thomas, the apostle preferred by Gnostics, and later, by the Manicheans, inspired in the same way acts in which the horror of certain sects for marriage is set forth with the utmost energy. Thomas arrived in India while the nuptials of the daughter of the king were in preparation. He so strongly persuaded the fiancés as to the inexpediency of marriage, the wicked sentiments which result from the fact of having begotten children, the crimes which are the consequence of esprit de famille, and the troubles of housekeeping, that they passed the night seated by the side of one another. On the morrow their relations were astonished at finding them in this position, full of a sweet gaiety, and free from any of the ordinary embarrassments incident to such circumstances. The young couple explain to them that bashfulness has no longer any meaning for them, since the cause of it has disappeared. They have exchanged the transient nuptials for the joys of a never-ending paradise. The strange hallucinations to which these moral errors gave scope, are all vividly depicted throughout the entire book. The first outline of a Christian hell, with its categories of torments, is found traced there. This singular writing, which constituted a part of certain Bibles, recalls the theology of the pseudo-Clementine romance, and that of the Elkasaites. In it the Holy Ghost is, like as with the Nazarenes a feminine principle, the mother misericordiæ.' Water represents the purifying element of the soul and of the body; the unction of oil is then the seal of baptism, like as with the Gnostics. The sign of the cross already possesses all its supernatural virtues, as well as a sort of magic.

The Acts of St Philip have also a theosophic colouring, and a very pronounced Gnosticism. Those of Andrew were one of the parts of the compilation of the pretended Leucius, who merits the most anathemas. The orthodox Church was at first a stranger to these fables; then she adopted them, at least for popular use. Iconography especially found in them, as in the apocryphal Gospels, an ample repository of subjects and of symbols. Almost all the attributes which have been made use of by imaginative writers to distinguish the apostles, comes from the apocryphal Acts.

The apocalyptic form served also to express how much there existed in the heterodox Christian sects of insubordination, of unruliness, and of dissatisfaction. An ascension or anabaticon of Paul, which set forth the mysteries that Paul was reputed to have seen in his ecstasy, was in great vogue. An apocalypse of Elias enjoyed considerable popularity. It was amongst the Gnostics in particular that the apocalypses, under the name of apostles and prophets, germinated. The faithful were on their guard, and the moderate Church party, who at once feared the Gnostic excesses and the excesses of the pious, admitted only two apocalypses--that of John and of Peter. Nevertheless, writings of the same kind, attributed to Joseph, Moses, Abraham, Habakkuk, Zephaniah, Ezekiel, Daniel, Zacharias, and the father of John, were in circulation. Two zealous Christians, preoccupied with the substitution of a new world for an old world, excited by their persecutions, greedy, like all the fabricators of apocalypses, of the evil news which came from the four corners of the earth, took up the mantle of Esdras, and wrote under that revered name a number of new pages, which were joined to those which the pseudo-Esdras of 97 had already accepted. It has also been thought that the apocalyptic books attributed to Enoch received in the second century some Christian additions. But this appears to us little probable; those books of Enoch, formerly so esteemed, and which Jesus had probably read with enthusiasm, had fallen, at the time of which we now speak, into universal discredit.

The Gnostics, in like manner, could show psalms, pieces of apocryphal prophets, revelations under the name of Adam, Seth, Noria, the imaginary wife of Noah, recitals of the nativity of Mary, full of improprieties, and great and small interrogations of Mary. Their gospel of Eve was a tissue of chimerical equivocations. Their Gospel of Philip presented a dangerous quietism, clothed in a form borrowed from Egyptian rituals. The ascension or anabaticon of Isaiah was made up of the same stuff, in the third century, and was a true source of heresies. The Archonties, the Hieracities, the Messalians, proceeded from that. Like the author of the Acts of Thomas, the author of the Ascension of Isaiah is one of the precursors of Dante, by the complaisance with which he expatiates upon the description of heaven and hell. This singular work, adopted by the sects of the Middle Ages, was the cherished book of the Hogomites of Thrace and of the Cathares of the West.

Adam had likewise his apocryphal revelations. A testament addressed to Seth, a mystic apocalypse borrowed from Zoroastrian ideas, circulated under his name. It is a clever enough book, which recalls many of the Jeschts, Sadies, and Sirouzé of the Persians, and also at times the books of the Mendaites. Adam therein explains to Seth, from his recollections of Paradise and the signs of the angel Uriel, the mystic liturgies of day and night which all creatures celebrate from hour to hour before the Eternal. The first hour of the night is the hour of the adoration of demons; during that hour they cease to annoy man. The second hour is the hour of the adoration of fish; then comes the adoration of abysses; then the thrice holy of the seraphim: before the Fall men heard at that hour the measured beating of their wings. At the fifth hour of the night the adoration of the waters takes place. Adam at that hour heard the prayer of the great billows. The middle of the night is marked by an accumulation of storms, and by a great religious terror. Then all nature reposes, and the waters sleep. At this hour, if one takes water, and if the priest of God mixes it with holy oil and anoints with this oil the sick who cannot sleep, the latter are cured. At the time the dew falls, the hymn of herbs and grain is sung. At the tenth hour, at the full early dawn, comes the turn of men, the gates of heaven are opened, so as to let enter the prayers of all living beings. They enter, prostrate themselves before the throne, then depart. Everything that one asks at the moment when the seraphim are beating their wings and when the cock crows, one is sure to obtain. Great joy is shed over the world when the sun shines forth from the paradise of God upon creation. Then comes an hour of expectation and of profound silence, until the priests have offered incense to God.

At each hour of the day the angels, the birds, every creature, rises up in like manner to adore the Supreme Being. At the seventh hour there is a repetition of the ceremony of entering and retiring. The prayers (Priéres) of all living beings enter, prostrate themselves, and walked out again. At the tenth hour the inspection of the waters takes place. The Holy Spirits descends over the waters and springs. Without this, in drinking the water, one would be subject to the malignity of the demons. At this hour again water mixed with oil cures all manner of sickness. This naturalism, which recalls that of the Elkasaites, was attenuated by the Catholic Church, but the principle it contained was not entirely rejected. The exorcisms of water and of the different elements, the division of the day into canonical hours, the employment of holy oils, conserved by the orthodox Church, had their origin in ideas analogous to those which the Adamite Apocalypse has complaisantly developed.

The Christian Sibyl women do little more than repeat without comprehending the ancient oracles. Those of the Apocalypse, in particular, she never ceases vatianating, though, and announcing the near destruction of the Roman Empire. The favourite idea at that epoch was that the world, before it came to an end, would be governed by a woman. The sympathy of the old sibyllists for Judaism and Jerusalem is now changed to hatred; but the horror for the Pagan civilisation is no less. The domination of Italy over the world has been the most fatal of all dominations: it will be the last. The end is near. Wickedness springs from the rich and the great, who plunder the poor. Rome is to be burned; wolves and foxes are to live amongst its ruins; it will be seen whether her gods of brass will save her. Hadrian, when the Sibyllists of the year 117 saluted with so much expectation, was an iniquitous and avarcious king, a despoiler of the entire world, wholly occupied with frivolous devices, an enemy of true religion, the sacreligious instituter of an infamous cult, the abettor of the most abominable idolatry, Like the sibyllists of 117, he of whom we have been speaking asserts that Hadrian could have but three successors. Their names (Antonine) recall that of the Most High (Adonai). The first of the three will reign a long time, and this evidently refers to Antoninus Pius. This prince, in reality so admirable, is treated as a miserable king, who out of pure avarice despoiled the world and heaped up at Rome treasures which the terrible exile, the assassin of his mother (Nero, the Antichrist), will abandon to the pillage of the peoples of Asia.

Oh! how thou shalt weep then, despoiled of thy brilliant garments and clad in habits of mourning, O proud queen, daughter of old Latinus! Thou shalt fall, no more to rise again. The glory of thy legions, with their proud eagles, will disappear. Where will be thy strength! what people will be allied to thee, of those whom thou hast overcome by thy follies.

Every plague, civil war, invasion, and famine announces the revenge that God prepares on behalf of his elect. It is towards Italy especially that the judge will show himself severe. Italy will be reduced to a pile of black volcanic cinders, mixed with naphtha and asphalte. Hades will be its portion. Then finally equality will exist for all; no longer will there be either slaves or masters, or kings, or chiefs, or advocates, or corrupt judges. Rome will endure the ills she has inflicted on others: those whom she has vanquished will triumph in their turn over her. That will take place in the year in which the figures cast up will correspond to the numerical value of the name of Rome, that is to say, in the year of Rome 948 (195 of J. C.).

The author calls this the day which he longs for. He employs epic accents to celebrate Nero, the Antichrist, preparing in the shades or beyond the seas the ruin of the Roman world. The contests between the Antichrist and the Messiah will come to pass. Men, far from becoming better, will only grow more wicked. The Antichrist is to be finally vanquished, and shut up in the abyss. The resurrection and the eternal happiness of the just will crown the apocalyptic cycle. Attached to the initials of the verses which express these terrible images, the eye distinguishes the acrostic ΙΗΣΟΥΣ ΧΡΙΣΤΟΣ ΘΕΟΥ ΥΙΟ ΩΓΗΡ ΣΤΑΥΔΟΣ; the initial letters of the first five words give in their turn ΙΧΘΥΕ "fish," a designation under which the initiated were early accustomed to recognise Jesus. As people were persuaded that the acrostic was one of the processes which the old sibyls had employed to make known their secret meaning, people were struck with astonishment to see so clear a revelation of Christianity delineated upon the margins of a writing that was thought to have been composed in the sixth generation which followed the deluge. There was an old translation of this singular production in barbarous Latin verse, which gave rise to another fable. It was pretended that Cicero had found his Erythrean fragment so beautiful that he had translated it into Latin verse before the birth of Jesus Christ.

Such were the sombre images which, under the best of sovereigns, assailed the sectarian fanatics. We must not blame the Roman police for treating such books at times with severity; they were now puerile, then full of menaces: no modern state would tolerate their like. The visionaries dreamed only of conflagrations. The idea of a deluge of fire, in contradistinction to the deluge of water, and distinct from the final conflagration, was accepted by many amongst them. There was also a talk about a deluge of wind. These chimeras troubled more than one head, even outside of Christianity. Under Marcus Aurelius an impostor attempted, in making use of the same species of terrors, to provoke disorders which might have led to the pillage of the city. It is not wise to repeat too often Judicare seculum per ignem. People are subject to strange hallucinations. When the tragic scenes which he imagined were slow in coming, he sometimes took upon himself to realise them. At Paris the people formed the Commune because the fifth act of the siege, which had been promised, did not come to pass.

The Antichrist continued to be the great preoccupation of the makers of apocalypses. Although it was evident that Nero was dead, his shadow haunted the Christian imagination -- people continued to announce his return. Often, however, it was not Nero that people saw behind this fantastic personage; it was Simon Magus.

From Sebaste was to issue Belial, who commands the high mountains, the sea, the blazing sun, the brilliant moon, the dead themselves, and who was to perform numerous miracles before men. It is not integrity, but error which will be in him. He will lead astray many mortals, both of the Hebrew faithful and of the elect, and others belonging to the lawless race who have not yet heard tell of God. But whilst the threats of the great God are being put into execution, and whilst the conflagration will roll over the earth in huge floods, fire will also devour Belial and the insolent men who have put their faith in him.

We have been struck, in the Apocalypse, with this mysterious personage of the False Prophet, a thaumaturgic seducer of the faithful and the Pagans, allied to Nero, who follows him to the region of the Parthians, who must reappear and perish with him in the lake of brimstone. We are led to surmise that this symbolical personage designates Simon Magus. In seeing in the Sibylline Apocalypse "Belial of Sebaste" playing an almost identical part, we are confirmed in that hypothesis. The personal relations of Nero and Simon Magus are perhaps not no fabulous as they appear. In any case, this association of the two worst enemies that nascent Christianity had encountered, was well adapted to the spirit of the times, and to the taste for apocalyptical poetry in general. In the Ascension of Isaiah Belial is Satan, and Satan assumes in some sort the human form of a king, the murderer of his mother, who is to reign over the world, in order to establish the empire of evil. The author of the pseudo-Clemen tine romance believes that Simon will reappear as Antichrist at the end of time. In the third century a still greater trouble was introduced into that order of fantastic ideas. People distinguished two Antichrists, the one for the East, the other for the West--Nero and Belial. Later, Nero finished by becoming, in the eyes of the Christians, the Christ of the Jews. The suppulations of the works of Daniel came to complicate these chimeras. St Hippolytus, in the time of Severus, is wholly engrossed with them. A certain Juda proved by Daniel that the end of the world was to come about the year 10 of Septimus Severus (of J. C. 202-203). Every persecution appeared to be a confirmation of the dismal prophecies which had accumulated. From all these confused data, the Middle Ages drew the grandiose myth which remains, amidst transformed Christianity, as an incomprehensible relic of primitive Messianism.

# APPENDIX I

It is admitted pretty generally that the Jewish war under Hadrian entailed a siege and a final destruction of Jerusalem. So large a number of texts represent this view, that it at the first glance rash to call the fact in question. Nevertheless, the chief critics who have considered it--Scaliger, Henry de Valois, and P. Pazi--had perceived the difficulties of such an assertion, and rejected it.

And to commence with, what is it that Hadrian should have besieged and destroyed? The demolition of Jerusalem under Titus was entire, even exceeding that usual to military operations.

In admitting that a population of so many thousands of persons was able to dwell within the ruins which the victor of 70 left behind, it is clear in such a case that this heap of ruins was incapable of supporting a siege. Even while admitting that from the time of Titus to Hadrian some timid attempts of Jewish restoration might have been brought about, in spite of the "Legio Xa. Fratensis" who encamped on the ruins, one is not inclined to suppose that these attempts were of such a nature as to give the place any importance whatever in a military point of view.

It is also very true that a great many savants, with whose opinions we coincide, think that the restoration of Jerusalem, under the name of "Ælie Capitolina," began in the year 122 or thereabouts.

It is of no use to the adversaries of our theme to lay great stress on that argument, because they unhesitatingly admit that Ælia Capitolina was not commenced to be built till after the last destruction of Jerusalem by Hadrian. But no matter! If, as we think, Ælia Capitolina had been in existence for about ten years at the time that the revolt of Bar-Coziba broke out, about 133, how can one conceive that the Romans would have had occasion to take it! Ælia would not again have possessed walls capable of sustaining a siege. How, moreover, suppose that the "Legio Xa. Fratensis" had left their positions knowing that it would be obliged to reconquer them. It may be said that the same thing occurred under Nero, when Gessius Florus abandoned Jerusalem, but the situation was totally different.

Gessius Florus found himself in the midst of a great city in revolution. The "Legio Xa. Fratensis" was situated in the midst of a population of veterans and squatters, all friendly to the Roman cause. Their retreat would not have explained itself in any fashion, and the siege which would have followed would have been a siege in a manner without purpose.

When one examines the texts, very scarce, which relate to the War of Hadrian, it is necessary to make a large distinction. The texts really historical not only do not speak of a capture and a destruction of Jerusalem, but by the style in which they are couched, they exclude such an event.

The oratorical and apologetic texts, on the contrary, where the second revolt of the Jews is cited, "non ad narrandum, sed ad probandum," for the purpose of serving the arguments and the declamations of the preacher or of the polemic, imply that all the events that happened under Hadrian were as if they happened under Titus. It is clear that it is the first series of texts that deserves the preference. Criticism has for a long time refused to trust to the precision of documents drawn up in a style whose essence is to be inaccurate.

The historical texts reduce themselves unhappily into two in the question which concerns us, but both are excellent. There is, to commence with, the narrative of Dion Caasius, who appeared not to have been here abridged by Xiphilin; there is in the second place, that of Eusebius, who copied Ariston de Pella, a contemporary writer of events, and living close at hand to the seat of the war. These two narratives are in accord with one another. They do not speak a single word of a siege, nor of a destruction of Jerusalem. For an attentive reader of the two tales cannot admit that such a fact would have passed unnoticed. Dion Cassius is very particular; he knows that it was the construction of Ælia Capitolina which occasioned the revolt; he gives well the character of the war, which happened to be a war of little cities, of fortified market towns, of subterranean works--or rural war, if one is permitted thus to express oneself.

He insists on facts so secondary as that of the ruin of the pretended tomb of Solomon. How is it possible that he could have neglected to speak of the catastrophe of the principal city?

The omission of all notice about Jerusalem is still less understood in the narrative of Eusebius or rather of Ariston de Pella. The great event of the war for Eusebius is the siege of Bether, "the neighbouring town to Jerusalem;" of Jerusalem itself not a word. It is true that the chapter of the "Historie Ecclesiastique" relative to that event has for the title: Ἡ κατὰ Ἀνδριανὸν ὑστάτη Ἰουδαίων πολιορχίας, as the chapter relative to the war of Vespasian; and of Titus has for title (I. III. C.V.) Peri tes meta ton Christon hustates Ioudaion πολιορχίας; but the word adapts itself well to the whole of the campaign of Julius Severus, which consisted in sieges of little cities. In section 3 of the chapter relative to the war of Adrian, the word πολιορχία is used to designate the operations of the capture of Bether.

In his "Chronique" Eusebius follows the same plan. In his "Demonstration Evangélique," and in his "Theophaive," on the contrary, he points to that fact, and when he is no longer borne out by the very words of Ariston de Pella, he allows himself to be led away by the resemblance which has deranged nearly all the Jewish and Christian tradition. He pictures the events of the year 135 on the model of the events of the year 70, and he speaks of Hadrian as having contributed with Titus to the accomplishment of the prophecies on the annihilation of Jerusalem. This double destruction doubly serves him to realise a passage of Zacharias, [2] and to furnish a basis for the theory which he advances of a Church of Jerusalem lasting from Titus to Hadrian. [3] St Jerome presents the same contradiction. In his "Chronique," mapped out on that of Eusebius, he follows Eusebius as an historian. Then he forgets that solid base, and speaks, as do all the fathers of the orator school, of the siege and destruction of Jerusalem under Hadrian. [4] Tertullian [5] and St John Chrysostom [6] express themselves in the same way. One knows how dangerous it is to introduce into history these vague phrases, well known to preachers and to apologists of all times. Still less is it necessary that we should examine the passages in the Talmud where the same assertion presents itself, mixed up with those historical monstrosities which destroy the value of the mentioned passages. In the Talmud the confusion of the war of Titus and that which took place under Hadrian is constant. The description of Bether is copied from that of Jerusalem-- the duration of the siege is the same.

Is not this the proof that he had not separate mementoes of a new siege of Jerusalem, for the good reason that there had not been one. When the tale was started of a siege by a sort of argument a priori, it is possible that one a posteriori should be started also to give it in history a basis which it had not. Naturally, for it is on the first siege on which one falls back for that. That confusion has been the trap where the whole popular history of the Jewish mishaps has suffered itself to be taken. How can we prefer such blunders to strong arguments which, drawn from solitary historical evidence, we now have in the question Dion Cassibus or Ariston de Pella?

Two grave objections remain for me to solve: only can they smooth away the doubts on the theory which I maintain. The first is derived from a passage of Appius. This historian, enumerating the successive destructions which overthrew the walls of Jerusalem, puts one before the other, and on the same line the destruction of Titus and that of Hadrian.

The passage of Appius furnishes in every case a strong inaccuracy--he supposes that Jerusalem was walled under Hadrian. Appius foolishly supposes that the Jews, after Titus, re-erected their town, and fortified it. His ignorance on that point shows that he is not guided by the aforesaid comparison, but by the coarser similarity which has deceived every one. The difficulties of the campaign, the numberless πολιορχίαι of which it is full, show that even a contemporary who had not proof of the facts was able to commit a like error.

Assuredly more grave is the objection derived from the study of the old coins. It is certain that the Jews during the revolt did not coin nor stamp money. Such an operation seems at the first glance not to have been possible at Jerusalem. The types of these moneys lead to that idea. The "legend" is most often, "For the liberation of Jerusalem;" on some others, the figure of a temple surmounted by a star.

Jewish coin study is full of uncertainties, and it is dangerous to oppose it to history; it is history, on the contrary, which serves to throw a light upon it. Besides, the objection about which we speak has emboldened certain numismatic students of our days to deny absolutely the occupation of Jerusalem by the followers of Bar-Coziba. One will admit that the insurgents were able to coin money at Bether quite as well as at Jerusalem, if one thinks of the miserable plight in which in that supposition Jerusalem was. On the other hand, it seems that the types of coins of the second revolt had been imitated or taken directly from those of the first revolt, and on those of the Asmoneans. There is here an important point which deserves the attention of numismatists; for one could find here a means of solving the difficulties which yet hover over the entire groups of the autonomous coinage of Israel.

We wish to speak chiefly of the coins with the "impression" of Simeon Nasi of Israel. We fall into the greatest misrepresentation when we seek to find this Simeon in Bargioras, in Bar-Coziba, in Simeon, son of Gamaliel, etc. None of these persons could coin money. They were revolutionaries, or men of high authority, but not sovereigns. If one or the other had placed his name on the money, he would have marred the republican spirit and jealousy of the rebels, and so, up to a certain point, their religious ideas.

A similar matter would be mentioned by Josephus in the first revolt, and the identity of that Simeon would not be so doubtful as this is. It is never asked if the French Revolution had any coins with the effigy of Marat, or of Robespierre. This Simon, I believe, is no other than Simon Maccabeus, the first Jewish sovereign who coined money, and whose coins ought to be much sought after by orthodox persons. As the aim which they established was to overcome the scruples of the religious, such a counterfeit would suffice for the exigencies of the time. It had also the advantage of not putting into circulation only those types acknowledged by all. I think then, that neither in the first nor in the second revolt, that they had money struck in the name of a person then alive. The "Eleaser-Hac-Cohen" of certain coins ought probably to explain this in an analogous manner, which the numismatists will hit upon. I strongly think that the latter revolt had not a proper stamp, and they could best imitate the earlier ones. A material circumstance confirms that hypothesis. On the coins in question, in fact, one never sees שמעון--one frequently sees שנעש or שמצ. These two forms are so frequent that one can see a simple fault as to the position of the letters. In the second, in a great many cases, we cannot help thinking that the last two letters have disappeared. It is not impossible that the alteration of the name of Simeon was made expressly to imply a prayer,--"Hear me" or "Hear us." It is, at all events, contrary to all probability that one sees in the name of Simeon the true name of Bar-Coziba. How is it that this royal name of the false Messiah, written on an abundant coinage, would remain unknown to St Justin, to Aristion de Pella, to the Talmudists, who clearly speak of the money of Bar-Coziba. Still less can on see any president of the Sanhedrim whose authority would have been recognised by Bar-Coziba.

So anyway, one is led to think that the coinage of Bar-Coziba did not consist but in impressions done from a religious motive, and that the types which bear these impressions were of the ancient Jewish types, which I conclude were for the rebellion of the time of Hadrian. By this are raised some enormous difficulties which the Jewish numismatism presents:--Firstly. That these persons unknown to history or these rebels should have coined money like sovereigns. Secondly, The unlikelihood that there is that these miserable insurgents caused issues of money so handsome and so considerable. Thirdly, The employment of the archaic Hebrew character, which was out of use in the second century of our era. Supposing that it had been attempted to bring back the national character, they would not have given them fashioned so grand and handsome. Fourthly, The form of the temple tetrastyle surmounted by a star. This form does not correspond either more or less to that of the temple of Herod. For one knows the scrupulous nicety that the ancient masters took to reproduce the features of the principal temple of the city exactly, by slight but very expressive touches.

The temple of the Jewish money, on the contrary, without the triangular pediment, and with its gate of a singular fashion, represents the second temple, that of the time of the Maccabees, which appears to have been tolerably shabby. If we reject that hypothesis, and which must belong to the second revolt, the types which bear the figure of the temple, and the era of "the liberation of Jerusalem," we say that the deliverance of Jerusalem, and the reconstruction of the temple, were the only object of the revolts. It is not impossible that they portrayed these two events upon their money before they were realised. One takes for a fact that which one aspires to with such efforts. Bether, before all, was a sort of provisionary Jerusalem, a sacred asylum of Israel.

The numismatism of the Crusades presents, besides, identically the same phenomena. After the loss of Jerusalem, in fact, the later authority, transported to St Jean de Acre, continued to mint money bearing the effigy of the Holy Sepulchre, with the words "+Sepulchri Domini," or "REX IERLM." The moneys of John of Brienne, who never possessed Jerusalem, present, also the image of the Holy Sepulchre. "This markedly characteristic type," says M. de Vogüé, "seems to be on the part of deposed kings a protestation against the invasion, and a maintenance of their rights in misfortune and exile." There are also moneys with the title Tvrris Davit, struck a long time after the taking of Jerusalem by the Mussulman. It must be admitted, however, that much of the Jewish money of the second revolt was struck away from Jerusalem. Every one, in fact, agrees that if the revolted were masters of Jerusalem, they were quickly driven out. One finds coins of the second and third year of the revolt. M. Caxdoni explained by this difference of the situation, the difference of the legends ysr'l lchrvt, and סלשורי תורחל, the second only answering to the epoch when the rebels were masters of Jerusalem.

Be that as it may, the possibility of a coinage struck at Bether is placed beyond doubt.

That at one moment of the revolt, and amidst the numberless incidents of a war which occupied two or three years, the revolted occupied Ælia, and were speedily driven out; that the occupation of Jerusalem, in a word, was a brief episode of the aforesaid war, is strictly possible; it is little probable nevertheless.

The "Legio Xa. Fratensis" which Titus left to guard the ruin, was there in the second and in the third century, and even to the time of the Lower Empire, as if nothing had happened in the interval. If the insurgents had been for a day masters of the sacred space, they would have clung to it with fury, they would have come running there from all directions; all the fighting men of Judea would above all bend their steps there; the height of the war would have been there; the temple would have been restored; the religion re-established; there would have been fought the last battle; and as in 70 the fanatics would have caused a general slaughter on the ruins of the temple, or, failing them, on its site. Now it is nothing of the sort. The grand siege operation took place at Bether, nigh to Jerusalem; no trace of the scuffle on the site of the temple in the Jewish tradition, not a memento of a fourth temple, nor of a return to the religious ceremonials.

It seems certain, then, that under Hadrian Jerusalem did not suffer a serious siege, did not undergo a fresh destruction.

How could it be destroyed, I again repeat?

On the supposition that Ælia did not begin to exist until 136, after the end of the war, how could one destroy a heap of ruins?

On the supposition that there was an Alia, dated either 122 or a little after, one would destroy the beginnings of a new city which the Romans would substitute for the old one. What good would such a destruction effect, seeing that, far from relinquishing the idea of a new Jerusalem as irreverent, the Romans resume that idea from that time with more vigour than ever? What has been carelessly repeated about the plough which the Romans had passed over the soil of the temple and city, has no other foundations than the false Jewish traditions, referred to by the Talmud and St Jerome, wherein Terentius Rufus, who was charged by Titus to demolish Jerusalem, has been confounded by Tinlius Rufus, the imperial legate of the time of Hadrian. Here again the error has arisen from the historical delusion which has transferred to the war of Hadrian, which one knows is a trifle, the circumstances much better known of the war of Titus. It has often been attempted to find in the two bulls which are on the reverse of the medal of the foundation of Ælia Capitolina, a representation of a "Templum Aratum." These two bulls are simply a colonial emblem, and they represent the earnest hopes which the new "Coloni " entertained for the agriculture of Judea.

Footnotes:

2. Zach. xiv. 1 et seq.
3. Euseb. H.E., iv. 5.
4. In Dan. xiv., Joel i., Habakkuk ii., Jerem. xxxi., Ezekiel v. 24., Zach. viii. 14.
5. Contra, Jud. 13.
6. In Judæos, Homil. v. 2. Opp. 1, pp. 64-5 (Montf.) Cf. Seudas at the word βδελυγμα; Chronique d'Alex, year 119.

# APPENDIX II

The epoch when the book of Tobit was composed is very difficult to fix. In our time, the distinguished critics M. M. Hitzig, Volkmar Grætz, have ascribed that writing to the time of Trajan or of Hadrian. M. Grætz connects it with the circumstances which followed the war of Bar-Coziba, and in particular to the interdiction which according to him was made by the Romans as to the interment of the corpses of the massacred Jews. But besides the fact of a similar interdiction is not founded except upon that of passages of the Talmud stripped of serious historical value, the characteristic importance attributed in our book to the good work of interring the dead, explained itself in a manner much more profound, as we are just now going to show.

Three great reasons, in our opinion, preclude us from accepting the Book of Tobit as being at a date so early,--forbid us to descend, at least for the composition of the book, beyond the year 70.

Firstly, The prophecy of Tobit (xiii. 9 et seq., xiv. 4 et seq.), which ought naturally to be taken as a "prophetia post eventum," clearly mentions the destruction of Jerusalem by Nabuchodnosor (xiv. 4); the return of Zerubabel; the construction of the second temple, a temple very little to be compared to the first, very unworthy of the divine majesty (xiv. 5). But the dispersion of Israel would have its end, and again the temple would be rebuilt, with all the magnificence described by the prophets, to serve as a centre for the religion of the whole world.

For the old prophet there was no destruction of the second temple; that temple would be the advent of the glory of Israel, would not disappear, except to give place to the eternal temple. M. Volkmar, M. Hitzig observe, it is true, that in the Fourth Book of Esdras, in Judith, and in much of the apocryphal book, the destruction of the temple by Nabuchodnosor is identified with the destruction of the temple by Titus, and that the reflections which are placed in the mouth of the fictitious prophet are those which happen after the year 70.

But this opinion, besides being of such secondary application, is not here admissible. Evidently the verse 5 xiv. refers to the second temple. The remark that the new temple was very different from the first--for it was anything but majestic--is an allusion to Esd. iii. 12, told in the style of Josephus, Ant. xi. iv. 2. Still more this important passage would lead one to think that at the time when the Book of Tobit was written, Herod had not as yet put forth his hand on the second temple in order that he might rebuild it, an event which took place the 19th year before J.C.

The critics whom I now am fighting apply here the system, getting greatly into fashion, which seeks to base upon a passage of the pseudo Epistle of Barnabas, and according to whom there had been under the reign of Hadrian, a commencement of the rebuilding of the temple undertaken by consent with the Jews. It is to this reconstruction that may apply the passage of Tobit xiv. 5. But I have shown elsewhere that the interpretation of the false passage of Barnabas is wrong.

Were it true, it would be singular that an abortive attempt, which would not be without interruption, should become thus the base of the whole apocalyptic system.

Secondly, the verse xiv. 10 furnishes another proof of the composition, relatively old, of the Book of Tobit. "My Son, see what Aman did to Ahkiakar, who had nourished him, how he cast him from the light into darkness, and how he repaid him; but Ahkiakar was saved and Aman received the chastisement that he deserved; Manasse likewise gave him alms, and was saved from the deadly snare which Aman had spread for him; Aman fell into the snare and perished." This Ahkiakar was a nephew of Tobit's father, who figures in the book as the steward and maitre d'hotel of Esarhaddow. The part he plays is incidental and peculiar.

The fashion in which he is spoken of, seems to show that he was known by some other means.

The verse we are quoting does not explain this, unless one admits, parallelly to the Book of Tobit, another book where an infidel, called Aman, who had for foster-father a good Jew named Ahkiakar, that he repaid him with ingratitude and thrust him into prison, but Ahkiakar was saved and Aman was punished.

This Aman was evidently, in the Jewish romances, the man who played the part of offering to others snares into which he himself fell, seeing that in the tales to which Tobit made allusion, the same Aman suffered the fate which he intended a certain Manasses to undergo. Impossible, in my opinion, not to see here a parallel of the Haman of the Book of Esther hung from the gallows where he hoped to hang Mordecai, foster-father of Esther.

In a book composed in the year 100 or 135 of our time, all this is inconceivable. One must refer it to a time and to a Jewish society where the Book of Esther would exist under an entirely different form than that of our Bibles, and where the part of Mordecai was played by a certain Ahkiakar, also a servant of the king.

Now the Book of Esther certainly existed, just as we have it, in the first century of our era, since Josephus knows of its being interpolated.

Thirdly, an objection none the less grave against the method of M. Grætz is that, if the Book of Tobit was posterior to the defeat of Bar-Coziba, the Christians would not have adopted it. In the interval between Titus and Hadrian, the religious brotherhood of the Jews and the Christians is sufficient to account for the fact that books newly brought to light in the Jewish community, such as that of Judith, the apocalypse of Esdras, and that of Baruch, would pass without difficulty from the synagogue to the Church. After the intestine broils which accompanied the war of Bar-Coziba, there would be no room for this. The Jewish and Christian faiths are henceforth two enemies; nothing passed from one side to the other of the gulf which divide them. Besides, the synagogue really no longer created such books, calm, idyllic, without bigotry, without hate.

After 135, Judaism produces the Talmud, a piece of dry and violent casuistry. The religious views are all profane, and of Persian origin, as that of the healing of demoniacs and of the blind by the viscera of fishes. This moderation of the marvellous, in consequence of which the two are cured, without miracle, by the prescriptions whereof those privileged of God have the secret, all this does not belong to the second century after J. C.

The condition of the people at the time when our author wrote, was comparatively happy and tranquil, at least in the country where he composed it. The Jews appeared wealthy, they were in domestic service under the nobles, acting as go-betweens in all purchases, and occupying places of confidence, being employed as stewards, major-domos, butlers, as we see in the Books of Esther and of Nehemiah. In place of being troubled by the rain, dreams, and passions which engrossed every Jew at the end of the first century of our era, the conscience of the author is serene in a high degree. He is not exactly a Messianist. He believes in a wonderful future for Jerusalem, but without any miracle from heaven, or Messiah as king. The book then is, in our opinion, anterior to the second century of our era. By the pious sentiment which there reigns, it is far behind the Book of Esther, a book from which all religion sentiment is totally absent. It might be imagined that Egypt was the spot where such a romance could possibly have been composed, if the certainty that the original text was written in Hebrew had not created a difficulty. The Jews of Egypt did not write in that language. I do not think, however, that the book was composed at Jerusalem or in Judea. What the author intends is to cheer up the provincial Jew, who has a horror of schism, and abides in communion with Jerusalem.

The Persian ideas which fill the book, the intimate acquaintance which the author possesses of the great cities of the East, although he makes strange mistakes as to the distances, bring one to imagine that he is in Mesopotamia, particularly at Adiabene, where the Jews were in a very flourishing condition in the middle of the fast century of our era.

In supposing that the book was thus composed about the year 50 in Upper Syria, one can, it seems to me, satisfy the exigencies of the problem. The state of the usages and of the ideas of the Jews; above all, that which concerns the bread of the Gentiles, recalls the time which preceded the revolt under Nero. The description of the eternal Jerusalem seems based upon the Apocalypse (ch. xxi.), not that one of the authors had copied from the other, but that they drew from a source of mutual imaginations. The demonology, especially the circumstance of the devil bound in the deserts of Upper Egypt, recall the Evangelist Mark. Lastly, The form of the personal memoirs, which the Greek text presents, at least in the opening pages, makes one think of the Book of Nehemiah: that form was no longer in use in the apocryphas posterior to the year 70. The inductions which lead one to assign the date of the composition to an anterior date, inductions which we have not dissembled, are demolished by the considerations which prevent us, on the other side, attributing to the book a great antiquity. One important fact, indeed, is that one does not find, neither amongst the Jews nor the Christians, any mention of the Book of Tobit before the end of the second century. Now it is necessary to confess that if the Christians of the first and second century possessed the book, they would have found it in perfect harmony with their sentiments. Let it be Clement Romain, for example; certainly if he had had such a writing at hand, he would have quoted it, just as he quotes the Book of Judith. If the book had been anterior to Jesus Christ, one cannot comprehend that it would have remained in such obscurity.

On the contrary, if one admits that it was composed in Oschoene in Adialene a few years before the grand catastrophes of Judea, one may suppose that the Jews engaged in the struggle would have had knowledge of it. The book was not yet translated into Greek: the greater part of the Christians could not read it. Lymmachus or Theodosius would have been found in possession of the original, and they would have translated it. In that case, the fortunes of the book amongst the Christians would be commenced.

One leading element of the question, which has not been used here by the interpreters, are the analogies which a sagacious criticism has discovered between the Jewish narrative and that collection of tales which have gone round the world, without distinction of language or race. Studied from this point of view, the Book of Tobit seems to us like the Hebrew and godly version of a tale which is related in Armenia, in Russia, amongst the Tartars, and the Higanes, and which is probably of Babylonian origin. A traveller finds in the roadway the corpse of a man which had been refused sepulture because he had not paid his debts. He stopped to bury him. Soon afterwards, a companion, clothed in white, offers to journey with him. This companion gets the traveller out of a bad scrape, procures riches for him, and a charming wife, who wrests him away from the evil spirits. At the moment of parting, the traveller offers him the half of all that which he had gained, thanks to him, save and except his wife, and naturally so. The companion demands his half share of the woman: great perplexity arises! At the moment when he is about to proceed to make that strange division, the companion reveals himself--he is the ghost of the dead man whom the traveller had buried.

No doubt that the Book of Tobit is an adaptation according to Jewish ideas of that old narrative, popular throughout the whole of the East. It is this that explains the fantastical importance assigned to the burial of the dead, which constitutes a remarkable feature of our book. Nowhere else in the Jewish literature is the burial of the dead placed on the same footing as that of the observance of the Law. The resemblance to the tales of the East confirms thus our hypothesis concerning the Mesopotamian origin of the book. The Jews of Palestine did not listen to these pagan tales. Those of Oschoene would be more open to the talk of those outside them. We most add that the Book of Esther could not have existed in that country in the form which it was known in Judea: this will explain the strange passage concerning Aman and Ahkiahkar.

Our hypothesis then is that Book of Tobit was composed in Hebrew in the north of Syria, towards the year 40 or 50 after J.C.; that it was at first little known by the Jews in Palestine; that it was translated into Greek towards the year 160 by the Judeo-Christian translators, and that it was immediately adapted by the Christians.

**THE END**